AF795337

Sport and Doping

Eike Emrich/Werner Pitsch (eds.)

Sport and Doping

The Analysis of an Antagonistic Symbiosis

PETER LANG
Frankfurt am Main · Berlin · Bern · Bruxelles · New York · Oxford · Wien

Bibliographic Information published by the Deutsche Nationalbibliothek
The Deutsche Nationalbibliothek lists this publication in the Deutsche Nationalbibliografie; detailed bibliographic data is available in the internet at http://dnb.d-nb.de.

ISBN 978-3-631-63078-5

© Peter Lang GmbH
Internationaler Verlag der Wissenschaften
Frankfurt am Main 2011
All rights reserved.

All parts of this publication are protected by copyright. Any utilisation outside the strict limits of the copyright law, without the permission of the publisher, is forbidden and liable to prosecution. This applies in particular to reproductions, translations, microfilming, and storage and processing in electronic retrieval systems.

www.peterlang.de

"It is interests (material and ideal), and not ideas which have directly governed the actions of human beings. But the "worldviews" that have been created by "ideas" have very often, like switches, decided the lines on which the dynamic of interests has propelled behaviour." (Weber, 1988, Vol. 1, 252)

"The 'idea' always disgraced itself insofar as it differed from the 'interest'." (K. Marx, The Holy Family, MEW (Marx Engels Werke) 2, 85)

Foreword by the editors

In the run-up to the 2008 Olympic Games in Beijing, the scientific and media debate surrounding the doping issue "hotted up" in many corners of the world. Saarland University was no exception. At the suggestion of the former Director of the Federal Institute of Sports Science, Dr Martin-Peter Büch, a cycle of lectures was planned, starting with a lecture on doping in elite sport from the sociological perspective. This was followed by other lectures that examined the problem from the economic, legal and medical perspective. The lecture cycle concluded with an inter-disciplinary panel discussion held within the context of Saarland University's Open Day, in which representatives from the fields of law, economics and medicine, as well as the head of the German Anti-Doping Agency (NADA), Mr Armin Baumert, participated.

An intensive exchange of ideas, in the meantime perpetuated within the context of the Economics Seminar and a number of research projects concerned with the doping issue, ensued among representatives from the fields of law, economics and sociology as a side effect of these activities. This brief history of the book also explains why the editors are also authors and co-authors of several articles included. The present volume is a reworked and partially completed edition of an anthology which was first published in German in 2009. It presents the transcripts, in some cases enhanced versions of the lectures, and also some additional thoughts to the international scientific community.

In conclusion, we would like to point out that the authors of this anthology will continue their cooperation with the aim to shed more light on the phenomenon of doping. It is to be hoped that after reading this book, the interested reader will not perceive this as a threat.

The editors of the present volume would finally like to express their grateful thanks, also on behalf of the remaining authors, to Professor Dr Dr Manfred Messing for his meticulous proofreading of the manuscript and critical and constructive suggestions for improvement, as well as to the Ministerium für Inneres und Sport des Saarlandes (Saarland Ministry of the Interior and Sport) and the

Landessportverband für das Saarland (Saarland Sports Federation) for their material and immaterial support during the project. Both the minister concerned and the president of the Landessportverband are actively engaged in combating doping, and without their assistance the present volume would not have been written. We also thank the translator Mrs. Jan Wheeler for the accurate and diligent translations.

Saarbrücken, July 2011

Eike Emrich and Werner Pitsch

Contents

Introduction

In sociology, Max Weber applied the term levels of adequacy. Analysis of these adequacy levels concerns itself in particular with the degree of elective affinity of concrete structural forms of social action with concrete economic forms, that is, "concerning whether and how strongly they mutually favour one another's continuance or, conversely, hinder or exclude one another – are "adequate" or "inadequate" to one another" (Weber, 1968, 341). Elite sport and doping may well be a case in point, since the phenomenon of doping has probably gone hand in hand with modern professional sport – performed for a monetary reward – from its very beginnings to the present day. Olympic sport could arguably only be considered "doping-free" at the time of its modern-day revival, when it was exclusively performed by moneyed aristocrats who could afford to dedicate themselves to practising it – real amateurs in the classic sense of the word. Be that as it may, a multi-perspective approach to the phenomenon of "Doping in elite sport" suggests that different social processes in their mutual interaction, i.e. in a specific figuration (Elias, 1986, 139 ff.), are initially responsible for producing, promoting and supporting this frequently problematically perceived phenomenon, and that social actors both contribute to its existence and profit from it.

In the more recent past, doping studies that take a system- and actor-theoretical approach have examined structural links between the sport system and other systems. The fundamental ethos of sport becomes entwined with that of various other systems, such as economics, the media, politics, and as a result the socially acquired orientations of actors in the sport system take a specific direction. Thus ultimately the social system of sport is primarily impacted by monetary interests of both the economic and the media system, as well as interests of the political system for national representation – which potentially indirectly and directly influences political campaigning.

For athletes and officials alike, this gives rise to a single-dimensional ethos geared towards winning and outperformance and encompassing all central roles, which imposes prescriptive behavioural norms (cf. Bette & Schimank, 2006) upon athletes that impel them to orient their behaviour exclusively towards this ethos. Consequentially, it becomes increasingly unlikely that actors will voluntarily commit to acting contrary to the normative expectations resulting from the ethos, for example in order to comply with the rules of fair play.

The system structures or their sociological interpretation thus become social facts that can significantly influence behaviour and drastically reduce individual freedom of decision. This places the actors in the unusual situation where they are generally expected to conform to the enhancement-oriented imperative to succeed and exceed, while at the same time respecting the normative ideals of the institution of sport. The culturally constructed idea and organized practice –

beset as it is with human weaknesses and egotisms as well as non-intended effects – thus drift apart and produce considerable normative tensions at actor and system level.

At the same time, the positively connotated social functions of professional and elite sport derived from the idea of the institution serve to legitimize the supply of material and nonmaterial resources to national and supranational sports organizations. This also includes the notion of the self-governing amateur, who apart from being norm setter and controller in one person, also lives *for* sport, but not *from* it. Originating in the idea of the institution of elite sport, this "noble amateur" finds a new raison d'être in the classical – inherently desirable – elite sport model by taking on the role of the nobleman of our meritocracy who respects the principles of equality, merit and competition. In this spirit, today's elite athletes should achieve their sporting records exclusively on the basis of talent and effort in a rule-governed competitive environment impacted by no other factors; that at least is the idea anchored in the formal and informal rules of the institution of elite sport.

Doping, as an unobserved breach of the norm, enhances peak performances and records, thus increasing the attraction of and helping to legitimize the use of such substances. Given the basic idea of sport, doping is as a matter of principle dysfunctional; for sports practice, however, this is only the case when it is detected. By the same token, when detected it demonstrates that sport is not a haven of happiness, that deviant behaviour as described by Durkheim (1999, 181) is a normal phenomenon, that cheats do not stop at sport and that bare-faced, vested interests determine behaviour. For its consumers, however, the enthrallment of elite sport today rests on the achievement of peak sporting performances within the rules, and a continued raising of the bar in line with the drive to succeed and exceed. This raising of the bar is inhibited by doping controls and forces not only athletes, but also associations and other (co-)producers of the commodity elite sport into an organized pathology (on the term pathology in the organizational context cf. Türk, 1976; on the divergence of individual and collective goals cf. Etzioni, 1961, 24 f.). Despite the drive to improve and exceed spurred by the cultural sphere of sport, associations and athletes must show restraint by voluntarily abstaining from doping or agreeing to doping tests. However, the more top performances are linked to material income and nonmaterial attention, which is then exchanged for money in the attention market, the more difficult it is to close the gap that exists between the production and legitimization function; this is currently only manifest in cases of doping-related breaches of the norm (on organized hypocrisy, cf. Brunsson, 2002): in the public sphere, there is obviously a clash between ideas and interests. The point is: Wherever individuals engaging in sport have been lured by the attention-enhancing, reputational and financial incentives sport offers, there have always been deviators.

This process is reported and commented on at arm's length by part of the press, at times adopting a clear stance against doping, but at times also by another, in this regard more ambivalent part of the press that is hungry for the kind of sensations continuously bred by the divide between idea and practice. As a deviation from the norm with high entertainment value, doping is either treated in the media on the grounds of its proliferation as the main scourge of sport, or alternatively they report on the more or less successful efforts in the battle against illicit drug use. In general, once they go beyond a certain level, public debates on the doping issue force sports organizations to react by taking a position on the media coverage in order to "keep the idea of sport alive". This, in turn, in itself gives rise to a self-perpetuating cycle.

The present scientific preoccupation with doping also exhibits lines of tension and a number of associations to doping in elite sport. As applied sciences, disciplines such as biochemistry and pharmacy are expected to solve the problem of the effectiveness of doping controls by developing corresponding testing methods; yet at the same time, precisely these same sciences continuously produce substances that can be consumed for doping purposes which are (as yet) untraceable. The more doping offenders are caught, in other words the more effective the controls are, the more pressing the extent of the problem becomes. In light of the general suspicion, the more dopers are detected, the more widespread testing methods need to become in order to convict a greater number of offenders. The absence of a greater number of doping convictions can then always be attributed to the successful deterrent effect of the conducted tests. As a result of the gap between the development and the dissemination of suitable verification methods, doping controls and discussions about which substances should be banned and how to enforce testing are therefore also part of a perpetuum mobile, since from the perspective of those who promulgate clean sport, the race between the innovative forces in the doping market and the controllers inevitably has to lead to a permanent crisis. In this context, the position of the doping controllers reminds us rather of the fate of Sisyphus, who was compelled to repeat forever the task of rolling a huge boulder up a hill, only to see it roll down again. Whether, as Camus surmised, he was a happy man or not, is beside the point; one thing is certain: his labour was definitely crisis-proof. Contrary to Sisyphus, however, doping controllers have chosen their assignment voluntarily and earn their living from it.

Philosophers, economists, sociologists, psychologists and educationalists also have a fascination with the phenomenon of doping, thus implicitly confirming the controversy in the "Fable of the Bees", according to which "the basest and vilest behaviours (in this case of dopers, eds.) produced positive economic effects" (translated from Mandeville, 1980, 43). Doping offers a whole generation of present-day researchers, including the authors of this book, plenty of opportunity for scientific study. The results of exclusively sociological, economic or educational analyses, which serve as a basis for the discussion on recommendations for reducing doping, do not in essence provide empirically proven measures against doping in the sense of "if A then B" implications. In urging all stakeholders to take concerted action against doping they appear rather lame and, in blunt terms, are a bit like a doctor telling an alcoholic to give up drinking. Indeed, at times the intensity and moral force of the appeal simply obscure the lack of scientifically based interventions. Above all the many educational anti-doping initiatives fall into this category and urgently require evaluation. The constant appeal to athletes to uphold the principles of fair play quite possibly even leads to an erosion of underlying moral values. They exhort individuals in an international competitive environment to maintain ethical standards in competition, where frequently their only defence against the exploitation attempts of others is to bend the rules. On the assumption that athletes live from sport, expecting them to prejudice their own chances of earning a living is in itself highly questionable. But even where individuals are drawn to elite sport and in this context are forced to react to the exploitation attempts of others, they are always faced with the choice of either taking illicit drugs to enable them to pursue a career as a professional athlete, or refusing to consume them and thus saying goodbye to the dream of practising their sport on a professional level.

All in all, doping indeed turns out to be a phenomenon in which – in line with the adequacy levels approach – individual acts of athletes, collective decisions in associations, media exploitation interests, scientific analyses and organized control efforts are intertwined. Given the assumption of rationally behaving actors whose decisions are aimed at maximizing their respective benefit, the balance that emerges from this interaction corresponds to the non-intended effect of many unrelated rational individual decisions, each under given restrictions and each with different opportunities. Beyond this analysis of the situation, a look at (organizational and legal) efforts at regulation shows that these, too, focus on the rational decision-maker. Otherwise any attempt at control via the level of sanctions and via the probability of detection of doping consumers as well as providers would be predisposed to failure. However, even these efforts have not in the past led to doping representing a marginal phenomenon in elite sport, nor being capable of being considered as such.

So what basic parameters in the sense of individual incentives and restrictions are needed to allow individuals to pursue their interests and at the same time not violate the normative expectations of the institution? The answer to this relatively simple question is in fact extremely complex, as it requires a combination of economic and legal analysis.

Doping violates the principle of fair play in sporting competition. The idea of elite sport is eclipsed by the dominant motive of competitors' self-interest. In the economic sense, the social order of sport is a public commodity that for instance in the case of doping is suppressed by inferior commodities, namely a deficient order. The rule violator in the form of the unobserved doper not only violates equal opportunities, he or she also capitalizes on violating the rules. Hence they are the ones who at the same time must have a vested interest in upholding the order, since only if it has validity do they stand to profit from violating it. On the normative level, sporting competition is in this sense per se a zero-sum game in which the personal advantage of one player is based on the opponent's disadvantage. Yet even in this area dilemma structures are increasingly emerging as the current legal framework and control structures permit individual deviators to impose their will on others and ultimately derive advantages within and outside sporting competition (on this and the following remarks cf. Emrich, 2008; 2006).

What stands out from all this is that basing the ethics of moral desirability exclusively on the idea of sport, especially on Olympic ideals, demands too much both of the IOC as an organization and, obviously, of internationally competing athletes, who are exposed to market-driven competition that is largely dependent on their sporting success. The question about an appropriate social order therefore also encompasses the following considerations:

- How can we prevent individuals in sporting competitions imposing their will on others and, in doing so, systematically undermining fair play in the sense of adherence to the rules (within rules, cf. Brennan & Buchanan, 1985)?
- Does the idea of elite sport lose its credibility if associations are unable to guarantee fairness in sporting competition?
- What marginal ethics can the IOC and the international sports associations afford to espouse in comparison with other sport providers?

A social order in the form of a contract between sports associations and as a contract between athletes and associations must weigh up and constantly rebalance the associated marginal benefit between preserving traditional rules on the one hand and continuous further development of the social order on the other. This gives rise to a fourth question, namely:

- What structure of the social order, i.e. what arrangement of the rules, can ensure that in their mutual interaction both sports associations and athletes accept the binding character of the rules of the social order?

This is only likely to be the case on a sustained basis if it is more in the individual's interest to comply with the rules than to break them. These self-serving interests must therefore be the starting point for applying sanctions to reinforce the rules.

Summing up, the question is therefore how, given the increasing marketability of sport products – including Olympic sport – we can successfully preserve the essential idea of elite sport, and in particular Olympic sport, in a social order that is valid for everyone and upheld by everyone, avoid "sacrificing" its moral fabric to commercial interests, protect sporting competition and its diversity, and at the same time widely permit the IOC, its member associations and athletes to pursue their entrepreneurial interests.

In this, we need to consider whether there is a specific synthesis path between the two apparent extremes market and temple, or rather economics and ethics, and if so, what this might look like. The disciplines most suitable to answering this question are first and foremost law and economics, although their contributions towards addressing the phenomenon are necessarily limited, to the extent that the incidence frequency of doping in the collective, individual doping motives, and possibilities and limits of detection, including non-intended side effects, are incorporated a priori in the analysis and not inferred a posteriori from empirical analyses. The articles in this volume are therefore mainly recruited from the fields of economics and law, supplemented by other key references from empirical sociology.

References

Bette, K.-H., Schimank, U. (2006). *Doping im Hochleistungssport: Anpassung durch Abweichung.* 2nd extended edition. Frankfurt: Suhrkamp.

Brennan, G., Buchanan, J. M. (1985). The Reason of Rules. Cambridge: Cambridge Univ. Press.

Brunsson, N. (2002). *The Organization of Hypocrisy: Talk, Decisions and Actions in Organisations.* Copenhagen: Business School Press.

Durkheim, E. (1999 [orig. 1895]). *Die Regeln der soziologischen Methode.* 4th edition. Frankfurt am Main: Suhrkamp.

Durkheim, E. (1893). De la division du travail social. Paris: Alcan.

Elias, N. (1986). *Was ist Soziologie?* Munich: Juventa.

Emrich, E. (2006). Zur Kommerzialisierung der olympischen Idee – einige grundlegende Anmerkungen (pp. 39-55). In Kutschke, F. (Ed.). *Ökonomie Olympischer Spiele.* Schorndorf: Hofmann.

Emrich, E. (2008). Markt oder Tempel? Zwischen Moral und Eigennutz: Was können wir von der Bienenfabel für die Ökonomie der Olympischen Spiele lernen? In Wacker, C., Marxen, R. (Eds.): *Olympia – zwischen Ideal und Wirklichkeit. Festschrift commemorating the 60th birthday of Norbert Müller* (pp. 103-132). Berlin: LIT.

Etzioni, A. (1961). *A Comparative Analysis of Complex Organizations. On Power, Involvement, and their Correlates.* New York: The Free Press of Glencoe.

Marx, K., Engels, F. (1972). Die heilige Familie oder Kritik der kritischen Kritik gegen Bruno Bauer und Konsorten. *Werke (Works), Volume 2* (pp. 3-223). Berlin: Dietz Verlag.

Mandeville, B. (1980). *Die Bienenfabel. Mit einer Einleitung von Walter Euchner.* Frankfurt am Main: Suhrkamp (Part 1 1705, quoted here from the 3rd edition, published 1724).

Pitsch, W., Maats, P., Emrich, E. (2008). Skizzen zu einer Ökonomik des Dopings. In Müller, N., Messing. M. (Eds.). *Olympismus – Erbe und Verantwortung* (pp. 381-418). Kassel: Agon.

Türk, K. (1976). *Grundlagen einer Pathologie der Organisation.* Stuttgart: Enke.

Weber, M. (1968 [orig. 1922]). *Economy and Society. An Outline of Interpretive Sociology.* New York: Bedminster Press.

Weber, M. (1988 [1920]). Wirtschaftsethik der Weltreligionen. In Ders. *Gesammelte Aufsätze zur Religionssoziologie* (pp. 237-573). 3 volumes, 9th edition. Tübingen: Mohr Siebeck.

Werner Pitsch, Peter Maats, Eike Emrich

The frequency of doping in elite sport – a replication study

1 Introduction

Apart from speculations in the press and reports by "inside observers" of the sport scene (translated from Bette, Schimank, Wahlig & Weber, 2002, 11) about a purported rise in the number of dopers, there have to date been very few serious attempts to empirically examine the actual prevalence of doping among German squad athletes. Given the methodological problems inherent in studying an issue deemed as socially undesirable as doping, this in no way comes as a surprise.

The Randomized Response Technique (in the following: RRT) inhibits inferences about the behaviour of the respondent, guarantees 100% anonymity and therefore proves particularly suited for analyzing sensitive data. This technique was first used to examine the proportion of dopers among German squad athletes by means of an online survey in 2005 (Pitsch, Emrich & Klein, 2005, 69). The results showed a reliable rate of athletes who had used prohibited substances to enhance their performance at least once during their sporting career totalling between 25.8% and 48.1%. In the 2005 season, the prevalence of doping was rated at between 20.4% and 38.7%. For their entire athletic career up to the point of the survey, we must therefore assume a proportion of 51.9% 'honest non-dopers' and for the 2005 season a proportion of 61.3% 'honest non-dopers' (ibid., 63).

The results show that prevailing theoretical attempts up to that point in time to explain the prevalence of doping do not hold up. If the survey is to be believed, by far the majority of German squad athletes do not succumb to the pressure to succeed anchored in the structures of a sport system geared to winning and outperformance (cf. Bette & Schimank, 2006). Also surprising is the finding that on the whole a comparatively small sample stated their coaches as having incited them to engage in illegal doping practices (5.1%), while family members and friends were stated by 6.5%. Doping also proved to be far more a problem of the "second tier" than of athletes competing at international level (cf. Pitsch, Emrich & Klein, 2007).

2 Problem

The main criticism of the study conducted by Pitsch, Emrich and Klein (2005; cf. 2007) related to using the RRT in an online survey, which, it was claimed, was not suitable for obtaining honest answers to embarrassing questions. For a number of years, the comparability of written and Internet-based surveys has been controversially discussed, above all in the field of market research (cf. in the overview Batinic et al., 1999; Reips & Bosnjak, 2001; Batinic, Reips &

Bosnjak, 2002). The latest state of the art in survey techniques, however, does not give a uniform picture of how the factual and perceived anonymity of the respondents linked to the different forms of questionnaire actually affects the way they respond. Preserving anonymity is important when investigating doping prevalence, however, since it can be assumed that the identification of honest dopers would lead to a livelihood-threatening loss of income and standing. Compared to standardized written questionnaires, online surveys are seen as a considerably less reliable research tool because they are likely to require higher costs of trust. This debate is further fuelled by cases of data abuse (cf. the data privacy abuse by Google Employees in September 2010) that have been controversially discussed in the public arena. Moreover, not only the instrument itself, but also the way in which the target group is addressed is important for obtaining honest responses and influences the results.

In response to the problem concerning the validity of web survey techniques, the 2005 study was replicated in 2008. The population of German squad athletes was divided by random into two samples (randomized). Subsequently, in order to methodologically analyze any differences in response behaviour and thus permit a systematic comparison of the two approaches, one subgroup was requested to fill out a paper-based questionnaire and the other was asked to participate in an online survey. It was also intended to compare the findings of the 2005 survey with those of the 2008 study, giving consideration to possibly changed basic parameters and a somewhat differently composed sample.

3 Method

In surveys on forms of deviant behaviour there is always the possibility that the results will be heavily biased. The degree of bias is assumed to be influenced by the degree to which the sensitive behaviour is observable to the researcher, by the relevance of the behaviour to the interviewee, and by the degree to which the answer to a sensitive question is publicized (Esser, 1986). Alongside well-known and generally applied methods for guaranteeing anonymity of data and compliance with data protection provisions, an attempt was made to control this tendency towards bias by using the randomized response technique (RRT). This interview technique can help to obtain more reliable responses to questions related to illicit and/or illegal practices than direct questioning and the associated bias effects resulting from supposed social desirability by the interviewees (cf. Lensvelt-Mulders et al., 2005, 340 ff.). As well as the question relating to the sensitive attribute, an additional instruction is given, which, depending on the outcome of a randomizing process, encourages the respondent to answer the question honestly or with “Yes”, irrespective of whether they display the respective attribute or not. This process is usually illustrated using the example of a die, whereby surveys sometimes also work with other methods, for example the interviewee's month of birth.[1] An example is drawn on to illustrate the process.[2]

- Question: Have you ever used banned drugs or methods in order to enhance your sporting performance?
- Additional instruction: If you were born in the months from January to April, please answer "Yes"; if you were born in any other month, please answer honestly.

Since the researchers do not know the interviewee's month of birth they cannot infer from an individual "Yes" answer whether the respondent has actually consumed doping substances or not. All that is known is the relative frequency of occurrence of births in the months January to April, as well as the distribution of "Yes" and "No" answers among all respondents. The distribution of births across the months of birth produces the probability p with which an interviewee received the instruction "answer yes". From the distribution of "Yes" and "No" answers and the known probability p, it is possible to calculate the proportion of people in the population π who display the sensitive attribute (here: the number of dopers) (cf. Figure 1).

However, RRT surveys have also been shown to suffer from a bias produced by interviewees who for no explicable reason fail to follow the instruction (cf. Locander, Sudman & Bradburn, 1976; Shimizu & Bonham, 1978). This kind of "cheating" has to be distinguished from deliberately dishonest answers arising from biased responses in direct questioning as a result of suppositions of social desirability. In cases where interviewees for example do not trust the anonymization process, they will answer "No" even if they were instructed to answer "Yes", whether they display the sensitive attribute or not, because in either case reidentification would incriminate them. For the RRT, this would mean that among the share of the population π of those who have resorted to performance-enhancing substances there would also be some "No" answers, and among the share of the population β the proportion of "Yes" answers would be lower than anticipated on the basis of the randomized attribute.

---

[1] The literature mentions the use of various other randomization devices (e.g. Scheers, 1992; Tracy & Fox, 1981; Shimizu & Bonham, 1978) or other randomly distributed attributes such as the last digits of telephone numbers (Stem & Steinhorst, 1984; Goodstad & Gruson, 1975). For a web-based survey, however, it cannot be assumed that all respondents will have a randomization device such as a coin or a dice readily available at the precise moment when they participate in the survey. Other randomly distributed attributes, such as the last digits of a randomly selected telephone number, presuppose knowledge about the distribution of telephone numbers according to their final digits.

[2] This example presents the forced response technique for qualitative attributes according to Boruch (1971), which was used in the online survey. On the Warner model as well as two variations of the unrelated question model also for quantitative attributes, cf. for example the overview in Scheers (1992).

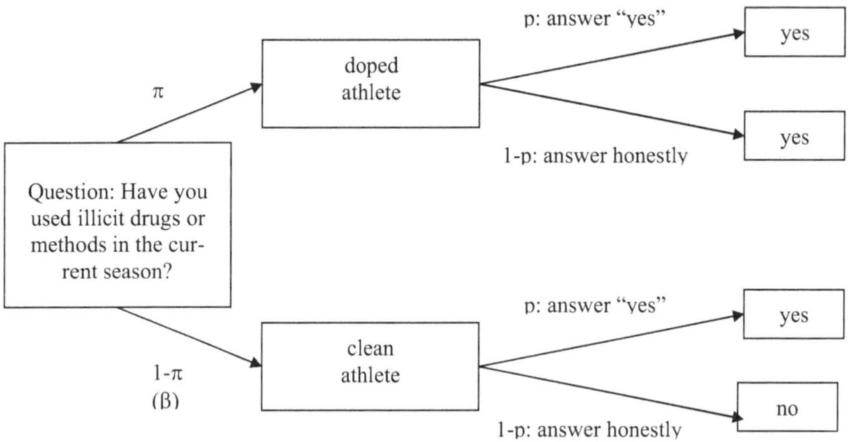

Fig. 1: Basic structure of the "forced answer" model

In an effort to control such biases, Clark & Desharnais (1998) developed the so-called "cheater detection model", which also in web-based surveys on forms of deviant behaviour permits more reliable estimates[3] than direct questioning about such behaviour (cf. the application of Musch et al., 2001, using the example of tax evasion). In the "cheater detection model", the interviewees are randomly distributed between two different instruction conditions, whereby the additional instruction "answer yes" is stated with different probabilities p1 and p2 (usually 1-p1). In this case, the proportions of "honest dopers" π, "honest non-dopers" β as well as "cheaters" γ are calculated from the proportion of those who have answered the question under the condition p1 and p2, the probabilities p1 and p2, as well as the number of "Yes" and "No" answers (cf. Figure 2). Even with this technique the RRT still has the shortcoming that systematic biases arising from "Yes" answers when interviewees have been instructed to answer "No" remain undetected. This can occur where deliberate wrong answers are given, but also where utilized in deviant subcultures in which the use of banned substances and methods in order to enhance performance represents a subcultural norm.[4]

---

[3] Here and in the following text the term "estimation" will be used as a statistical technical term: An estimator is a value which is calculated basing on a sample in order to characterize a population. The term "estimation" may therefore not be intermixed with the connotation of a reduced accurateness as any result of statistical analyses of samples are "estimators".

[4] To also enable application of the RRT in such cases as these, the basic methodological and mathematical principles of "Yes-and-no cheater detection" have been developed in a cooperation between the Sport Economy and Sport Sociology departments at Saarland University (Dr Werner Pitsch) and the Fraunhofer Institute for Technical and Industrial Mathematics in Kaiserslautern (Dipl.-Mathematiker Sascha Feth). To be published separately.

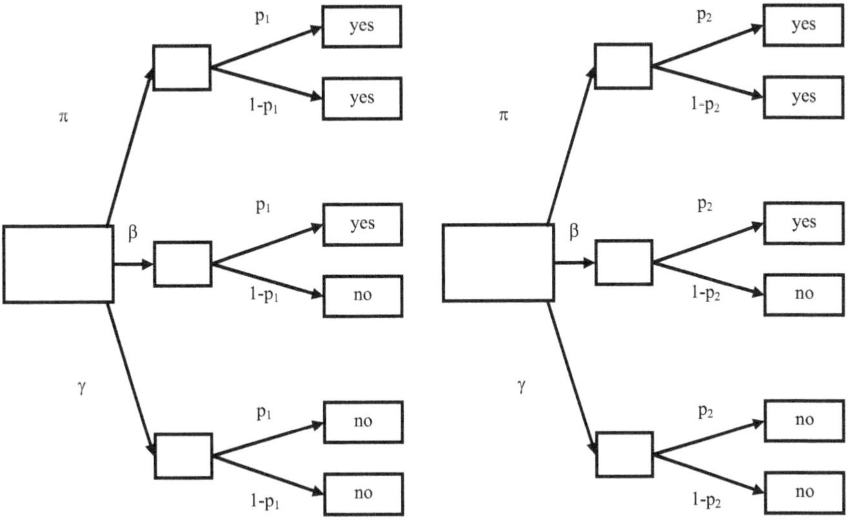

Fig. 2: Randomized Response Technique with "cheater detection" based on Clark & Desharnais (1998)

4 Sample

The basis for application of the RRT in 2008 was the population of German squad athletes drawn from the list of national squad athletes which the German Olympic Sports Federation (DOSB) had provided in 2006 (5,409 addresses), randomized into two subgroups. Sample 1 was requested by post to fill out a paper-based questionnaire, while sample 2 was contacted by post and asked to participate via an Internet link in an online survey.[5] In order to protect the anonymity of the sample population, the online survey was carried out on the basis of similar security standards to those used in online banking. The athletes were made aware of this.

The response rate for the online survey was 639 and for the paper-based survey 863 data records, corresponding to an overall response rate of 27.77%. Bearing in mind that among experts elite sport is a field which is considered over-investigated and athletes are very frequently asked to participate in surveys, this response rate was satisfactory. Compared to their representation in the population, participation of women was significantly higher in both survey forms than that of men (only data records by gender: $\chi^2=32.71$, df=1, $p<0.001$),

[5] For example, they are obliged to inform the National Anti-Doping Agency (NADA) regularly by computer of their whereabouts for the purposes of unannounced doping tests (Anti-Doping Administration and Management System). Biases in response behaviour due to 'Internet illiteracy' can therefore be neglected.

but the contingency coefficient C=0.06 revealed that this effect was rather weak and was significant only because of the high population count.

The distribution of respondents by gender (see Table 1) did not differ significantly between the two survey forms (χ^2=0.23, df=1, n. s.). With a share of 7.04%, item non-response was significantly higher among online respondents than in the paper-based survey (cf. Table 1).

Tab. 1: Distribution of respondents and population by gender

Gender	Postal survey	Online survey	Population
Item non-response	2.2	7.0	-
Male	49.3	48.2	57.8
Female	48.5	44.8	42.2

Tab. 2: Distribution of respondents and population by birth cohort

Birth cohort	Postal survey n=863	Online survey n=639	Share of the cohort in the population
Item non-response	n=19 (2.2%)	n=43 (6.7%)	n=19 (0.3%)
<1960	--	--	n=173 (2.8%)
1960-1969	1.5%	3.2%	2.3%
1970-1979	11.3%	10.2%	15.7%
1980-1989	78.7%	76.8%	75.6%
1990-1999	8.5%	9.7%	6.4%

With respect to the decade of birth, there was no difference between the two survey forms (χ^2=5.31, df=3, n. s.); however, here again there was a significant difference between the participants in the survey and the population (χ^2=31.70, df=3, $p<0.001$, cf. Table 2), which by analogy with the gender effect is also to be seen as very weak (Tschurpow contingency coefficient C'=0.05, cf. Bortz, 1985, 287).

Due to the low number of records in the different kinds of sport, the data could not be evaluated at that level. For this reason, the disciplines were categorized according to the scheme developed by Emrich, Pitsch and Papathanassiou (2001, 153 ff.; cf. Pitsch, Emrich & Klein, 2005, cf. Table 3). Categorizing led to sufficient replications for athletes in the games to make initial evaluations. In the artistic-compositional sports and in the combat sports, the replications were too low to evaluate specific effects.

Tab. 3: Distribution of respondents by discipline category and survey form

Discipline category	Postal survey n=863		Online survey n=693		Population N=5409	
	no.	percentage	no.	percentage	no.	percentage
Games	127	19.9	118	21.4	1,194	22.1
Cgs sports[6]	354	55.5	309	56.0	2,688	49.7
Combat sports	54	8.5	53	9.6	490	9.1
Artistic-compositional	57	8.9	52	9.4	757	14.0
Without classification	46	7.2	20	3.6	280	5.2
Item non-response	225	26.1	87	12.6		

The distribution of respondents over the discipline categories did not differ significantly between the two survey forms (χ^2=7.69, df=3, n. s.), but did differ significantly, although with only a weak effect size, between the total sample and the population (χ^2=25.58, df=3, p<0.001, C'=0.04).

The respective achievement level, measured in the categories "up to regional level", "up to national level", "international level, European" and "international level, worldwide" did not differ significantly between the two samples (χ^2=5.63, df=3, n. s.). 93.3% of the respondents in the paper-based survey had participated in competitions at least at the European level during their career (63.2% international level, worldwide; 30.1% international level, European); in the online survey, the rate of respondents who competed at European level or higher reached 90.3% (58.8% international level, worldwide, 31.5% international level, European). The level of achievement in the 2008 season did not differ significantly either between the two survey forms (χ^2=2.55, df=3, n. s.), however, the level of competition participation was noticeably lower with 49.4% up to national level and 50.4% at European level or higher.

5 Results

5.1 Results of the method comparison

In the following, some central results of the survey conducted using the RRT method are first presented and discussed from the method comparison angle, as this permits direct inferences to be made about the reliability of the data. In a next step, the results, where they at least appeared to indicate a reliable trend, are analyzed in detail and in comparison with other surveys.

---

[6] Disciplines where the performance is measured typically in centimetres, grams, or seconds.

The analysis of the response rate already revealed that participants in the online survey showed a higher item-based non-response rate. 83 respondents (accounting for 13.0% of online interviewees) did not complete the survey and failed to fill out the questionnaire in full. The rate of item non-responses relating to the four RRT questions about the phenomenon of "doping" showed values of between 8.8% and 13.0%, while in the paper-based survey these values were between 0.3% and 1.0%.

This observation already permits the cautious conclusion that the response behaviour of the interviewees in the online survey may – despite application of the RRT – be subject to other, possibly stronger biases than is the case in the paper-based survey. The evaluation of the RRT survey relating to doping in the course of the career as well as in the current season produced the values shown in Table 4. To estimate the parameters in the online survey, it was necessary to draw on the maximum likelihood estimate method briefly outlined by Clarke and Desharnais (1998, 163). This revealed significant discrepancies between the online survey and the paper-based survey not only in the number of respondents who completed the questionnaire, but apparently also in the number of dopers as well as cheaters.

Tab. 4: Estimated proportion of honest "Yes" and honest "No" respondents and cheaters based on the RRT survey

Question	Method	Honest "Yes"	Cheaters	Honest "No"
Have you ever...?	Postal	14	28	58
	Online	0	18	82
Have you in the current season...?	Postal	13	29	58
	Online	0	15	85

By looking at the way in which respondents were recruited in the different surveys, it is hoped to shed light on possible bias effects not controlled by means of the RRT, which, consequently, might partly account for these discrepancies in the results. In the 2005 online survey, athletes were contacted by email by the athlete spokesperson for the sports concerned and asked for their cooperation. In 2008, they were written to personally and were either directly sent the questionnaire with a stamped addressed envelope or referred to the link for the online questionnaire.

In the 2005 online survey, which was organized according to the pyramid principle, the participants remained anonymous except to the seed persons of the pyramid system, the athlete spokespersons; while in 2008 the athletes must have been aware that their identity was known to the researchers, as they were addressed directly by post. This necessarily entails higher costs of trust than in the first study. There is also a difference between the postal and the online survey in terms of costs of trust with respect to the transfer of data on the Internet. An overview of the different costs of trust of the respective survey forms is presented in Table 5.

Tab. 5: Overview of costs of trust

Form of survey	Population	Response rate	Costs of trust		Result
			Approach	Response	
		2005			
Online pyramid system (only knowledge of the seed persons)	Theoretically known (total population of all German squad athletes)	448	low	high	20-25% honest dopers, 18-22% cheaters
		2008			
Paper-based; contacted by post by name	2006 squad list – approx. 2,700 usable addresses (50% share of total population of 5,409)	863	high	low	10% honest dopers, 25% cheaters
Online; contacted by post by name	2006 squad list – approx. 2,700 usable addresses (50% share of total population of 5,409)	639	high	high	0% honest dopers, 18% cheaters

Due to the lower anonymity in the recruiting process, the costs of trust of potential respondents in the current online survey were significantly higher than in the postal survey and also higher than in the 2005 online survey. Despite the fact that the recipients of the data are a team of university researchers, the costs of trust can be so high that especially where interviewees display sensitive attributes, there is a higher probability that they will refuse to participate in the survey altogether. Among those who do participate, there is a similarly likelihood of a higher proportion of item non-responders, especially on questions relating to sensitive attributes. Apart from these structural differences between the various survey forms, the more intensified discussion about Internet data security and protection from unauthorized access by third parties over the past few years may additionally have contributed to the differences noted. Moreover, since 2008 Internet providers in Europe have a duty to retain communication data (EU directive 2006/24/EC), which undermines the anonymity of the respondent as required by the randomized response technique.

Based on these methodological considerations, in the following analysis the online survey is not evaluated any further because the data appeared biased, most likely due to a response bias exhibited in the non-participation of doped athletes.

5.2 The rate of dopers in elite sport

By adding the rate of honest dopers to that of cheaters, whose behaviour with regard to the attribute the researchers know nothing about, one can calculate the interval which should include the true score of dopers in the population. The lower limit of the interval is the estimated proportion of honest dopers. The difference to the upper interval limit represents the proportion of cheaters.

The paper-based survey resulted in a lower interval limit of 9.6% and an upper limit of 35% across all sports disciplines for the question *"Have you ever knowingly used illicit drugs or methods in order to enhance your performance?"* (cf. Figure 3). For the athletes' whole career, we calculated a proportion of 65.2% *honest non-dopers;* in the 2008 season the estimated rate of *honest non-dopers* was 65%.

Referring to the 2008 season, the question *„Have you knowingly used banned doping substances in the current season?"* elicited an interval in the paper-based survey of 10% to 35%. This would tend to confirm the results of the 2005 survey, whereby the results of the current survey fall even further below the global estimate of 42 to 84% of doped athletes postulated by Plessner and Musch (2002).

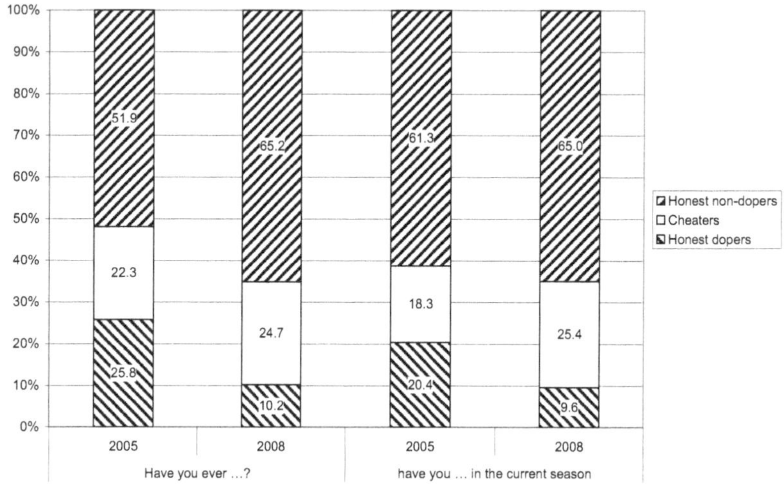

Fig. 3: Estimated proportions of "honest dopers", "honest non-dopers" and "cheaters" in the population throughout their career and in the current season in the 2005 and the 2008 study

For the athletes' whole career, the proportion of *honest non-dopers* in games is significantly higher with 83.6% (16.4% *cheaters*) than that for the cgs *disciplines* with 56.3% (14.2% *honest dopers*; 29.5% *cheaters*, cf. Figure 4). For the 2008 season, the proportion of *honest non-dopers* was at roughly the same level as the values for the athletes' whole career (cf. Figure 5). Differences were also found when comparing athletes according to their level of competition participation in the previous season and in the ongoing season at the time of the survey. Both the question concerning whether they had ever used banned doping methods and the question concerning doping in the current 2008 season largely concurred in their results that doping is less prevalent at international level than at national level, thus confirming the outcome of the 2005 study (cf. Figure 6).[7]

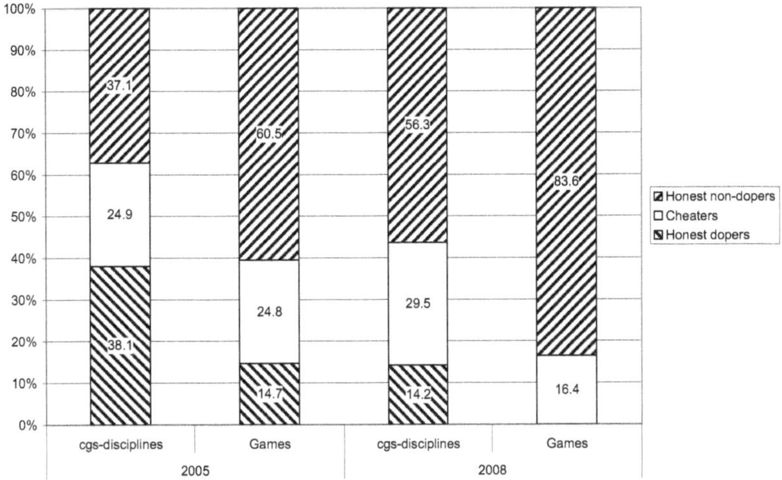

Fig. 4: Estimated proportions of "honest dopers", "honest non-dopers" and "cheaters" in different sport categories throughout their career

The studies also looked at whether the athletes' social environment, both sporting and private, had an active stimulating influence on their decision not to engage in illicit doping practices. The question[8] *"Have you ever been incited by your coach, other supervisors and officials to use illicit drugs or methods in order to enhance your performance?"* was answered in the negative by 99.5% of respondents in the paper-based survey. Comparable values were elicited by the question *"Have you ever been incited by family members and/or friends to use illicit drugs or methods in order to enhance your performance?"*: 99.4% answered in the negative.

[7] An analogue evaluation to the 2005 study was not possible due to the low number of respondents who had at best reached national level (n=57, 6.6%).

[8] The following questions were asked directly and not with the help of the RRT.

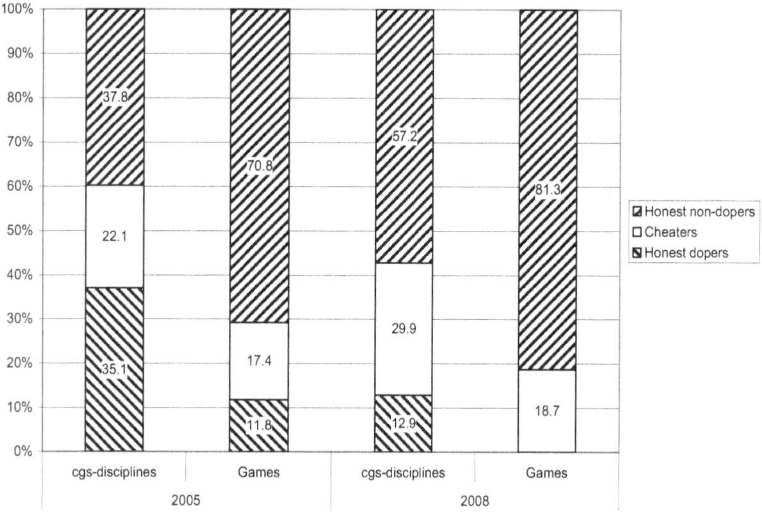

Fig. 5: Estimated proportions of "honest dopers", "honest non-dopers" and "cheaters" in different sport categories in the current season

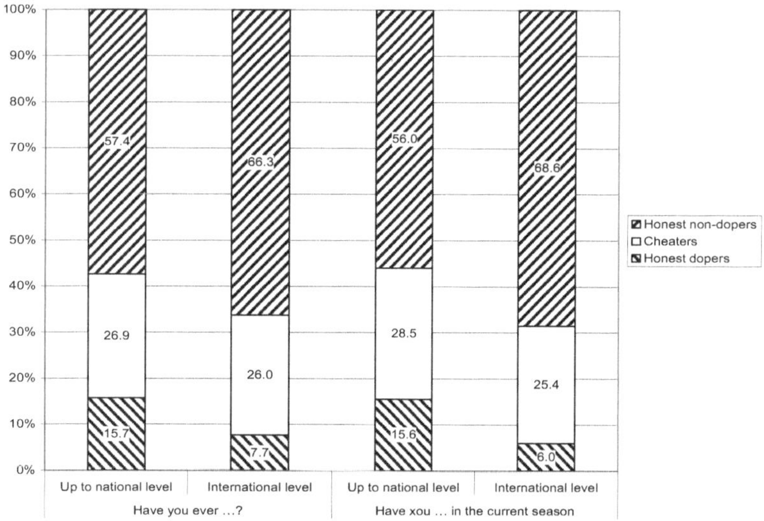

Fig. 6: Estimated proportions of "honest dopers", "honest non-dopers" and "cheaters" by levels of competition in the current season

The question, *"Have you ever been penalized for using banned doping substances?"* produces a rate of 11% *cheaters* across all sporting disciplines (cf. Figure 7). The rate of 0% honest confessors concurred with the findings of the 2005 online survey (cf. Pitsch, Klein & Emrich, 2007). However, a much higher proportion of athletes stated they had not been sanctioned after being tested positive for doping. It remains to be seen whether these findings continue to be stable in subsequent studies.

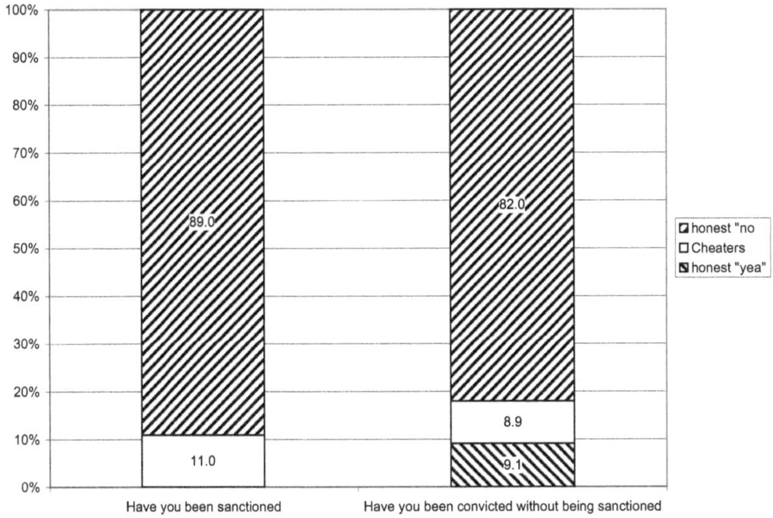

Fig. 7: Estimated proportions of "honest confessors", "honest deniers" and "cheaters" in the population who have been convicted of doping with and without being penalized

On average, 6.26% of athletes proceed from the assumption that there are cases of positive but unsanctioned doping behaviour. As Table 6 shows, the results vary significantly, however, between the different discipline categories.

The question "*In your opinion, how many of your opponents are using banned substances this season?*" produces a relatively homogeneous estimate of an average 7.6% (standard deviation 12.51%) across all sporting disciplines. Responses vary from 5.12% for games to a maximum of 9.17% for *cgs sports* (cf. Table 7).

Tab. 6: Incidences of cases of known but unsanctioned doping in the respective sports association of the athlete [%]

Discipline category	Yes	No
Item non-response	2.9	97.1
Games	3.1	96.9
Cgs sports	8.1	91.9
Combat sports	3.8	96.2
Artistic-compositional	1.5	98.5
Without classification	13.5	86.5
Total	6.3	93.7

A similarly homogeneous estimate is given for the probability of detection. The response to the question "In your opinion, what percentage of the athletes in your sport category who use banned doping substances are actually convicted of doping?" produced an estimate averaging 16.9% (standard deviation 30.3%, cf. Table 8).

Tab. 7: Athletes' estimate of proportion of doped athletes according to sport category [%]

Discipline category	Average	Standard deviation
Item non-response	4.28	6.61
Games	5.12	7.93
Cgs sports	9.17	14.28
Combat sports	9.08	15.45
Artistic-compositional	5.31	10.58
Without classification	8.14	10.21
Total	7.64	12.51

6 Discussion

The 2008 paper-based survey shows that the upper limit of the rate of dopers among German elite athletes is estimated at 35%, thus tending to corroborate one central result of the 2005 survey, namely that in 2008 more than half the number of athletes do not resort to illicit drugs. Compared to the measured frequency of doping in German elite sport of up to 35%, the extent of doping prevalence estimated by the athletes themselves is vastly underestimated. They assume an average rate of 7.6% (standard deviation 12.5%) of dopers amongst their rivals, of whom the athletes believe on average around 16.9% are detected. This does not permit any convincing conclusion pointing to a social pressure anchored in the structures of a sporting system geared towards winning and outperforming which athletes are more or less forced to succumb to.

Tab. 8: Athletes' estimate of probability of detection

Discipline category	Average	Standard deviation
Item non-response	17.32	30.96
Games	14.68	30.36
Cgs sports	18.59	30.80
Combat sports	12.00	25.70
Artistic-compositional	14.17	29.23
Without classification	16.16	30.71
Total	16.89	30.32

Furthermore, athletes did not seem to be exposed in 2008 to any direct stimuli in their immediate environment that incited them to use banned doping substances. In the present study, by analogy with the 2005 survey, doping again appears to be a "second tier" problem, which would suggest athletes behave rationally. For a top international first-tier athlete, the loss of standing and income they would suffer if they were to be discovered using illicit drugs would be significantly higher, and the benefits of doping on the other hand significantly lower by comparison, because these athletes have already achieved a high level of performance and success. Added to this is the higher risk of detecting doping practices resulting from the higher number of controls compared to the second tier (Pitsch, Emrich & Klein, 2005, 73).

By analogy with the 2005 study, doping is also shown in the 2008 survey to be more prevalent in the cgs sports than in games. The established differences could again be explained by assuming a rational choice approach. By contrast with games, enhanced performances in the cgs sports are directly reflected in competition results. The individual benefit immediately pays off, whereas in games, success usually does not become apparent until the end of the season and entails greater uncertainties due to the greater complexity of the sporting performance (cf. Pitsch, Emrich & Klein, 2005, 74; Loland, 2004).

References

Bortz, J. (1985). *Lehrbuch der Statistik für Sozialwissenschaftler*. 2nd ed. Berlin: Springer.

Batinic, B., Werner, A., Gräf, L., Bandilla, W. (Eds.) (1999). Online Research. Methoden, Anwendungen und Ergebnisse. Göttingen: Hogrefe.

Batinic, B., Reips, U.-D., Bosnjak, M. (Eds.) (2002). *Online Social Sciences*. Göttingen: Hogrefe and Huber Publishers.

Bette, K.-H., Schimank, U. (2006). *Doping im Hochleistungssport: Anpassung durch Abweichung*. 2nd extended edition Frankfurt: Suhrkamp.
Bette, K.-H., Schimank, U., Weber, U., Wahlig, D. (2002). *Biographische Dynamiken im Leistungssport. Möglichkeiten der Dopingprävention im Jugendalter*. Cologne: Sport und Buch Strauß.
Boruch, R. F. (1971). Maintaining Confidentiality of Data in Educational Research: a Systemic Analysis. *The American Psychologist, 26*, 413-430.
Clark, S. J., Desharnais, R. A. (1998). Honest Answers to Embarrassing Questions: Detecting Cheating in the Randomized Response Model. *Psychological Methods, 3*, 160-168.
Emrich, E., Pitsch, W., Papathanassiou, V. (2001). *Die Sportvereine. Ein Versuch auf empirischer Grundlage*. Schorndorf: Hofmann.
Esser, H. (1986). Können Befragte lügen? Zum Konzept des „wahren Wertes" im Rahmen der handlungstheoretischen Erklärung von Situationseinflüssen bei der Befragung. *Kölner Zeitschrift für Soziologie und Sozialpsychologie, 38*, 314-336.
Goodstadt, M. S., Gruson, V. (1975). The Randomized Response Technique: A Test on Drug Use. *Journal of the American Statistical Association, 70*, 814-818.
Lensvelt-Mulders, G. J. L. M., Hox, J. J., van der Heijden, P. G. M., Maas, C. J. M. (2005). Meta-Analysis of Randomized Response Research. Thirty-Five Years of Validation. *Sociological Methods and Research, 33*, 315-348.
Loland, S. (2004). The Vulnerability Thesis and its Consequences: A Critique of Specialization in Olympic Sport. In: J. Bale & M. K. Christensen (Hrsg), *Post-Olympism? Questioning Sport in the Twenty-first Century* (S. 189–199). Oxford, New York.
Locander, W., Sudman, S., Badburn, N. (1976). An Investigation of Interview Method, Threat and Response Distortion. *Journal of the American Statistical Association, 1976*, 269-275.
Musch, J., Bröder, A., Klauer, K. C. (2001). Improving Survey Research on the World-Wide Web Using Randomized Response Technique. In U.-D. Reips, M. Bosnjak (Eds.). *Dimensions of Internet Science* (pp. 179-192). Lengerich et al: Pabst.
Pitsch, W., Emrich, E., Klein, M. (2005). Zur Häufigkeit des Dopings im Leistungssport: Ergebnisse eines www-surveys. *Leipziger Sportwissenschaftliche Beiträge, 46* (2), 63-77.
Pitsch, W., Emrich, E., Klein, M. (2007). Doping in elite sports in Germany: results of a www survey. *European Journal for Sport and Society, 4* (2), 89-102.
Plessner, H., Musch, J. (2002). Wie verbreitet ist Doping im Leistungssport? Eine www-Umfrage mit Hilfe der Randomized-Response-Technik. In B. Strauß, M. Tietjens, N. Hagemann, A. Stachelhaus. (Eds.), *Expertise im Sport* (pp. 78-79). Cologne: Strauß.

Reips, U.-D., Bosnjak, M. (Eds.) (2001). *Dimensions of Internet Science*. Lengerich, Papst Science Publishers.
Scheers, N. J. (1992). Methods, Plainly Speaking. A Review of Randomized Response Techniques. *Measurement and Evaluation in Counselling and Development, 24*, 27-41.
Shimizu, I. M., Bonham, G. S. (1978). Randomized Response Techniques in a National Survey. *Journal of the American Statistical Association, 73*, 35-39.
Stem, D. E., Steinhorst, K. (1984). Telephone Interview and Mail Questionnaire Applications of the Randomized Response Model. *Journal of the American Statistical Association, 79*, 555-564.
Tracy, P. E., Fox, J. A. (1981). The Validity of Randomized Response for Sensitive Measurements. *American Sociological Review, 46*, 187-200.

Jens Flatau, Frank Schröder

Motivations of elite athletes for and against doping substance use

1 Problem definition

For sporting competition, a collective and binding system of rules that apply to all contenders is constitutive.[9] By entering into competitive sport, athletes formally recognize and accept these rules. However, this says nothing about the degree to which they *genuinely* accept and comply with the rules, as is illustrated by the habitual tendency to break them and the need for umpires and referees. A well-known example is that of the foul in games. Whereas the complementary case, faking a foul on the part of an opponent – so-called diving – is generally perceived, at least by the opponent and the spectators, as illegitimate, a foul – at any rate when the referee inflicts a penalty – is accepted as part of the game. By contrast with a thief, for example, who – if caught – in addition to being prosecuted and receiving a "fair punishment" also suffers an enormous loss of social standing, a foul in sport is something quite normal and a perfectly legitimate "tactical move". By the same token, a so-called tactical foul in football, for instance, which prevents an opponent from scoring a goal but is not penalized with a yellow or red card, is seen as a good foul and is positively sanctioned by fellow team players, team officials and fans of the fouling player. So-called rough play that is perpetrated purely out of a lack of self-control and not for any rationally calculated reason, and results in the player being sent off, is felt to be a bad tactical move that is internally negatively sanctioned (for more about this cf. Emrich & Papathanassiou, 2003). Ultimately, what it comes down to is obtaining a competitive advantage that is not based on any sporting achievement through the rationally calculated use of tactics – regardless of whether they turn out to contravene the rules.[10]

Doping is another form of behaviour that runs counter to the rules. One of the main arguments in favour of establishing anti-doping rules is the principle of equal opportunity, which is constitutive for sporting competition. With the help of Merton's anomie theory (1968, 185 ff.), the occurrence of doping is relatively easy to explain (cf. also Emrich, 2004, 309 ff.). Only a very small proportion of competition participants enjoy a high degree of social recognition as a result of their ranking. In some disciplines, this goes hand in hand with a financial aspect that works in the same way. In Olympic Games, this recognition focuses on the three medallists in a contest, whereby – and this also applies to other tourna-

[9] In this respect the monopolies of the professional associations are functional inasmuch as they provide a set of rules that are valid for all contenders.
[10] This only applies provided the view is not taken that good and bad tactical moves with breaches of the rules are part, possibly even a constitutive part, of the respective sport.

ments – the winner is nearly always disproportionately rewarded, both materially and immaterially (cf. Emrich & Prohl, 2008).[11] At the same time, social recognition and material wealth represent generally accepted, institutionalized goals in every society in the world. If, for purely statistical reasons as explained above in the case of sport, a relatively high percentage of the population is not able to achieve these goals, this means that a relatively high percentage is in an anomic state inasmuch as the institutionalized goals are not or cannot be achieved with the institutionalized means – chiefly talent and training. The more individuals are in an anomic state, the more will decide to attain the institutionalized goal with non-institutionalized, i.e. illegal means, if these promise to significantly enhance their performance. Anabolic steroids, growth hormones and EPO can be said to have such a performance-enhancing effect.

Referring to numerous published statements by insiders in the field of elite sport (e.g. Jörg Jaksche[12], Kelly White[13], Angel Heredia[14]), as well as empirical studies in the field of sports science (Pitsch, Emrich & Klein, 2006 as well as Pitsch, Maats & Emrich in this volume), it can be assumed that in some disciplines at least, a substantial and thus significantly higher proportion of top-level athletes than are actually caught use doping substances (cf. the article by Emrich & Pitsch in this volume). A high proportion of norm breakers, in other words clearly non-existent norm validity, leads us first of all to question the legitimacy of the norm. Just as in a democratic system laws are (should be) made for citizens, so too in sport – a system constituted in principle from the bottom up – rules should be made for athletes. If a high proportion of citizens contravene a law, the *first* question to be asked is whether – with all due consideration of the consequences – the law in question should be abolished. As one example of such an adaptation of the law to reality, we can cite the opening of one-way streets for cyclists in some German towns and cities. Of course, apart from purely pragmatic considerations, such decisions must also take account of ethical issues such as human rights and for sure (often-neglected) human duties, where these are affected. Last but not least, the abolition of a law should actually reflect the will of the majority of those concerned.

Such a will to abolish the anti-doping framework obviously does not exist (in Germany), at least not if association officials, sponsors, the media and spectators are included in this circle, which – given the real decision-making powers of the associations when it comes to setting and changing rules – is to be strongly rec-

---

[11] An exception that confirms the rule is the Swiss sports media, where athletes ranked in the so-called "Diplomrängen" enjoy a high level of public recognition. One example is Swiss gymnast Ariella Kaeslin, who placed fifth at the Olympic Games in the vault event final and was voted "Swiss Sportswoman of the Year" for her achievement.

[12] In "Der Spiegel" dated 30.6.2007

[13] In the WDR TV production "Blut und Spiele" ("Blood and Games"), shown on 8.8.2007

[14] In "Der Spiegel" dated 11.8.2008

ommended.[15] The generally accepted illegitimacy of deviations from the norm, hand in hand with a perceived high rate of deviation, means that this represents a social problem.[16]

This automatically raises the question about suitable measures to mitigate, or ideally, to solve the problem. In principle, both positive and negative institutional sanctions designed to influence individual incentive structures (cf. Blum et al., 2005, 28) are conceivable here. At the moment, however, this is done exclusively via negative sanctions (competition bans) imposed on athletes who test positive for a prohibited substance. The situation described above relating to a (presumed) high estimated number of unknown cases however directly illustrates the inefficacy of this sanctioning system.

Firstly, since ingestion of doping substances (by contrast to sporting performances) is not directly observable, proof of their use – insofar as we are referring to drugs, the most commonly consumed prohibited substances – can only be obtained indirectly, i.e. by analyzing body fluids.

Secondly, this is confounded by the fact that precisely the above-mentioned, highly potent doping substances do not need to be taken in competition in order to be effective and – depending on the respective "detection window" – if discontinued in time prior to the tournament can no longer be detected in competition testing. This in turn leads to the separate problem of a system of out-of-competition testing, which, based on the postulate of equal opportunity in sport, will be discussed below.

Thirdly, knowledge about detection windows suggests that doping athletes, in cooperation with doping substance producers, dealers, physicians and coaches – who all profit from doping – do not act innovatively in the Merton sense merely by virtue of the fact that they resort to doping, but because in the sequential game against anti-doping investigators they, as rational actors, are continuously looking for new ways to avoid their violation of the norm being detected (cf. on this the articles by Daumann, Pitsch & Emrich as well as Emrich & Pitsch in this volume). This is often compared metaphorically to a race. On the part of the investigators, in addition to the already mentioned out-of-competition testing, this race encompasses refined methods of analysis or, most recently, long-term storage of doping samples in the hope that new analysis methods might subsequently be developed. Athletes and their entourage, on the other hand, either avail themselves of new substance derivatives (for which no means of detection as yet exist) or new methods of deception.

[15] The question as to the degree to which it contradicts the original idea of sports associations to orient decisions towards other stakeholders than the athletes themselves, and to what extent this requires hypocrisy, shall be discussed elsewhere.

[16] In light of the value-based doping discussion often also engaged in by sports scientists, we would like to point out that the present study aims to be free from value judgements in the meaning of Weber. We are therefore concerned with explaining phenomena, i.e. solving problems from a scientific and not from a definitional or judgemental perspective.

We can note that the assumed very low detection rate detracts significantly from the intended deterrent effect of the negative "ban from competition" sanction.

Given the inefficacy of the current anti-doping incentive system, we are forced to ask what alternative, institutionally settable selective incentives might exist. One problem here is that – as with the detection of doping usage – it is generally not directly observable. While a positive doping test at least delivers a relatively high degree of certainty that the tested athlete has actually consumed doping substances, given the deception methods described above a negative doping test does not necessarily prove the opposite (cf. the article by Pitsch as well as Pitsch & Emrich in this volume). Thus a structural uncertainty always remains with respect to how "clean" an athlete really is; whereby positive sanctions, such as honouring and awarding prizes to athletes who with almost 100 percent certainty are not doped, are eliminated as incentive mechanisms. And even where athletes attempt on their own initiative – for example by voluntarily agreeing to regular testing – to deliver credible proof of their compliance with the norms, the interest this generates on the part of the general public and sponsors and, linked to this, the social and monetary earnings prospects of these athletes (in more general terms: the explicit recognition for norm-compliant behaviour within a group with a high deviator rate) are likely to be pretty limited.[17] This raises the question of whether additional institutional incentives are conceivable at all (on a variant of this situation, namely rational investment in the semblance of honesty as opposed to genuine honesty cf. Emrich & Pitsch in this volume).

Incentives are directed at people's preferences, which are in turn based on their needs. Apart from the anomie theory, there are of course others, such as the systems theory, that for the most part logically describe the conditions that lead to the usage of doping substances (Bette & Schimank, 1995). However, because of their collective approach, they are not able to explain why it is that some athletes take performance-enhancing drugs, while others don't. This suggests athletes behave disparately regarding the question of illicit drug use, especially given that individuals have several and – at least with respect to their characteristics – interindividually different preferences (cf. Alchian & Allen, 1964, 12, 15). Only from knowing about these preference structures, i.e. the motivations for and against doping substance use, can incentive systems in the fight against doping practices be developed. This is a classic area of study of psychology and – given in this case the significant socio-economic context – in particular the social sciences. As is generally the case in the study of deviant behaviour, it is a difficult field of research to access because, as we know, test subjects tend to display socially desirable and hence (correlated across all answers) biased response behaviour. This is compounded by the fact that even if we in principle

---

[17] As an example for this, we can cite the German "Zehnkampf-TEAM" ("decathlon team"), who in this respect earn less compared to medallists.

assume a consciously and rationally deciding actor, there may be a non-intended tendency to conceal subconscious motives. Especially in the case of doping, which is reinforced by relatively high sanctions, the question is therefore to what extent it is possible to determine the true motives of elite athletes using conventional scientific methods. The answer to this question once again first requires epistemological explanation.

2 Popper's thesis of the three worlds

According to Popper's (1972, 154) philosophy, "three ontologically distinct subworlds" can be distinguished:

1. The "physical world" (the world of physical states)
2. The "mental world" (wishes, hopes, thoughts …)", i.e. the subjective world of self-conscious awareness (including sensory perceptions of the world)
3. The "world of intelligibles" (man's objectivised perception of the world; ibid.)

The second world is therefore the world we experience directly with our senses, that each of us subjectively perceives as everyday reality. Constructivism stressed that this perception represents a construct that may differ significantly from individual to individual. To Popper, however, by contrast with the constructivist approach, this neither means that knowledge about the first world is of little significance, nor that such knowledge is non-existent. According to Popper's theory, "the third world of mathematical and scientific theories" (ibid, 155) and the intersubjective provability using scientific methods represents cognitive knowledge about the first world. Although – fully in line with the Popperian concept of fallibility – the third world can only ever represent a non-completive map of reality with numerous as yet undiscovered flaws, nevertheless this map claims to be objective and finds application in the form of the methods (which in general function very well), with which human beings influence the first world. Although created by human beings, the objective status of the third world derives from the intersubjectivity of the research process as well as the multitude of individual scientific findings (of a multitude of scientists) that constitute it.

3 Methodological conclusions from the existence of the third world

Referring to the introductory problem of determining the truth in connection with doping, we arrive at the following generalized problem formulation: How, based on a scientific method that must satisfy the criterion of intersubjective verifiability, can we make the sub-conscious perceptible in order to obtain objective knowledge about the subject of analysis? We are not primarily concerned at this point with the question of whether doping is involved or not, but with what motives, as objects of World 3, directed the decision for or against doping.

By contrast, above all hermeneutical or so-called qualitative research methods in the social sciences are in general oriented towards generating knowledge by "empathizing" with the test persons and how they subjectively relate meaning to their perception and action. This, however, means that as "a subjective state of understanding" (ibid, 163), they move on the level of the non-objective second world. Rather than these psychological states, Popper (ibid, 186 ff.) believed the objective problem situation, underpinned by a "metatheory", should be the focus of analysis. Hermeneutics in Popper's view thus means understanding problems objectively and with critical-rational means through the reconstruction of situation-appropriate actions.

The only hermeneutical methodology we are aware of that claims to meet Popper's requirements – intended to mean here: striving for knowledge belonging to the third world – is the "objective hermeneutics" approach developed by Oevermann (2002) as a method to "explain typical, characteristic structures of new, little known developments and phenomena in little investigated fields of research and shed light on the underlying rules behind these phenomena" (translated from Oevermann, 2002, 1). This refers to the "objective meaning structures" and "latent sense structures" (ibid) of a case, which manifest themselves in – mostly written, but in principle also acoustic or image-based – observation protocols (data collected specifically for the analysis), as well as in "natural" documents and the "expressive forms" they contain (ibid). The objectivity thus derives from placement of the observation subject in a social and at the same time case-specific structural relationship which, while it can be exclusively reconstructed on the basis of the subjective expressive forms by the researcher with his knowledge of structural rules (or in more general terms: with the help of his theoretical knowledge) – for example of language or family relationships – must by no means necessarily be conscious to the subject as such. Objective hermeneutics therefore differs categorically from those methods that aim to reconstruct actions subjectively.

As a result of the logical-reconstructional approach, this method tends to be applied in so far little investigated and therefore non-prestructured fields of research. The inductive approach (on the problem of induction in general cf. Popper, 1959, 27 ff.), which, while essential for exploration is principally flawed when it comes to obtaining widely proven findings, is combined with deductive hypotheses analysis, in other words applying Peirce's (1965) "abductive" reasoning, i.e. inference of new rules. Hypotheses about rules are generated in the course (in the case of temporally prestructured material) of the sequential and extensive analysis and afterwards critically validated in the sequentially subsequent part of the observation protocol on the basis of the falsification principle. It is quite possible for several of these hypotheses, sometimes also known as "readings" (translated from Oevermann, 2002, 24), to compete with each other for validity; although this has to be qualified in the case of equal plausibility (generation) and evidence (falsification) by giving preference to the reading that requires the fewest additional assumptions ("economy principle"; translated from Oevermann et al., 1980, 25).

The sequentiality of objective-hermeneutical analysis derives from the fundamental (temporal) sequentiality of human existence. In the determination of sequences, sequential analysis makes a basic distinction between two quite different parameters. The first of the two parameters consists "in the totality of sequencing rules through which at any given location in the sequence the meaningfully possible connections are generated and also the possible meaningfully compatible previous actions are in each case identified and can be developed accordingly" (translated from Oevermann, 2002, 7). This parameter is to be understood as a set of algorithmic generative rules of very different types. These generative rules quite rudimentarily include, for example, the rules of linguistic syntax, but also the pragmatic and logical rules of speech acts and the logical rules for formal and material-factual plausibility. This totality of sequencing rules repeatedly generates at each location in the sequence a new scope of options and possibilities from which the causal agents present in this practice space then have to select an option. Which selection is actually made is determined by a second parameter that encompasses all components and elements of the predispositions of the different life practices or causal agents (ibid). The totality of predispositions of any given life practice is what determines its originality or character, indeed its objective "case structure uniformity" (ibid, 8).

The text sequences of the interview records are first analyzed according to the rules of objective hermeneutics for their purely linguistic meaning and hence detached from their case-specific context. This concentrates on the empirical material, "pure" language as an object of the third world, and not on related (speculative) intentions of the speaker, which are assigned to the second world.

At the beginning of a sequence-analytical case reconstruction, the text is interpreted with a high degree of extensiveness. Even the smallest expressive particles are examined for their meaning content. In the course of a sequential analysis, as well as on the level of the various cases, this extensiveness tends to decrease, providing that even after detailed analysis no new findings of importance for the case or the field of study impose themselves. However, within any one case reconstruction, it is always possible to analyze several, not directly sequentially linked segments with a high initial extensiveness.

In the present research context, the method of objective hermeneutics was applied in order to draw on the analyzed rule-based case structures to identify contexts of justification (belonging to the third world) that could help explain the phenomenon of doping in sport.[18]

[18] Of course, case structures also contain subjective parts (belonging to the second world) which also have to be taken into account in the analysis of case structure uniformities. However, they are *not the goal* of the analysis.

4 Method

Data was collected from nine interviews. One of the main goals of objective hermeneutical analysis – as with many other qualitative methods – consists in discovering ideal types characteristic for the field of study, which as it were act as the outer poles demarcating the borders of the field. Experiences with objective hermeneutics show that "in general, ten to twelve case reconstructions are adequate to obtain sufficiently reliable responses [to the research question, eds.], even in the case of more complex investigation questions" (translated from Oevermann, 2002, 17).

Each of the interviews is a non-standardized interaction. The rationale behind this is on the one hand to ensure in the interests of research field exploration that no findings are "missed" as a result of a predefined structuring of the interview (scripted questions). On the other hand, given the "sensitivity" of the topic, the aim is to create an atmosphere that as closely replicates a natural dialogue as possible.[19] The interviews were recorded with the help of a dictaphone and fully transcribed taking paralinguistic utterances into account.

The sample was composed based on the criterion of maximum contrast, whereby the contrasting characteristics listed below were partly derived from foregoing theoretical considerations, partly from the results of the preceding case analyses:

- *Use/non-use of doping substances (inasfar as known beforehand),* resulting from the underlying basic question of the study, namely what motivations lead to the choice of respective behaviour options.
- *Gender*, as a basic physical category of differentiation, given the mainly physical (performance- and health-related) effects of doping substances.
- *Structure of the sport-specific delivery of performance*, given that the performance-enhancing potential offered by doping is related to the contribution of individual condition-based skills in producing the performance results and therefore ultimately also the success.[20]
- *Degree of commercialization of the attained level in the respective sport*, to enable assessment of the significance of material motives in doping-related behaviour.

---

[19] One aspect of this is not launching into the interview with the topic of doping, but with a general, innocuous question about the interviewee's sporting career, thus allowing the interviewer to home in more implicitly on the topic of interest later.

[20] This correlation results first of all from the fact that the most potent as yet known active substance groups can boost endurance and (anaerobic) strength, while comparatively effective substances that enhance coordinative and mental skills do not (yet) exist. With team sports this is additionally compounded by the fact that the perception of individual performance is reduced. Thirdly, in the case of team *games*, it is not possible to exactly identify and measure the contribution of individual performance in the overall performance and fourthly, here the delivery of performance is also governed by (predominantly cognitively determined) interpersonal coordinative skills.

Table 1 presents the structure of the sample based on these characteristics.

Tab. 1: Study sample and interindividual contrastive characteristics

Athlete	Use of doping substances	Gender	Discipline	Degree of commercialization of the discipline
1	yes	male	American football	high
2	yes	male	Track and field (middle distance)	low
3	yes	male	Cycling (road)	high
4	no	male	Wrestling	low
5	no	female	Triathlon	low
6	no	female	Track and field (throw)	low
7	no	female	Rowing	low
8	no	male	Football	very high
9	no	male	Badminton	low

The evaluation took place within the scope of joint meetings of the concerned researchers.[21] This modus operandi increases the objectivity and reliability of the analysis because it generates more readings and several interpretations of expressive forms at the same time and non-applicable readings can, where appropriate, be more quickly falsified.

5 Results

In the following, we first present synopses[22] of three of the nine case reconstructions undertaken within the scope of the project, which adequately represent the ideal types determined in the study. In the first case, the biographical-structural details of the interviewed athlete are included in the interpretation, as they are relevant. Following this, we provide an overview of the essential results of the entire study.

[21] The interview material was evaluated partly within the scope of a research project run by Ulrich Oevermann himself.

[22] When presenting results obtained using the objective-hermeneutical method, we are faced with the problem that – especially if, as here, the intention is to present an entire project with several case reconstructions – the extensiveness of the interpretation would require an equally extensive written presentation of a complete case reconstruction, which is not possible within the scope of a collection of articles. Neither is the presentation of individual interview passages – as frequently used to illustrate and interpret qualitative research findings – meaningful, since on the background of the contingent sequentiality of objective-hermeneutical analyses they always build on what went before. Objective hermeneutics therefore to some extent defies conventional scientific publication and presentation forms.

5.1 Synopsis of the case reconstruction of athlete 1

Athlete 1 is raised with one sister and two half-brothers in a protestant Franconian family. The father, himself a businessman, demands a lot from his children, which not least because of their relationship status leads to a competitive situation between them. Athlete 1 drops out of secondary school in grade 9 (at age 14/15), starts training in the same field of business as his father and leaves home. After his training, he actually works for a short while in this field, but then becomes a full-time player with a German second-league American football team, for which he plays for two years, during which time the team is promoted to the first Bundesliga. He then moves to an NFL Europe team, which for him represents a further personal advancement. He plays there for several years, only later, after a number of injuries, to end his career in a lower division, where at the time of the interview he is working as a junior coach.

From the simple knowledge of these biographical details, we can already surmise the first case structure hypothesis that athlete 1, motivated by his failure in the eyes of his father, is very success-driven in American football in order to gain access to the "tough-guy male community" of American football players. Sport thus provides an ersatz communal relationship as well as an ersatz field for proving himself via his performance.

For athlete 1, the main incentive to dope lies on the conscious level in the comparatively high monetary reward or in the possibility to be able to earn a living from his income from sport, in the expectation of obtaining a future contract with a higher-placed club/franchise. The decision to take performance-enhancing substances as a means of increasing his chances of being admitted to such an organization is in athlete 1's eyes a perfectly rational one to achieve his goal of autonomy from the family home and at the same time prove to his family that he has made it professionally.

In the course of the interview, athlete 1 is at pains to show solidarity towards his ersatz community of American football colleagues (many of whom in his opinion use doping substances at professional level) and defend them against moral criticisms – which, though neither explicit nor implied by the interviewer, are obviously anticipated by the interviewee – by pointing out that illicit drug use is also common in other sports and is not a phenomenon in American football alone. He also points to the working environment, where illegal drugs are also consumed in order to enhance performance.

With respect to his own undetected violations of NFL Europe's anti-doping rules, athlete 1 argues exclusively in the logic of "getting caught". He does not see his behaviour as violating the fair play principle or cheating on his colleagues, and additionally points out the wide prevalence of doping.

On the subconscious level, athlete 1 decides in favour of a career in American football, and subsequently in favour of illicit drug use, because he needs the affiliation to the all-male community of American football players he has admired from the outside in order to compensate for his dysfunctional relations with his primary communal relationship, his family of origin.

The fact that consumption of doping substances poses a risk to his health personally plays no role in this decision. He justifies this to himself with the argument that he has only taken Ephedrine and rates the health risks associated with use of this drug as being very low. Football players who also resorted to higher-risk drugs, according to statements made by athlete 1, suppressed the health risks associated with their consumption and consequently did not allow these risks to deter them from using such drugs. By pointing out that we all take very high risks in our daily lives, for example when we drive along the motorway at 200 kilometres an hour, athlete 1 tries to relativize the risk athletes take when they consume such drugs and that critics accuse them of as irresponsibly gambling with their health, in the same way as the consumption of performance-enhancing substances in general. However, in this he forgets structural differences in the respective risks taken by the groups he compares. This is a further illustration of his attempt to defend the "guild" of American football players, with whom he still feels solidarity even beyond the end of his career, against anticipated outside attacks.

5.2 Synopsis of the case reconstruction of athlete 5

Athlete 5 can professionally pursue a career as a triathlete within the scope of the government-funded sport promotion schemes offered to employees of the German armed forces (Bundeswehr), from which she is mostly on release for training purposes. Her main motive for pursuing a professional career is her passion for the sport. She sees her Bundeswehr commitment as being limited to the duration of her elite sporting career; it is purely instrumental in nature.

Athlete 5 on principle personally rejects the idea of doping as being unethical; however based on her own observations, she assumes that the majority of her sporting colleagues use doping substances, as the requirement profile of the triathlon event suggests. She stresses that the decision of whether or not to consume performance-enhancing drugs is taken by every athlete autonomously and that even in a field with a (presumed) high rate of dopers, such as professional cycling, every individual has the possibility to abstain from doping. On the whole, we can observe in her a strong internalization of the fair play principle (here in the sense of abstinence from doping), which is based on her family social situation.

Apart from her value-based fundamental rejection of doping, she states that the fear of possible health-damaging side effects is enough to prevent her from consuming illicit drugs. She claims the extraordinary rush of ecstasy she feels when a sporting competition has gone well compensates her for any privations that go along with sporting success.

5.3 Synopsis of the case reconstruction of athlete 6

The main reason for athlete 6 not to take doping substances lies in the possible health risk associated with doping. For her, this includes the ability to bear healthy children, which she sees jeopardized among other things by the consumption of doping substances. She is also primarily intrinsically motivated to practise her sport and as a second motive against doping states a strong need to achieve success on her own merits.

She states that the prospect – after testing positive for doping – of having to face all those whom she knows through sport and to whom she has continuously expressed her negative stance towards doping would be intolerable for her. She would also consider the credibility of sport in general jeopardized if she were to test positive for doping and is also concerned to meet the expectations placed in her exemplary behaviour on the part of the association.

Additional motives for athlete 6 not to consume performance-enhancing drugs are her internalized fair play principle as well as what she sees as the elementary rules of ethics.

5.4 The three typologies

For all of the interviewees, the sequential analysis of the interview protocols in each case showed a passionate solidarity with the sport they practised. On the basis of this solidarity, athlete 1 continues to consume Ephedrine although it has already become clear to him that a financially highly lucrative career in the NFL is beyond his grasp. Having realized this, he is motivated to take the drug on the conscious level on the sole motivation that it enables him to continue to belong to an NFL Europe team. Subconsciously, he needs the affiliation to the outwardly admired all-male community following the breakdown of his relationship with his family of origin. Athlete 1 is still consuming Ephedrine at this time in the hope of meeting the performance requirements in the training camps for a place in the team squad. The camps are held before the start of the season and are a contest between roughly twice as many hopefuls as there are places in the team squad. The predominant motive for refraining from doping in the interim is the anticipated ban on competition that would result from a positive doping test. This would be tantamount to an at least temporary exclusion from the team communal relationship.

While violation of the anti-doping rules that apply in the respective sports does not cause athlete 1 to feel that he has committed a morally reprehensible breach of the rules or violated the constitutive precept of sporting fair play, athlete 5 could, in this respect, not be more of a contrast. Based above all on the values instilled in her by her parents, she could not conceive of taking performance-enhancing drugs, because this would mean she would be forced to lie to friends, colleagucs and the general public. Living such a lie would be intolerable to her.

The same motive is in principle to be found with athlete 6. Her negative attitude towards doping is, however, dominated by the fear of long-term detrimental effects on health, which anabolic steroids taken by some colleagues in her sporting discipline in the past have been proved to possibly cause. Added to this is a high desire for authentic, merit-based performance, which could not be satisfied through illicit drug use.

Both athlete 5 and athlete 6 state that sport gives them extraordinary euphoric experiences that they have not experienced in any other area of life. These may on the one hand be brought about intrinsically through competitive success and achieving a personal goal or extrinsically through the cheering and support of the spectators.

While athlete 6 has in the past considered the use of performance-enhancing drugs, but decided against it for the reasons mentioned, the triathlete categorically rejects the idea of consuming doping substances, above all on the grounds of the principle of honesty internalized in the course of parental socialization. The results of further interviews suggest that communication of corresponding values by coaches is less effective (cf. on this also Emrich & Klein, 2008, 131).

6 Discussion

The epistemological interest of the present study was firstly an impartial and fundamental one. The intention was to make a contribution to the understanding of elite athletes' individual decision whether to dope or not. Secondly, it was hoped this would produce findings for an application in the sense of an institutional sanctioning arrangement. The obtained findings are discussed against the background of these two aspects.

It comes as no surprise that the interviews analyzed within the context of the project reveal a strong financial motive for illicit drug use in elite sport. Nevertheless, the incentive to take performance-enhancing drugs appears to be almost as high in sports in which a fairly average income is earned even at top international level as in highly commercialized sports. The reason for this would appear to be the apparently strong desire to make sport a full-time career. This desire in turn results from a great passion for their sport, which characterizes all interviewed elite athletes, giving rise to the wish – at least for a certain time[23] – to make it their central purpose in life.

Doping thus not only becomes attractive where peak sporting performance goes hand in hand with exceptional earnings opportunities, but also where on the national level a small proportion of athletes are nurtured by public bodies, in other words above all in Olympic disciplines, which are supported out of national interest. As a consequence, this sponsorship leads to the situation that the institutional endorsement of sport with its claim "make sport your career" creates a strong incentive for illicit drug use.

As well as this individual motive, a social motive for doping was also established. This reflects the wish to belong to a group with the character of a communal relationship, which on the other hand is a perfectly natural human desire

[23] The observation that many athletes attempt to continue to make their sport the main focus of their lives even after the end of their active career, for example as full-time coaches, supports this interpretation.

(Maslow, 1943, 380 f.). In our modern society, in which extended families, tribes and clans barely play a role any more, the core family and peer groups represent the main forms of communal relationship. The latter are particularly important for adolescents and young adults – in other words at the same age as the majority of top athletes – when it comes to the process of flying the nest and overcoming the crises of adolescence (cf. Piaget, 1932). In this process, subcultural values and norms can develop within peer groups that conflict with those outside the group. Doping can, therefore, on the one hand occur as a rationally calculated act resulting from the need to belong to a community in situations where the level of doping-free performance jeopardizes membership. On the other hand, doping can be a social act because it conforms to intra-group norms.

On the side of motivations against doping, the study similarly identified the a priori very plausible anticipated negative side effects on health athletes ascribed to performance-enhancing drugs. Three points have to be made here. Firstly, the potential health-damaging effects vary considerably from one drug to the next. Since only certain drugs have a performance-enhancing effect in the individual sports, the threat doping has on health also varies depending on the sport. Secondly, all drugs can have different effects interindividually, which applies equally to doping substances and their side effects. Severe damage to health can, but must not necessarily, occur. Thirdly, subsequent damage to health caused by doping, like all future costs and benefits, is subject to discounting of the future (Elster, 1983).

The health motive appears to be more pronounced among women than men. We should note that this claim needs to be substantiated by quantitative surveys. Nevertheless, it is known from studies relating to various other areas of life that women are generally more averse to risk than men and consequently are less likely to act in a way that is detrimental to their health. It can be assumed that one reason for this lies in the responsibility that is inexorably linked to their own body to procreate, or at least a corresponding awareness for this, as mentioned by athlete 6.

As a further individual motive against doping, a "need for achievement" as described by McClelland (1961, vii) was established, whereby this achievement only enhances one's self-esteem if it is authentic, i.e. achieved on one's own merits (doping-free). According to Lenk (1992, 7, translated), this type of "merit-based achievement" is an expression of personal freedom of action. Following on from this, the rejection of doping in elite sport can also be interpreted as an individual freedom vis-à-vis the obligation imposed by the system to conform to doping (on this conformity with the system cf. Bette & Schimank, 1995), in other words as a conscious escape from maximum competition success as the exclusive goal.[24]

[24] Whether this motive only has prospects of action validity if the athlete, as in the given case, is in a position to practise the sport professionally even without the performance-

A further motivation against doping is a deeply internalized orientation of one's own actions towards the values and norms of fair play, which are in principle deemed as being violated by doping, even if a high rate of dopers can be presumed among colleagues and competitors.

This last, strictly value-rational action type is the only one within the scope of the present study that genuinely appears to be immune to doping, that rejects it on principle and at all costs. For all other types and their motivation constellations, the evaluation prior to the decision to act corresponds to that of the rational homo oeconomicus, albeit with individually different and above all not exclusively material desiderata. Knowledge about their motives and awareness of the rational choices behind their decisions make these types in principle susceptible to the right incentives.

Two additional groups of types with unambiguous preferences would also be logically conceivable within this scheme. Each of these is characterized by purposive-rational action[25] and values internalized during their socialization which, consequently, are virtually unalterable. Nevertheless, they immunize against non-doping, providing the sport concerned is one in which doping has a high probability of remaining unobserved and significantly enhances performance (type A). In sports for which no effective doping substances exist, actors abstain from their use, since all this does is generate costs (type B). This type of immunization differs from that described above, however, in that it does not last a lifetime, and contradictory decisions can occur on the action level if certain parameters change, for example in the case of type A the perceived probability of detection significantly increases or effective doping substances are developed for the sport practised by type B.[26]

One value that forms the basis for such purposive-rational action types could, for example, be winning as an exclusive goal, described by Gardner (1974, 51) as "the ethic of winning", whereby purpose and value would coincide.

The fact that type A as described above could not be established within the present research project might at first glance lead us to suppose that empirically it rarely occurs. It is, however, far more plausible to assume that doping as a "complex" object of research shows the limits of objective hermeneutics – on two levels. Firstly, even this approach is unable to solve the problem of sample selectivity which is inherent in any research on deviant behaviour – to the extent this depends on the "voluntary" cooperation of its test subjects. What is meant by this is that individuals who consciously behave in a socially undesirable way will not participate in such studies in the first place, not least because their par-

---

enhancing effect of doping substances is unclear, but given the ascertained strength of the motive to be a professional athlete can be assumed.

[25] The following is an *ideal-type* description for analytical purposes. Weber himself (1968, 26) already noted on the empirical existence of the purposive-rational action type that it was "essentially only a limiting case".

[26] This would thus be the sporting complement to the neoclassical variant of homo oeconomicus in economic theory as reacting exclusively to material incentives.

ticipation does not deliver any benefit in the sense of unambiguous preference; on the contrary, it is more likely to incur costs (e.g. opportunity costs such as training time or rest periods), and would not, in other words, be purposive-rational. If, on the other hand, (secondly) action types of this category do take part in studies, but for rational reasons make untrue statements, unless they entangle themselves in linguistic contradictions and thus lie, their untruths cannot be proved even with the help of objective hermeneutics.

This as a matter of principle raises the question of the expectations and reality of the method applied here. In particular, we need to ask whether the comparatively high amount of time invested in the sequential analyses is worthwhile in terms of actually significantly higher returns. It is certainly too soon to answer this question conclusively, especially since it can be assumed that the returns vary depending on the research question. It will ultimately only be possible to draw final conclusions on the basis of research focused on a comparison of different qualitative methods, where possible from a number of different fields of research.

7 Implications for combating doping

As observed in the introduction, the aim is to reduce the incidence probability of doping on the institutional side by creating positive and negative incentives (via corresponding sanctions). The survey of athlete's motives was intended to shed light on possible effective incentives.

It has already been noted that in light of the strong motive to make sport their main purpose in life, athletes are more likely to see performance-based endorsement as an incentive to dope where it would not be possible because of a low commercialization level to practise their sport on a full-time professional basis without backing by the government or the Stiftung Deutsche Sporthilfe (German Sports Aid Foundation). In this respect, use of illicit substances is the only way for athletes to attain the international peak performance level required for such sponsorship. This widens the range of sports in which doping becomes attractive. This situation once again illustrates the dilemma facing sport promotion: the desire and need on the one hand to enhance performance and at the same time to fight against (performance-enhancing) doping.

A functional positive incentive in the interests of combating doping in this context would be public recognition for athletes who abstain from doping. The problem with this, however, is the same as with the conviction of dopers: given the low selectivity of doping controls, it is almost impossible to publicly prove that no illicit drugs have been used.

On the assumption that actors weigh up the costs and benefits of doping, as proved to be the case for most of the interviewed elite athletes, then – on the premise that the probability of being caught cannot be raised in the short term – increasing negative punishments in the case of doping convictions is an effective method. However, in this connection sport encounters legal problems that go along with its professionalization. Neither longer bans on competition, which for professional athletes is the same as an occupational ban, nor higher penalties can hold up before an ordinary court if they violate the principles of non-discrimination and proportionality, especially when compared to existing rules for other occupational groups (cf. on this the article by Senkel in this volume). In general, similar legal problems exist in connection with the sanction approach of high claims for damages, which in the same way must from a legal point of view be proportional to the level of sanctions generally imposed in other social areas and may not threaten athletes' livelihood.

Attempts, for example on the part of the World Anti-Doping Agency (WADA), to raise the probability of detection by introducing corresponding guidelines for a more rigid testing system have been very inconsistently implemented in different countries, which when comparing sport on an international level has only further served to reduce equality of opportunity on this dimension (cf. the article by Senkel, Emrich & Momsen in this volume). Concrete measures to be cited here in particular include a higher number of out-of-competition tests and athletes providing uninterrupted prospective details of their whereabouts. As we know, athletes especially consider the latter to be a significant curtailment of their personal freedom. This is not just a question of subjective reservations, but also moves in the direction of unlawful or even unconstitutional measures. If tightened further, anti-doping measures would certainly come up against legal limitations in this area, too – provided these have not already been exceeded and it is simply a case of nobody having brought action yet.

Since, for the reasons stated above, it is virtually impossible to prevent doping by means of external incentives, the only deterrent for athletes where there is an excess of incentives in favour of doping is in all probability their own conscience. Based as it is on the internalization of the values of fair play, it is only possible to directly influence this immunization process in elite athletes to a very limited extent. This is because on the one hand they have generally already surpassed the sensitive phase for socialization of childhood and youth, and on the other hand socialization is only influenced to any appreciable extent by their original environment, and even there only by a few very close reference persons (particularly parents). Currently practised prevention measures do in fact also address children and youths. These include, for instance, educational brochures and the incorporation of anti-doping courses in coach licensing programmes; however, as we have seen above, the influence of coaches is comparatively low. A (theoretically considerably more effective) direct influence on parental upbringing from an early age is neither possible nor would it be ethically desirable. The only ascertained effective immunization against doping is therefore beyond institutional grasp and cannot be used as an anti-doping measure.

The socialization of an individual is a process that is influenced by other individuals, as well as (to some extent imparted through others) by cultural and economic factors. We can therefore assume that the international rate of athletes who are immune to doping varies, for example with alternative sources of income to professional sports or general lifestyle perspectives[27] – in other words: Morality is something one has to be able to afford.

The dependency of the rejection of doping on the internalization of ethical conceptions of competitive sport points to an approach already discussed in Emrich (2004, 327, translated) of a professional organization of sport "with a professional ethics that supports the value-rational and affectively legitimized order of the founding days, adherence to which is guaranteed by a corresponding internal social control system." Such a professional ethics in elite sport that rejects doping, based on the awareness that the collective – as the simple prisoner dilemma as a doping modelling illustrates – derives the greatest benefit without doping, could lead to a mutual and therefore more effective control of athletes. This could, for example, be achieved via the mechanism of "altruistic punishment" (Boyd et al., 2003), i.e. active negative sanctioning of deviators regardless of the individual costs incurred, for instance by publicizing obviously suspicious factors such as an abnormal improvement in performance or a change in voice pitch.

However, such practices also open the door for whistle-blowers. Added to this is the fact that the presumption of innocence is not only a legal, but in the broad population also a profoundly legitimate good, so that a conflict of values arises if doping cannot be proved beyond doubt. For the public – whether directly involved in sport or not – what follows from this is an urgent need for "hard" proof. Hence even internal controls do not get around the problem of the unobservability or difficult detectability of doping action, which ultimately merely means the problem would be redirected inwards.

8 Conclusion

The present study has delivered some insights into collective and individual conditions under which athletes decide whether to dope or not. On the one hand, this gives rise to a series of further research questions; it is therefore an exploration of the field of research in the intended sense. On the other hand, the expectation entertained at the beginning – that effective institutional measures to combat doping could be inferred from knowledge about motivations for action – could not be fulfilled.

In conclusion, we can note that two aspects account for the difficulty in combating doping. The first is the necessarily purely circumstantial observation but lack of hard evidence of doping. This applies at least to the majority of dopers and can be explained by the insufficiency of the current doping investigation practice of testing urine and, more recently, blood samples. The second problem is linked to the first and consists in the fact that sport – especially because of its commercialization – cannot act autonomously from state legal institutions. At the latest with the so-called Bosman ruling, it thus became clear that where sport

[27] For example, professional sports in the former GDR was among other things so attractive because it offered the privilege of travelling to other countries.

is practised as a profession, the individual must be granted certain rights, in the same way as in other areas outside sport. Added to these are the more general rights related to human dignity and individual freedoms, which, in sport, too, are (or should be) beyond discussion.

Even if it may appear incomprehensible to some apologists of fair competitive sport, the doping problem is, when viewed from the outside, less dramatic than it is often made out to be and communicated by sporting bodies and not least also the sports media. A comparison with other social action systems puts the matter in perspective. Like this, doping becomes a problem like many others, a form of deviating behaviour which one has to accept after weighing up conflicting interests in favour of more important rights, until perhaps one day the development of appropriate methods finally makes it possible to reconcile the detection of deviating behaviour with the preservation of individual freedom.

References

Alchian, A. A., Allen, W. R. (1964). *University Economics.* 2nd print. Belmont (Ca.): Wodsworth.

Bette, K.-H., Schimank, U. (1995). *Doping im Hochleistungssport.* Frankfurt: Suhrkamp.

Blum, U., Dudley, L., Leibbrand, F., Weiske, A. (2005). *Angewandte Institutionenökonomik. Theorien – Modelle – Evidenz.* Wiesbaden: Gabler.

Boyd, R., Gintis, H., Bowles, S., Richerson, P.J. (2003). The evolution of altruistic punishment. *Proceedings of the National Academy of Sciences of the United States of America, 100,* 3531–3535.

Elster, J. (1983). *Sour Grapes: Studies in the Subversion of Rationality.* Cambridge: Cambridge University Press.

Emrich, E., Papathanassiou, V. (2003). Der Schiedsrichter als Regelüberwacher und –durchsetzer in der Institution Sportspiel. *Spectrum der Sportwissenschaft, 15* (2), 6-19.

Emrich, E. (2004). Doping im Sport aus soziologischer Sicht. In Messing, M., Müller, N., Preuß, H. (Eds.), *Olympischer Dreiklang: Werte – Geschichte – Zeitgeist* (pp. 285-321). 2nd edition. Kassel: Agon.

Emrich, E., Prohl, R. (2008). Agonalität: Wettkampfsport im Spannungsfeld zwischen Erfolg, Moral und Ästhetik. *Leipziger Sportwissenschaftliche Beiträge, 49* (1), 67-88.

Emrich, E., Klein, S. (2008). *Übungsleiter und Trainer als Werte(ver)mittler. Eine Handreichung für die olympische Erziehung in Sportorganisationen und Schulen.* Kassel: Agon.

Gardner, P. (1974). *Nice Guys Finish Last. Sport and American Life.* London: Allen Lane.

Lenk, H. (1992). *Leistung in Sport und Gesellschaft.* Friedrichshafen: Stadt Friedrichshafen.

Maslow, A. H. (1943). *A Theory of Human Motivation.* Psychological Review, 50, 370–396.
McClelland, D. C. (1961). *The Achieving Society.* Princeton (N.J.): Van Nostrand.
Merton, R. K. (1968). *Social Theory and Social Structure.* Enlarged edition. New York (N.J.): Free Press.
Oevermann, U. (2002). *Klinische Soziologie auf der Basis der Methodologie der objektiven Hermeneutik – Manifest der objektiv hermeneutischen Sozialforschung.* Accessed on 16 November 2006 at http://ihsk.de/publikationen/manifest.pdf
Oevermann, U., Allert, T., Konau, E. (1980). Zur Logik der Interpretation von Interviewtexten. In Heinze, T. & Allert, T. (Eds.), *Interpretationen einer Bildungsgeschichte: Überlegungen zur sozialwissenschaftlichen Hermeneutik* (pp. 15-69). Bensheim: päd.-extra-Buchverlag.
Peirce, C. S. (1965). *Pragmatism and Pragmaticism. Collected Papers, Vol. 5.* Cambridge, Mass: Belknap Press.
Piaget, J. (1932). *The Moral Judgment of the Child.* London: Kegan Paul, Trench, Trubner and Co.
Pitsch, W, Emrich, E., Klein, M. (2005). Zur Häufigkeit des Dopings im Leistungssport. Ergebnisse eines www-surveys. *Leipziger Sportwissenschaftliche Beiträge, 46* (2), 60-74.
Popper, K. R. (1959 [orig. 1934]). *The Logic of Scientific Discovery.* London: Hutchinson.
Popper, K. R. (1972). *Objective Knowledge: An Evolutionary Approach.* Oxford: Clarendon Press.
Weber, M. (1968 [orig. 1922]). *Economy and Society. An Outline of Interpretive Sociology*. New York: Bedminster Press.

Frank Daumann

Doping in elite sport from the economic perspective

1 Problem definition

Doping is not a new phenomenon and can be found in practically every type of sport. However, some cases appear particularly spectacular. At best, available data permit us to only roughly estimate the extent to which doping substances are really used, since on the one hand testing is not comprehensive and only targets substances are on the negative list, and on the other hand tests do not detect every case of doping abuse: for example it is currently being claimed that the so far undetectable substance aminoimidazole carboxamide ribonucleotide (AICAR) was used quite frequently in the Beijing Summer Olympics (author unknown, 2008a).[28]

According to the IOC, 4,770 doping tests (3,801 urine and 969 blood tests) were carried out within the context of the 2008 Summer Olympics in Beijing (IOC, 2008). These revealed eight cases of doping, corresponding to around 1.6 per mil (author unknown, 2008b, cf. the article by Pitsch in this volume). A similarly low rate of doping cases is to be found at earlier Olympic Games: in Sydney in 2000 a total of 2,359 doping tests were performed, 11 of which proved positive (around 0.5%). In Athens in 2004, 26 out of 3,667 tested positive, which corresponds to around 0.7% (IOC, 2007). At the Winter Olympics in Salt Lake City in 2002, 700 tests uncovered 7 violations (1%). In Turin in 2006, out of 1,200 tests only one case of doping was detected (IOC, 2007).

According to WADA (World Anti-Doping Agency) statistics, a total of 223,898 controls were carried out worldwide in 2007 in both Olympic and non-Olympic disciplines. These produced 4,402 positive results, in other words around 2 percent altogether (WADA, 2009; cf. the article by Emrich & Pitsch in this volume).

In the meantime, the use of doping substances appears to be quite widescale in popular sports, too (Daumann, 2008, 37 ff.).

This situation gives rise to two questions which this article will attempt to answer from the economic perspective:

1. Why does doping occur in elite sport?
2. What meaningful steps can be taken to prevent doping?

One critical problem in connection with the phenomenon of doping is how to define it. Put simply, doping could be described as the practice of using substances or methods to improve an athlete's performance which are considered

[28] On the spread of the share of dopers in the collective of German athletes cf. the article by Maats, Pitsch & Emrich in the present volume.

reprehensible from a sports ethics point of view.[29] The performance-enhancing effect, of course, depends on the one hand on the type of doping substance used and on the other on the respective individual constitution of the athlete concerned as well as, admittedly, on coincidence. Thus, even if every participating athlete resorts to such substances, doping can lead to a change in the athletes' original ranking. Furthermore, it is characteristic for the use of doping substances that it is impossible to tell simply by looking at someone whether they are doped or not. On the contrary, a competing athlete wanting to prove that a rival has resorted to doping is likely to face prohibitive costs, especially since the latter can also refuse to consent to the necessary personal tests. What athletes can observe, however, is one another's performance results.

2 An economic explanation for the occurrence of doping in elite sport

The economic behaviour model proceeds from the assumption that actors take rational decisions.[30] When faced with a decision, they weigh up the costs and benefits of individual behaviour options and select the option that offers the most favourable ratio. If we extrapolate this behavioural model to athletes in a competitive situation, then we can assume these actors will take doping substances when the benefits of doping outweigh the costs (Breivik, 1987, 83).

2.1 Costs and benefits associated with the decision to dope

In a competition situation, athletes are confronted with the cost and benefit categories shown in Table 1, whereby we shall for now assume that no penalty-carrying doping ban exists (Daumann, 2003c; 2008, 83 ff.). In the following, we shall examine these cost-benefit aspects in more detail.

Tab. 1: Cost-benefit categories of doping. Source: Daumann (2008, 84)

Decision criterion / Categories	Benefit	Costs
material	Prize money Earnings from sponsoring and endorsement contracts	Procurement costs Costs of possible damage to health
nonmaterial	Prestige Popularity "Fame and honour"	Moral scruples Loss of standing

[29] For a detailed discussion of the definition of the phenomenon of doping cf. Daumann (2008, 11 ff.). On the problems of operationalizing this definition cf. e.g. Hoberman (1992), Bird & Wagner (1997), Maennig (2002), Daumann (2003a) and Bette & Schimank (2006).

[30] On the economic behavioural model cf., for example, Becker (1976) and Brunner & Meckling (1977) as representative for many.

2.1.1 *Benefits of doping*

The purpose of utilizing doping substances is to improve performance. Assuming conditions are otherwise the same, enhanced performance improves the chances of winning for the athlete who decides to use doping substances. The benefit of doping thus results from an easily won competition victory. This, in turn, can bring the winning athlete a material and nonmaterial gain. The athlete's victory is first of all rewarded with prize money. In addition to this, their income from sponsoring and endorsement contracts improves, as sponsors are naturally interested in athletes who are successful.

The rapidly advancing professionalization and commercialization in many areas of elite sport have contributed to raising the amounts of prize money and the sums spent on sponsoring and endorsements. If we consider the development of prize money in the men's singles in tennis at Wimbledon, for example, we can note a jump from £ 100,000 (1984) to £ 850,000 (author unknown, 2009a) – almost tenfold. Similar developments can be observed for many other tennis tournaments (author unknown, 2009c; 2009d).

Golfers, too, play for very high prize monies: in the PGA World Tour, prize money totalling US $ 277 million is paid out (author unknown, 2009e). The prize money for the WGC Accenture Match Play Championship alone accounts for US $ 8.5 million of this (author unknown, 2009e).

Cycling also boasts comparatively good earnings possibilities: for the Tour de France there is a detailed bonus catalogue for the various winning categories, such as the yellow jersey; the overall winner in 2009 received prize money of EUR 450,000 (author unknown, 2009f).

Even in rather less prestigious sports such as the marathon, prize monies have in the meantime soarcd: for example the overall winner in the World Marathon Majors goes home with US $ 500,000 (author unknown, 2009g). The 2009 winner of the Boston Marathon received prize money of US $ 150,000 (author unknown, 2009h). This trend towards higher prize monies and sponsoring earnings can also be seen in a number of other sports.

Apart from these material categories, winning also entails nonmaterial benefits. Good performances also bring fame and recognition. This is especially the case where the competition concerned has a high historical and idealistic background as with the Olympic Games.[31] Thus, for example, the average level of recognition of the medal-winning athletes in an endurance discipline at the Turin Winter Olympics was raised from 47.2% (2005) to 61.6% (2006). Similar increases can be shown for popularity (Richter, 2006; 2007). However, due to

[31] Admittedly, a rise in recognition, popularity and standing in turn has economic consequences: the athlete's marketability increases and higher sponsoring earnings are quick to follow; in the best case accompanied by additional endorsement contracts. Even after the end of their active career, well-known and popular athletes often have the possibility to contribute their experience and knowledge as sports experts in various media.

increasing differentiation among sports, the nonmaterial benefits are probably no longer as high as they used to be.

Thus the commercialization and professionalization of sport have made it possible to realize considerable sums of prize money; furthermore, some sports offer very good possibilities to get hold of lucrative endorsement contracts (Tietzel & Müller, 2000, 280 f.). It can therefore on the whole be assumed that the benefit of winning is very high. Seen like this, even a marginal improvement in the probability of winning can be very significant.[32]

2.1.2 Costs of doping

Doping incurs costs for the athlete, which again can be of a material or nonmaterial nature. Nonmaterial costs result because the athlete acts in violation of sports ethical norms and in doing so acquires a "guilty" conscience. Apart from these moral scruples, athletes also face a possible loss of standing, in other words, social sanctioning. These costs, however, are likely to play a less important role for athletes.

Apart from nonmaterial costs, athletes who dope face material costs. In addition to the consequential costs of damage to their health, these include costs for procuring the doping substances. Some doping substances can have a serious adverse effect on health. These health impairments usually do not set in immediately; generally they only become apparent much later. Athletes regularly ascribe low costs to these health risks because on the one hand they tend to underestimate the extent of the damage and the probability of it actually affecting them, and secondly because they have a very high preference for the present and therefore even if they did see things realistically, would still give costs they deem as relating to the remote future a low rating. In this context, Bird and Wagner (1997, 751) quote the American physician Goldman, who asked a number of elite athletes whether they would be prepared to accept subsequent death as the cost of five years of being undefeated. Fifty percent of the athletes answered in the affirmative. Although the results of such a survey can hardly be classed as valid, nevertheless they show the extent to which the risk to health resulting from doping and elite sport in general is gravely underestimated.

When it comes to procurement costs, the material earnings in commercialized sports can easily compensate any costs incurred. Thus the cost of one EPO injection at EUR 6 and an entire year's supply for EUR 100,000 is not really of any material consequence. When it comes to self-medication, the costs are much lower still: growth hormone pills and amphetamine tablets are available via the Internet at unit prices of just over $ 1 (author unknown, 2009b). A course of EPO – to achieve the desired performance enhancement three two-week courses are regularly taken – costs around EUR 1,000 (Gallbronner, 2007). Courses of

---

[32] This refers to the 'superstar effect' (Rosen, 1983), according to which even a marginal improvement in an athlete's performance can cause a significant material earnings increase due to strong ranking effects.

anabolic steroids lasting six weeks and longer can be procured over the Internet for less than EUR 100 (Daumann, 2008, 87 ff.).

Thus on the whole it can be assumed that athletes rate the costs incurred by doping as comparatively low.

2.2 Doping in a one-off competition

Put simply, the occurrence of the doping problem can be explained statically as follows: two athletes *i* (where $i \in \{1,2\}$) meet in a simultaneous competition in an individual sport without a penalty-carrying doping ban. The respective set of courses of action S_i contains the actions (strategies) doping d_i and abstinence from doping $\bar{d}_i$, so that $S_i = \{d_i, \bar{d}_i\}$ applies.

By winning, the individual athlete derives the above-mentioned benefit, which shall be described for athlete *i* as U_i. This win occurs with a probability of p_i, which depends on the choice of personal strategy $s_i \in S_i$, on that of the rival athlete $s_{-i} \in S_{-i}$ as well as on other factors such as relative personal fitness r_i and on coincidence – shown by the coincidence variable v: $p_i = p_i(s_i, s_{-i}, r_i, v)$. In this, it can be assumed that athlete *i*'s probability of winning decreases if rival *–i* takes doping substances.

(1) $$p_i(s_i, \bar{d}_{-i}, r_i, v) > p_i(s_i, d_{-i}, r_i, v)$$

therefore applies for all $i \in \{1,2\}$ and for all $s_i \in S_i$.

While the costs of pursuing strategy $\bar{d}_i$ are negligible for the given context ($C_i(s_i) = 0$, for $s_i = \bar{d}_i$), on opting for strategy d_i an athlete *i* incurs the costs explained above ($C_i(s_i) > 0$, for $s_i = d_i$).

Thus the overall benefit of an athlete *i* can be described as follows:

(2) $$E_i(s_i, s_{-i}) = p_i(s_i, s_{-i}, r_i, v)U_i - C_i(s_i)$$

where $C_i(s_i) = 0$ for $s_i = \bar{d}_i$, and $C_i(s_i) > 0$ for $s_i = d_i$.

Tab. 2: Payoff matrix for illicit drug use (based on Daumann, 2003b)

		Athlete 2	
		Abstinence from doping	Doping
Athlete 1	Abstinence from doping	$E_1(\bar{d}_1, \bar{d}_2) // E_2(\bar{d}_2, \bar{d}_1)$	$E_1(\bar{d}_1, d_2) // E_2(d_2, \bar{d}_1)$
	Doping	$E_1(d_1, \bar{d}_2) // E_2(\bar{d}_2, d_1)$	$E_1(d_1, d_2) // E_2(d_2, d_1)$

Given the mutual dependencies of the strategies chosen by the two athletes, the decision problem of both athletes can be represented with the help of a payoff matrix (Table 2). Rationally behaving actors will weigh up the costs and benefits of doping and select their strategy accordingly. The statements made above give reason to expect an overcompensation of the doping-related costs, and consequently of the doping-related increase in benefit, as a result of the improved probability of winning, i.e. for $E_i(\bar{d}_i, s_{-i}) < E_i(d_i, s_{-i})$ (for all $s_{-i} \in S_{-i}$). It can thus be assumed that in a world without a penalty-carrying doping ban, rationally behaving actors will give preference to the doping strategy. With $E_i(\bar{d}_i, s_{-i}) < E_i(d_i, s_{-i})$ for all $s_{-i} \in S_{-i}$ doping thus represents a predominant strategy for the given athlete i, so for a one-off competition the strategy cluster $[E_1(d_1, d_2), E_2(d_2, d_1)]$ is realized. Due to the costs inherent in practising the doping strategy, this cluster turns out to be suboptimal; in this comparative-static analysis, the cluster $[E_1(\bar{d}_1, \bar{d}_2), E_2(\bar{d}_2, \bar{d}_1)]$ would be preferable. The athletes thus find themselves in a prisoner dilemma (Breivik, 1987; Bird & Wagner, 1997; Eber, 2009).

2.3 Doping with changed parameters

In addition to the narrow reference framework of a one-off simultaneous competition in an individual sport with two actors, the following parameters seem worth considering:

1. repetition of thc competition,
2. removal of competition simultaneity in sports with precisely measurable results and
3. competition between teams.

The impact of these parameters on the choice of strategy is examined below in more detail.

2.3.1 Decision in the case of iterated simultaneous competitions

Repeated competitions could lead to implicit or explicit collusions between the rivals in the form of a mutual agreement to abstain from the doping strategy. By means of a supergame strategy, the suboptimal static Nash equilibrium $[E_1(d_1, d_2), E_2(d_2, d_1)]$ for both players could in this case be substituted by $[E_1(\bar{d}_1, \bar{d}_2), E_2(\bar{d}_2, \bar{d}_1)]$ (Friedman, 1971). This would, for example, be the case for identical rivals with a not-too-high preference for the present, who assume that the competition can be repeated an infinite number of times, and who can observe the actions of their respective rival. In reality, these conditions are in fact rarely met: on the grounds of their physical constitution, athletes must assume that the length of their career is inherently limited and, what's more, that sporting injuries may end it prematurely. Moreover, the individual athlete is constantly confronted with new rivals, since in most sports the pool of elite athletes is very large as a result of the growing level of competition internationalization (Breivik, 1987, 89). Finally, athletes are only able to inadequately gauge their rival's choice of strategy, since observable performance not only depends on the strategy, but also on other non-controllable influencing factors, which make clear inferences about the chosen strategy difficult (Wagner & Keck, 1990, 440).

Using the example of a repeated game with overlapping generations of players, Crémer (1986) is, however, able to show that, despite a finite number of games for the player and changing players, a subgame perfect strategy profile exists that leads to a higher individual payoff than the discounted payoffs in the static Nash equilibrium. This subgame perfect strategy profile, however, also allows for players who quit after the defined number of games to defect in their final game. Extrapolated to the problem of doping, this means that individual athletes, despite changing players in repeated competitions and a finite number of competitions, abstain from doping except in their last ever competition, provided the chosen action alternative can be observed ex post. The lack of ex post observability by the respective rival would be considered totally unproblematic if the chosen strategy could be inferred directly from the demonstrated performance, which is the case if the performance level of the athlete concerned were known and the effects of doping occurred deterministically. In reality, however, neither situation is likely; rather, the athlete's performance also depends on exogenous influencing factors that defy precise evaluation, so that at best there is a stochastic correlation between strategy and demonstrated performance.

Against this background, Green und Porter (1984) show – this time with identical actors – that a successful collusion between competitors can be realized with a trigger strategy. This trigger strategy, which is explained by the authors with the help of an oligopoly situation, in which the market price on the one hand depends on the non-observable output of the respective rival's performance and on the other on unpredictable fluctuations in demand, consists in an alternation between cooperative and punishment phases of fixed duration. The latter are triggered if the trigger price is not achieved. Extrapolated to the problem of doping, an individual trigger performance level could be agreed between athletes, which, if exceeded – irrespective of whether helped along by doping or not – would also entail a sanction phase. This, however, would presuppose that a doping-free trigger level can be determined for every athlete. However, even supposing such a level could be established, it would still not be possible to eliminate doping entirely, since the sanction phases would be triggered by random fluctuations in the performance level, and these in turn would result from the other competitors choosing the doping strategy for the duration of the sanction phase. A supergame strategy leading to a total abstinence from doping thus appears extremely improbable in light of the given parameters.

2.3.2 Decision in sports with precisely measurable results

So far we have looked primarily at sports where there was simultaneity of competition. If the results of the competition can be classified in a historical table of best performances, such as is the case in the 100 m sprint, for example, then the condition of simultaneity is no longer met. The individual athlete is not only competing against his or her rival, but also against previous successes of other athletes, with the aim of being added to the historical table of best performances. Such a ranking then permits the athlete to exploit exclusive temporary monopoly rent – for example as the reigning world champion in the 100 m sprint (Keck & Wagner, 1990, 109; Tietzel & Müller, 1999, 7; 2000). Consequently, the incentive to dope is likely to be considerably higher in sports with precisely measurable results than in other individual sports where single results cannot be measured in this way (Keck & Wagner, 1990, 109).

2.3.3 Decision in team sports

In competition between teams, the result has collective character and is thus an open invitation to take the free rider position. To the extent that, by analogy with Olson (1965), corrective measures in the form of social sanctions are unsuccessful, which is likely to be the case especially for team sports with large teams, the incentive to dope in such competitions is much lower (Tietzel & Müller, 1999, 6 f.). Here, however, competition over team positioning and a high separability of the team result can have a compensatory effect. Thus team sports such as baseball, which is characterized by its individuality in the collective, should show a significantly higher incentive to dope than team sports that require a high level of cooperation between the players and in which the contribution of the individual player to the overall result is barely ascertainable (cf. the findings of Pitsch, Maats & Emrich in this volume).

2.4 Intermediate result

Where there is a lack of preventive anti-doping instruments, athletes are shown to be exposed to very high incentives to use performance-enhancing substances. This incentive is likely to be highest in sports with precisely measurable competition results and in which historical tables of best performances play an important role. In team sports, the incentive is lower because of the collective-good character of the competition result. Presumably, however, all athletes in elite sport would resort to doping if no corresponding anti-doping measures were implemented.

3 Anti-doping instruments

These findings logically lead to two questions:

1. Is an intervention to prevent doping, irrespective of on what level, meaningful?
2. And if the answer to question 1 is "yes": What instruments prove appropriate in the fight against doping?

ad 1: In principle it can be assumed that doping reduces the quality of the entertainment service "sporting competition" (cf. the article by Emrich & Pitsch in this volume). Against this background, anti-doping interventions could at least appear meaningful to the organizers of sporting competitions.[33]

[33] On the discussion about the justification of (government) anti-doping measures cf. Daumann (2003a; 2008; 2009).

ad 2: An instrument to prevent doping should in the first instance match the objective, i.e. it should be capable of effectively preventing doping. Apart from this main purpose, other conditions exist, which should also be met (Bird & Wagner, 1997, 755; Wagner, 1994, 102, 120):

- Avoid degeneration of competition: the instrument should not lessen the incentive to win, which is inherent to sport, so that a high level of excitement is maintained.
- Low realization costs: implementing the instruments should involve as few costs as possible.
- Unambiguous results: the instrument should ensure that clear winners can be announced at the end of the competition and consequently subsequent annulations can be avoided.
- Uphold athletes' scope of freedom: any anti-doping measure should infringe upon athletes' freedom of action as little as possible.

Against the background of athletes' competition-based decision process, the anti-doping instruments that can be used (cf. Fig. 1) can be classified according to whether they focus on the benefit or on the cost category, or whether they increase collusion, i.e. cooperation between the athletes.

It has been shown that only a penalty-carrying ban with its combinations comes closest to meeting the requirements. For this reason, we dispense here with an evaluation of the other measures.[34]

A penalty-carrying anti-doping ban in elite sport on the one hand generates additional doping costs in the form of the expectancy value of the sanctions; and on the other hand the benefit of winning is reduced for the doping athlete. The original overall benefit of the athlete (2) changes if *F* is the level of sanction and q the probability of detecting doping, as follows (Dilger & Tolsdorf, 2004):

$$E_i^*(s_i, s_{-i}) = (1-q)p_i(s_i, s_{-i}, r_i, v)U_i - C_i(s_i) - qF \quad (3)$$
for $s_i = d_i$.

Implementing the ban requires tests in order to ascertain transgressions and impose sanctions where violations of the ban are detected. The detection probability q influences both the benefit of winning as well as the additional costs of doping, which are further determined by the level of sanctions *F*. The actual detection probability in turn depends on the quality of the tests and the size of the sample. The better the quality and the bigger the sample population, the higher the probability of detection under otherwise identical conditions will be. Sanctions can exist in material and nonmaterial form, whereby the latter cannot be employed in a targeted way. In a material sense, the "doping" strategy can be sanctioned by means of monetary penalties or competition bans. Competition bans hit successful athletes harder, because they would suffer higher opportunity

[34] An extensive discussion of the other measures can be found in Maennig (2002, 77 ff.) and Daumann (2008, 105 ff.).

costs as a result.[35] These are comparatively ineffective with athletes nearing the end of their career since their opportunity costs are relatively low if caught (Maennig, 2002, 78).

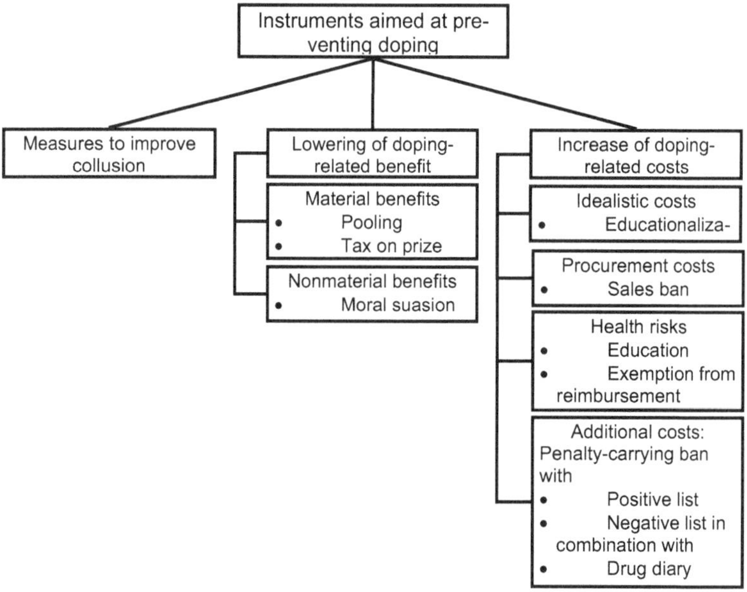

Fig. 1: Anti-doping instruments (based on Daumann, 2008, 108).

The disadvantage of every penalty-carrying ban based on anti-doping testing is the lack of unambiguous results: subsequent disqualification of drug cheats lessens the quality of the entertainment service because the winners cannot be determined until long after the competition is over. The problem of a lack of clear results is significantly reduced, however, the more the measures match the objective, because this would deter potential drug cheats and hence considerably reduce the number of subsequent disqualifications.

In this context, it should again be noted that the definition of doping presents an important stumbling block (Daumann, 2009): an abstract, i.e. essentialist definition of the term does not allow the phenomenon to be adequately described and reconciled with generally held conceptions; for example the regularly applied attributes detrimental to health, unfair, unnatural and non-transparent do not allow a clear-cut definition. In order to make doping litigable, we need,

[35] Nevertheless, staggered monetary penalties in line with performance capabilities would also be conceivable: In Berentsen's (2002) proposal, correspondingly higher sanctions would be imposed on higher ranking athletes, or tests should be carried out in such a way that the probability of detection is higher for these rankings.

therefore, to fall back on an enumerative definition: a list which contains either all permitted actions (positive list) or all prohibited actions (negative list).

A penalty-carrying ban based on the positive list would on the one hand lead to significant realization costs as a result of the many substances to be tested. Furthermore, athletes who fall sick would have to forgo a number of effective therapies and would only be able to participate in medical progress with considerable time lags (Keck & Wagner, 1990, 112; Wagner, 1994, 113). Against this background, a ban based on the positive list does not seem very suitable, above all because the high implementation costs would make across-the-board testing impossible.

The disadvantage of a ban based on the negative list lies in evading the list: it offers athletes strong incentives to consume performance-enhancing substances and methods that are not included on the list. This incentive is all the stronger, the more effective the controls and the higher the sanctions are (Keck & Wagner, 1990; Wagner, 2000, 294). The negative list thus not only initiates simple avoidance tactics, but also the development of doping innovations (Bird & Wagner, 1997, 754). The former reduce the productive efficiency of doping, as athletes switch to suboptimal, non-prohibited doping substances which in some cases entail an even greater health risk (Grupe, 1989, 10 ff.). The latter allow innovators for a comparatively long time to exploit an innovation rent in the form of improved chances of winning resulting from a negative list that is not up-to-date and a lack of detection methods. The extent to which a ban based on the negative list can effectively prevent doping depends to a large degree on how quickly the information asymmetry vis-à-vis doping innovators can be eliminated.

The introduction of an accompanying drug diary is onc possible method to reduce this innovation incentive. This drug diary records all drugs taken by the respective athlete (Bird & Wagner, 1997; Wagner, 1994; Wagner & Keck, 1990). Use of substances or methods that are either not listed in the drug diary or are on the negative list incurs sanctions. This necessitates extensive tests, which, however, entail very high realization costs (Wagner, 1994, 114). If, due to the considerable realization costs of this measure, testing intensity is reduced, doping innovations can continue to be covered up. If this were the case, there would be no significant reduction in the innovation incentive and the main disadvantage of a ban with sanctions based on a negative list would be largely the same.

An alternative approach is that of the innovation bonus, which is intended to provide an incentive to reduce the pioneering lead (Daumann, 2003a; 2003b; 2003c). This bonus is nothing other than a reward for athletes who register a doping innovation – irrespective of whether or not they are the ones who have developed the innovation.

This measure is intended to address a target audience as wide as possible in order to increase the probability that actors can be found who attach greater importance to the bonus than to keeping up the pretence.

An innovation in terms of the innovation bonus is characterized by the fact that it

- significantly enhances performance and
- is not yet included on the negative list.

A registered doping innovation is first tested for its performance-enhancing effect. If this can be established, the innovation is placed on the negative list and from then on its use can be penalized.

When deciding on the level of the bonus it should be ensured on the one hand that the amount paid out is high enough to constitute a real incentive for a larger number of actors with knowledge about such a doping innovation to come forward. On the other hand, the bonus should not bring about a misallocation in the field of research and development. Such a borderline situation exists in the pharmaceutical industry to the tune of several hundred million euros that is necessary for the development of every new drug.[36]

Furthermore, in order to ensure that ineffective innovations are not simply registered on a hunch, causing the costs of efficacy testing and the whole testing procedure to escalate, the registering actor should be called upon to contribute an appropriate amount towards research costs for proving their efficacy. Such an assumption of costs prevents rash registrations; however, the amount should not be so high that it too strongly outweighs the incentive to register individually effective doping innovations on the grounds of possibly risky upfront payments.

From the aspect of meeting objectives, a ban combined with the innovation bonus would relativize the main weakness of the conventional ban solution: the innovation bonus would mean that the negative list would be regularly updated, shortening the time lead of those athletes who utilize the innovation. Still unsolved, however, is the problem that the development of low-cost detection methods often lags considerably behind, as the example of EPO demonstrates.

Combining a ban with the innovation bonus would completely eliminate a degeneration of competition; athletes would also still have the same scope of freedom as with the orthodox ban solution. However, this instrument would also mean accepting disadvantages in terms of unambiguous results, because subsequent disqualifications cannot be completely ruled out.

However, the combined solution appears to entail significantly higher costs than the conventional solution. Since the costs for implementing the controls are similar for both methods, the cost ratio on the one hand mainly depends on the level of the innovation bonus and the proportional costs for the proof of efficacy, and on the other on the necessary research costs for compiling the negative list. Given that anti-doping research in the conventional solution is carried out for the most part blindly, it can be assumed that, given identical ex post quality of the negative list, the research costs for updating the negative list are higher for the

[36] Di Masi et al. (2003) estimate the research and development costs for the development of a new authorized drug at an average US $ 800 million; these vary significantly, however, depending on the area of indication (Adams & Brantner, 2006).

conventional solution than the updating costs for the combined solution. In this respect, a ban combined with the innovation bonus not only gains the advantage from the perspective of the reduced innovator lead, but also from the cost perspective.

The innovation bonus would have an additional interesting side-effect: it would improve the quality of doping. Less effective and ineffective "doping substances" are edged out, because due to efficient updating and given corresponding rewards of the bonus system athletes must assume that all effective doping substances are included on the negative list. Substances and methods that are sometimes advertised as secret tips, but are not on the list, do not possess this quality attribute. They can therefore be identified by the athletes as ineffective, because otherwise a corresponding provider would have registered this supposed doping substance and collected the innovation bonus. Against this background, the innovation bonus is a considerable improvement over the simple penalty-carrying ban.

4 Conclusion

The present study has shown that the elite sport framework provides strong incentives to use doping substances. These incentives are greatest for sports with precisely measurable results, since the athlete is not only competing against his or her current rival, but is also fighting for a placement in the historical table of best performances. By contrast, the incentive proves weakest in the case of team sports, because here the competition result has a collective-good character and therefore adopting the free rider position can seem a meaningful strategy. On the whole, it can be assumed that forgoing anti-doping measures would lead to an across-the-board utilization of doping substances.

There is a wide range of measures available to combat doping, which turn out to be variably suitable. A penalty-carrying ban based on the negative list comes closest to the objective; however it also offers strong incentives to evade the negative list, in other words in favour of doping innovation. One way out of this dilemma is presented by the accompanying innovation bonus, which rewards the registration of doping innovations. This makes it possible to somewhat reduce the time lead for doping innovators and update the doping list more regularly. This method, however, remains ineffective as long as practicable tests for the newly identified substances are not available.

The possibility of liberalizing doping for adult athletes should also not be totally ruled out: liberalization would presumably lead to across-the-board doping in elite sport, but not necessarily to higher health risks for athletes, since it would also permit better supervision and supply. The risks attached to new methods and substances with unknown side effects could be kept within bounds through accompanying medical supervision. Whether sport would thus lose its role model function is questionable, especially given that the role model argument is always based on a sporting ideal that in reality does not exist and never has existed.

References

Adams, C. P., Brantner, V. V. (2006). Estimating the Cost of New Drug Development: Is It Really $802 Million?, *Health Affairs*, 25, 420-428.

Author unknown (2008a). *Neues Dopingmittel AICAR*, accessible under: http://www.on-dope.de/, [retrieved on 22.11.2008].

Author unknown (2008b). *More Beijing drugs shame*, accessible under: http://www.timesonline.co.uk/tol/sport/olympics/article5114573.ece, [retrieved on 11.11.2009].

Author unknown (2009a). *Prize Money at Wimbledon (1968-2009)*, accessible under: http://aeltc2009.wimbledon.org/en_GB/about/history/prizemoney_history.html [retrieved on 12.11.09].

Author unknown (2009b). *Amphetmine Salt Combo Oral*, accessible under: http://www.medscape.com/druginfo/pricebrandimage?cid=med&drugid=32556&drugname=Amphetamine+Salt+Combo+Oral&monotype=pricebrandimage [retrieved on 12.11.09].

Author unknown (2009c). *2009 US Open Tennis Championship*, accessible under: http://www.altiusdirectory.com/Sports/us-open-tennis-2009.html, [retrieved on 18.11.09].

Author unknown (2009d). *2006 US Open Prize Money Tops Record $18.5 Million with Potential $21.1 Million Payout*, accessible under: http://www.tennisnews.com/exclusive.php?pID=12445, [retrieved on 18.11.09].

Author unknown (2009e). *2009 Golf PGA Tournaments Schedule*, accessible under: http://www.altiusdirectory.com/Sports/2009-golf-tournaments-schedules .html, [retrieved on 18.11.09].

Author unknown (2009f). *What is there to win?*, accessible under: http://www.letour.fr/2009/TDF/LIVE/us/reglements.html, [retrieved on 18.11.09].

Author unknown (2009g). *Prize Purse*, accessible under: http://www.worldmarathonmajors.com/US/series/article/21/, [retrieved on 18.11.09].

Author unknown (2009h). About the Boston Marathon, accessible under: http://www.worldmarathonmajors.com/US/events/article/27/, [retrieved on 18.11.09].

Becker, G. (1976). *The Economic Approach to Human Behavior*. Chicago: University of Chicago Press.

Berentsen, A. (2002). The Economics of Doping. *European Journal of Political Economy,* 18 (1), 109-127.

Bette, K.-H., Schimank, U. (2006). *Doping im Hochleistungssport: Anpassung durch Abweichung*. 2nd edition. Frankfurt am Main: Suhrkamp.

Bird, E. J., Wagner, G. (1997). Sports as a Common Property Resource. A Solution to the Dilemmas of Doping. *Journal of Conflict Resolution*, 41, 749-766.

Breivik, G. (1987). The Doping Dilemma – Some game theoretical and philosophical considerations. *Sportwissenschaft*, 17, 83-94.

Brunner, K., Meckling, W. H. (1977). The Perception of Man and the Conception of Government. Journal of Money, Credit, and Banking, 9, 70-85.

Crémer, J. (1986). Cooperation in ongoing organizations. *Quarterly Journal of Economics*, 101, 33-49.

Daumann, F. (2003a). Staatlicher Handlungsbedarf bei Doping im Hochleistungssport? *ORDO. Jahrbuch für die Ordnung von Wirtschaft und Gesellschaft*, 54 , 243-268.

Daumann, F. (2003b). Doping im Hochleistungssport aus sportökonomischer Sicht. *Sportwissenschaft*, 33, 174-190.

Daumann, F., (2003c). Doping im Hochleistungssport – Ursachen und Interventionsinstrumente aus ökonomischer Sicht. *Jahrbuch für Wirtschaftswissenschaften*, 54th volume, 214-230.

Daumann, F. (2008). *Die Ökonomie des Dopings*. Hamburg: Merus.

Daumann, F. (2009). Die drei Grundprobleme des Dopingphänomens: Plädoyer für eine Liberalisierung des Dopings, to be published soon.

Dilger, A., Tolsdorf, F. (2004). Doping als Wettkampfphänomen. In Horch, H.-D., Heydel, J., Sierau, A. (Eds.). *Events im Sport – Marketing, Management, Finanzierung* (pp. 269-280). Cologne: Institut für Sportökonomie und Sportmanagement.

DiMasi, J. A., Hansen, R. W., Grabowski, H. G. (2003), The Price of Innovation: New Estimates of Drug Development Costs, *Journal of Health Economics*, 22, 151-185.

Eber, N. (2009), The Performance-Enhancing Drug Game Reconsidered. A Fair Play Approach. *Journal of Sports Economics*, 9, 318-327.

Friedman, J. (1971). A non cooperative equilibrium for supergames. *Review of Economic Studies*, 38, 1-12.

Gallbronner, U. (2007). Doping – Der scheidende Sponsor der deutschen Radfahrer will künftig Epo vertreiben. *Bietigheimer Zeitung Online* (article dated 25 Sept. 2007), accessible under: http://www.bietigheimerzeitung.de/bz/html/news/brennpunkt.php4 [retrieved on 2 October 2007].

Green, E., Porter, R. (1984). Non cooperative collusion under imperfect price information. *Econometrica*, 52, 87-100.

Grupe, O. (1989). Doping und Leistungsmanipulation – Zehn Gründe für konsequente Kontrollen. *Olympisches Feuer*, 10-13.

Hoberman, J. (1992). Mortal engines: The science of performance and the dehumanization of sport. New York: The Free Press.

IOC (2007). *Factsheet: The Fight against Doping and promotion of athletes' health* (Update – February 2007), accessible under: http://multimedia.olympic.org/pdf/en_report_838.pdf [retrieved on 19.12.2007].

IOC (2008). *4,770 doping tests at the Beijing Games*, accessible under: http://www.olympic.org/uk/news/olympic_news/full_story_uk.asp?id=2782, [retrieved on 22.11.2008].
Keck, O., Wagner, G. (1990). Asymmetrische Information als Ursache von Doping im Hochleistungssport. *Zeitschrift für Soziologie*, 19, 108-116.
Maennig, W. (2002). On the Economics of Doping and Corruption in International Sports. *Journal of Sports Economics*, 3, 61-89.
Olson, M. jr. (1965). *The Logic of Collective Action: Public Goods and the Theory of Groups.* Cambridge: Harvard University Press.
Richter, N. (2006). Frauen vorn. *Horizont Sportbusiness*, 5, 8.
Richter, N. (2007). Die Hot Shots der Eiszeit. *Horizont Sportbusiness,* 5, 12-14.
Rosen, S. (1983). The Economics of superstars. *The American Scholar*, 52, 449-460.
Tietzel, M., Müller, C. (1999). *The Peculiar Economics of Doping,* Diskussionsbeiträge des Fachbereichs Wirtschaftswissenschaft der Gerhard-Mercator-Universität Gesamthochschule Duisburg, No. 266, Duisburg.
Tietzel, M., Müller, C. (2000). Wege aus dem Doping-Dilemma. Eine ökonomische Analyse. *Homo oeconomicus*, XVI (3), 277-286.
WADA (2009). *2006. Adverse Analytical Findings Reported by Accredited Laboratoires*, accessible under: http://www.wada-ama.org/Documents/Science_Medicine/WADA_LaboStatistics_2007.pdf [retrieved on 11.11.2009].
Wagner, G. (1994). Wie können die Doping-Zwickmühlen überwunden werden? In Bette, K.-H. (Ed.), *Doping im Leistungssport – sozialwissenschaftlich beobachtet* (pp. 101-130). Stuttgart: Naglschmid.
Wagner, G., Keck, O. (1990). Ein Weg aus der Doping-Zwickmühle – Stellungnahme zum Beitrag „The Doping Dilemma“ von Gunnar Breivik. *Sportwissenschaft*, 20, 439-446.

Werner Pitsch, Monika Frenger, Eike Emrich

The impact of anti-doping legislation in Europe – outlines for the development of model-based hypotheses[37]

1 Introduction

Concrete attempts to prevent doping have always oscillated between the extremes of making athletes' actions an offence prosecutable under the jurisdiction of sports courts – or meanwhile in the case of so-called wire-pullers and the athletes themselves of ordinary courts – and moral appeals serving a purely pedagogical purpose. If, as was not only pointed out by Digel (1994), but also proved from a decision-theory perspective by Bird & Wagner (1997), the probability of doping results from the system logic of elite sport, then both pedagogical efforts to put a stop to doping and general crime prevention would logically be generally unlikely to succeed. More recently, we have seen efforts Europe-wide to prevent doping by introducing institutionalized penalties; in Germany, too, for example within the scope of the anti-doping law. This has given rise to an intensive discussion on the rationale and expediency of implicating athletes in criminal jurisdiction. In response to protests primarily from the field of organized sports, the current German anti-doping law does not foresee such involvement. This confronts us squarely with the striking discrepancy between the widespread notion that penalties for athletes enshrined in law have a deterrent function and the scepticism towards such a function personally expressed by the German Olympic Sports Federation president (unpublished, 2006) when he states, for example, that he does not want to see athletes criminalized.

2 Theoretical background: The normative and empirical hypothesis of general prevention from the perspective of methodological individualism

When Bette & Schimank (1995, 285, translated by the authors) state that "as a result of ongoing commercialization athletes act as selfish utilitarians who, in light of their brief sporting career, naturally have a vested interest in maximizing their earnings and are under high pressure to perform in an environment conducive to doping", they are referring to a form of utilitarianism that was for a long time generally disapproved of and therefore disregarded in the theoretical discussion (Höffe, 1975, 8). Growing disillusionment concerning the measurable success of a concept aimed at prevention, resocialization and therapy, albeit one that led to a sustained rise in the earnings potential of those active in this field or of moral entrepreneurs, hand in hand with an economic approach to deviating

[37] The authors would like to thank Christian Pierdzioch for his valuable comments.

behaviour (Becker, 1974), served to reinforce a utilitarian reasoning behind penalties. This argument is pursued from two aspects:

a) in a normative sense, namely that the desired deterrent effect on potential deviators is to be seen as an end to legitimize government prosecution and
b) that government prosecution does actually have a subsequent deterrent effect (Vanberg, 1982, 7).

In his analysis, Vanberg (1982, 8ff.) points out with reference to Rawls (1975) the need to differentiate between two legitimization problems when it comes to justifying punishment:

a) justification of institutionalized punishment and
b) justification of a concrete criminal act.

The first point is concerned with the question of why the state should prosecute and how the institution that metes out the punishment is legitimized, while the second asks why a penalty should be imposed against a particular individual. The first case relates to the legal certainty that arises from a deterrent effect, as well as legitimization based not on divine will etc., but on internal consensus-building within a group; the second case assumes that the individual is actually guilty in the sense of having violated the law.

Rawls (1975, 98) in this context relates the two levels to two different official functions, namely that of the legislative body (i.e. parliament), which must give consideration to the future impact of its decisions, and that of the judge, who gives a verdict on past actions in a criminal act. A purely arbitrary deterrent, as is easily conceivable in despotism and also exists in the figure of the dictator in the Inspection Game in economics, would conflict with the deterrent function. If punishment could be meted out to everyone irrespective of how they have actually conducted themselves, there would be no incentive for anyone to refrain from infringing the law. As Pitsch (2009) and Emrich & Pitsch (2009) have shown, the questions this gives rise to are certainly relevant in the fight against doping insofar as fair doping tests do not exist, and investments in the appearance of honesty in sport production may be more rewarding than honesty itself in the sense of complying with the rules or abstaining from doping.

The fact that an individual mentally accepts a norm does not mean we can assume he or she will automatically act accordingly (Vanberg, 1982, 13). The economic discussion concerning the collective good problem makes it clear that the controversial issue is not that rules are sometimes violated, but is to be seen within the broader context of adherence to a system of rules, observance of which does not happen per se, but incurs costs.

So where do the advantages of a compliance with norms that aims at establishing social order lie? First ans foremost it alleviates uncertainty, because institutionalizing expectations rightly enables us to harbour reliable expectations about how the social environment behaves, as well as about how people will act in the future. However, the advantage of these expectations lies in the anticipated compliance of the other stakeholders, whereas self-compliance is definitely a disadvantage because, as Plato taught us, it limits behavioural alternatives; in short, rule-breakers only have an advantage to the extent that they can be relatively sure the other side does not break the rules. In other words, as long as by complying with the rules others do not bind themselves to the law or submit to the rules, rule-breakers risk disadvantages by, in turn, binding themselves to the law. So while people have a manifest interest in stability and guaranteed compliance with a normative order, they have no direct individual motive to submit to rules in their own behaviour, unless the stability of the order is guaranteed by institutions.

With the increasing size of the group, two factors come into play: first, in our individual expectations the probability of not being caught and sanctioned increases and second, the probability of our own infringements jeopardizing the social order and triggering a backslide into anarchy decreases (cf. Vanberg, 1982, 13ff.). In this context, systematic changes in the action situation change the weighting in the individual decision alternative, which by reason of cost-benefit calculations makes it appear expedient to choose compliance over deviation. This change in weighting consists in the organization of the state and the concept of law, which via changed earnings expectations, for example because of an institutionalized threat of penalties in the case of non-compliance, is intended to free individuals from the above-mentioned large number dilemma, which Buchanan (1977, 161) formulated as follows: "Each an every person may, of course, consider that he would be 'better off', in terms of his own evaluation, in a different world where the moral law is widely accepted as an overriding ethical rule. But privately and voluntarily there is simply no means through which the single individual can choose to make this alternative state of the world more nearly realizable."

Independent of sub-group-specific interests that come into play in the formulation of norms, we can therefore establish that the constancy of interindividual conflicts of interests makes a system of rules necessary in order to guarantee social order, and also that legal norms which show a general consensus need an implementation and enforcement apparatus in order to be effective. Voluntary normative self-commitments, generally subsumed under the term fair play, while certainly not expendable, by no means replace an enforcement and punishment apparatus.

2.1 The theory of general prevention as an empirical theory

Compliance and non-compliance each occur taking account of subjectively anticipated benefits and anticipated disadvantages (cf. Beccaria, 1966, 61; Bentham, 2000 [1781], 166). As Vanberg (1982, 18ff.) points out, the more recent economic theory of criminality postulated by the likes of Becker again ties in with the earlier conceptions of Beccaria and Bentham and deals with the problem in terms of the relationship between price and demand. If the price of a given conduct rises, for example because the risk of punishment brings higher penalties, demand, or the rate of deviating behaviour, declines accordingly.

Threats of punishment in terms of institutionalized rules therefore increase costs – which, however, presupposes economically rational behaviour (Becker, 1974, 9).

Consequently, numerous objections to the economic theory of criminality have been raised (cf. Vanberg, 1982, 22ff.), which in the main drew on an all too rationalistic concept of man. This was, however, significantly expanded in institutional economics, in which it is assumed that although different levels of information lead to asymmetrical information, individuals nevertheless act rationally even if only restricted or asymmetrical information is available. Thus rule-breakers may act on incomplete information; it is also quite possible that they fail to assess the risk of discovery and conviction, that they wrongly judge the long-term consequences of their actions, etc. But even if they calculate differently to conformers, this by no means implies that they do not calculate at all: "Moreover, the likelihood that an offender will be discovered and convicted and the nature and extent of punishment differ greatly from person to person and activity to activity. Yet, in spite of such diversity, some common properties are shared by practically all legislation [...]" (Becker, 1974, 1f.; cf. 11f.).

Moreover, general prevention does not, of course, make rule-breaking disappear; what changes is the frequency with which it occurs. In addition to this, it is perfectly conceivable for formal punishments in the institution of the law to overlap with other negative sanctions. State punishment is just one form in addition to physical, moral and religious punishment (Vanberg, 1982, 28 with reference to Bentham, 2000 [1781], 27), whereby the economic theory of state punishment is by no means incompatible with informal negative sanctions.

2.2 General prevention in doping

Assuming economics as a method of analyzing and predicting the behaviour of the average person, we can make the following conjecture: when it comes to compliance and non-compliance, people draw on certain resources. This brings all infringements to light, be they tax evasion, white-collar crimes, traffic violations, etc. (Becker 1974, 3). The optimum activity structure is determined by the relative advantageousness of alternative uses of resources. Changes in the expected benefit from observing the rules are reflected in changed activity patterns, in other words: if the expected benefit to be derived from complying with the rules declines, resources are diverted from compliance to non-compliance (ibid., 9). These considerations are in principle based on the subjective expected utility theory, according to which behavioural effects observed in collectives can be reconstructed on the basis of the subjective utility of a future event or situation (benefit, N) and the probability of its occurrence (p) for each element in the collective. Decisive variables in this context, according to Becker (1974, 11), are the level and risk of punishment, whereby the risk of punishment acts as a higher deterrent than the level of punishment[38]: or in the words of Bentham (2000 [1781], Chap. XIV, Of the Proportion between Punishments and Offences, 7th rule): “To enable the value of the punishment to outweigh that of the profit of the offense, it must be increased, in point of magnitude, in proportion as it falls short in point of certainty”. Using the choice between compliance and deviation as an example, the corresponding formalization according to Becker would be:

$$EN = p \cdot N(S) + (1-p) \cdot N(\gamma)$$

(EN = expected benefit from earnings with the help of deviant behaviour, - (1-p) = probability of escaping punishment, + benefit in the event of punishment – N(S) weighted with the likelihood of punishment p).

Taking Becker’s line (1974), this would initially have to be seen as a serious plea for more restrictive sanctioning, more investigative personnel and improved methods of prosecution (Becker, 1974, 14ff.)[39]. Factors influencing the expected benefit are: (first derivation).

a) $\frac{\partial EN}{\partial p} = N(S) - N(\gamma) < 0$

b) $\frac{\partial EN}{\partial S} = p \cdot \frac{\partial N(S)}{\partial S} < 0$

Raising the level of punishment and/or the probability of conviction would thus increase the price of violations and from a simple economic perspective reduce the number of infringements. A higher level of punishment combined with a higher likelihood of punishment could therefore also be seen by the doping market as a plea for much more restrictive sanctioning in the form of legislation that ideally penalizes both suppliers and consumers, more investigative personnel and improved methods of prosecution.

2.3 Specific assumptions about the doping ban from the economic perspective

Compared to other forms of deviating criminal behaviour, doping represents something of an anomaly. A bank robber, for example, loses any illegally ac-

[38] “The widespread generalization that offenders are more deterred by the probability of conviction than by the punishment when convicted turns out to imply in the expected-utility approach that offenders are risk preferrers, at least in the relevant region of punishments” (Becker, 1974, 11)

[39] Here, in particular government funds are used in order to introduce repressions intended to lower incidences of doping and thus “clean up” sport. This is tantamount to subsidizing, inasmuch as the collective good clean sport is produced with the help of public funds, making it possible to produce a signal effect with a positive impact on consumers in the sense of clean sport. This, however, gives rise to the question of whether athletes themselves should not provide – and finance – proof that they are “clean” (cf. seals of quality in other professions), given that it is the athletes who use sport (especially clean sport) as a vehicle for promotion and making money.

quired assets on discovery of the loot or through claims for compensation under civil law, in other words he has to relinquish any illgotten gains or make material compensation. Suppliers of doping substances or dopers, by contrast, do not lose any past earnings generated through doping or through dealing in doping substances. Voluntary consumption of doping substances rules out compensation claims against the supplier of those substances – unlike the forced consumption of doping substances in totalitarian regimes, which entitles consumers to lodge claims against the state. In addition, as a result of enhanced performance, the undetected doper increases the benefit of the "sport" good for all stakeholders (Emrich & Pitsch, 2009). With this in mind, when applied to the field of doping in elite sport, Becker's formalization requires specification on the one hand with respect to the ramifications of punishment. On the other hand, it can be assumed – and should be taken into consideration in the following formalizations – that the effects of the product of level and probability of punishment would not represent a linear function (cf. fig. 2) if the punishment were to also retroactively impact income earned with the help of doping in the form of a contractual penalty, claims for compensation or the like.

So far, the analysis of decision-making behaviour has been conducted strictly on the basis of methodological individualism. If, however, we wish to assess the thus calculated effects within a collective, we must bear in mind that unconnected individual actions can give rise to unexpected non-intended collective effects. Therefore we must also ask: Is, by analogy with prohibition in the USA, a state-imposed doping ban with tougher sanctions perhaps the non-intended motor of the doping market? If for dealers doping, or the sale of doping substances, were to become an act prohibited by law, they could be expected to react to such a ruling rationally. They would rationally weigh up the costs and benefits of the behavioural alternatives of dealing in prohibited substances versus giving up dealing against each other, whereby the level of sanctions and the probability of these being imposed here again essentially determine decision-making behaviour.

When an illegal supplier market is created, we can also expect an increased level of masking measures. For suppliers it is rational to offer specially designed masking techniques along with potential doping substances in order to minimize the likelihood of their customers getting caught and being exposed and subsequently punished as suppliers themselves. Government investments in crime fighting (e.g. by intensifying the government repression system) also influence the decision of course, as higher government investments also increase the probability of the risk of punishment. Since it is also in dopers' interests to lower the likelihood of detection, it can be assumed that an increase in the level and probability of sanctions on the supply side leads to rising doping prices and a lower probability of detection for consumers – and hence also for suppliers.

An increased level of sanctions for dopers as a result of criminal prosecution can likewise be expected to generate counter-investments, whereby the concrete level of these counter-investments is in turn influenced by the level and the risk of punishment as well as by the level of income that can be achieved through doping. The latter is strongly determined by the product of current annual earnings and expected remaining time during which an athletic career can be successfully pursued. Those investments a doper makes in order to avoid detection and punishment are thus a function of the level of punishment S (disadvantages), the probability of occurrence and the anticipated earnings from doping during the remaining career (advantages).

3 Problem specification

In terms of the theory of general prevention, it was assumed that higher penalties – given an unchanged or increased likelihood of discovery – lead to a reduction in doping abuse. In this context, the probability of detection has generally proved to be the factor to be given more weight in the product of the two variables. Even rationally acting players with restricted information react with counter-investments, with the help of which they influence or believe they can influence the probability of being discovered.

In the following formalization, we as a generalization assume risk-neutral suppliers in the market. The behaviour of risk preferers, who at least partly ignore any threat posed by repression and sanctions, can be implicitly derived from this. In the case of consumers, i.e. doping athletes, on the other hand, it is necessary to distinguish between risk takers and those averse to taking risks.

The present article aims firstly to model the supply and the demand side, taking into account actors who make counter-investments in obstructing criminal punishment, based on the recently tightened anti-doping law in Germany. Secondly, based on this model, we will attempt to estimate the effects for those countries in Europe with higher or lower penalties, while presupposing the same probability of detection for Europe in general. With the help of this comparison of higher and lower sanctions, it is possible to formulate hypotheses concerning the level of anticipated doping prevalence in these countries.

Legal provisions with respect to doping violations differ considerably from one European country to another. In a formalization of amendments to the law, Pitsch und Emrich (2009) already developed a model outlining the impacts of changes in legislation. This was based on an economic evaluation of a planned tightening of the law in Germany that could possibly influence the decisions of suppliers and consumers of doping substances.

4 Formalization of the basic model

The formalization presented in the following is based on an economic efficiency evaluation of the amendments to the legal situation in Germany in respect of the tightening of sanctions (Pitsch & Emrich, 2009). The model is outlined in a partly abridged and revised form.

4.1 Supply side

First of all it shall be assumed suppliers react rationally, in other words that they make counter-investments (I) that lower the probability (p) of being caught and punished.[40] The level of the counter-investment is, in addition to the probability of punishment (p), influenced by the level of punishment, government investment in direct obstruction and imposition of criminal punishment (in the following R = repression) and by the level of income from the sale or use of doping substances Nv.

In this, we assume a supplier who, if sanctioned, is not able to generate an income, whose opportunity costs in the case of sanctioning are the result of the product of the level of the sanction in years and his or her average income per year and who thus suffers no additional income losses from the possible but not compulsory – and to date only in absolutely exceptional cases (contractual penalties in professional cycling) subsequently imposed – confiscation of realized profits by the prosecuting authorities. In this respect, this argumentation targets both the small-scale businessman in the illegal doping market and well-organized illegal suppliers that generate a higher turnover. This allows small-scale black market dealers to be caught as well as larger-scale doping labs (e.g. "Balco") or developers of designer steroids. It does not, on the other hand, detect pharmaceutical companies that develop and manufacture products suitable for doping for other purposes.

In the following, functions such as the subjectively anticipated benefit EN as a result of the interaction of investments I in obstructing punishment, the level of sanctions (S), the level of repression (R) and the probability of detection (p) are considered. In this, the effects of the independent variables on the anticipated benefit are considered as follows:

- In order to establish whether it is feasibly possible to reduce the number of suppliers of doping substances or dopers, we analyze the conditions under which their anticipated benefit becomes negative.
- In order to see how exogenous parameters (e.g. the level of sanctions) interacting with endogenous parameters (e.g. the level of counter-investments) influence the anticipated benefit, it is necessary to consider the derivation of the function to one variable respectively. For example, the derivation of I to the variable S describes the increase of the function I at a point S. If this is always

[40] Kistner (2010, 34) reported in the German daily Süddeutsche Zeitung that a court ruling has upheld the right of doping expert Werner Franke to claim that racing cyclist Jan Ulrich paid 35,000 euros in one year for the procurement of illegal substances. According to the public prosecutor's office, between the years of 2003 and 2006, Ulrich visited the physician Fuentes 24 times in Madrid (sometimes for as little as 2 hours) and in the years 2004 and 2006 paid Fuentes a total of 80,000 euros. This on the one hand illustrates the costs of doping and on the other hand, it also demonstrates the illegal and illegitimate investment activity by small-scale businessman Ulrich in his performance potential.

positive with a growing parameter (strictly monotonically increasing), this means the value of I then increases. Conversely, if the derivation is consistently negative, the value of the function decreases with a growing parameter. Zero means the function is constant.

Assumption 1: Investments (I; which also include information costs, costs of trust and search costs), that a doping supplier makes in order to avoid being detected and punished are thus a function of the impending losses (level of punishment S and level of investments in prosecution R).

(1) $I = I(S, R)$

Whereby:

(2) $\frac{\partial I(S,R)}{\partial S} > 0$ and $\frac{\partial I(S,R)}{\partial R} > 0$

shall apply, i.e. (based on the above explanation): the higher the level of the sanction and the higher the investments of the collective actors (prosecuting authorities) in the detection of suppliers, the higher the level of the counter-investments. Counter-investments in this context may be the development and sale of unknown doping substances or those still in the process of development (such as S 107 that was presumably used in China), or the sale of doping substances together with masking agents. Other conceivable counter-investments could include bribe monies and the employment of paid "stooges" as vendors.[41]

The function of the counter-investments on the supply side is perforce also to lower the risk of the athlete's detection, since as an initial suspicion a detected case of doping would entail the risk of the supplier's own illegal behaviour being exposed. Any athlete already convicted as a dopers represents as a customer a higher risk for the supplier, which is likely to be reflected in higher prices or possibly in a refusal to supply the product. Supplier and consumer have only partially conflicting interests, inasmuch as suppliers are out to maximize their material benefit; at the same time, however, they can also be seen as having identical interests, since both parties have a vested interest in non-detection, in other words a specific form of antagonistic symbiosis (Emrich & Pitsch, 2009).

Assumption 2: The probability of detection is a function of the repressions and the counter-investments defined in (1):

(3) $p = p(R, I(S,R))$ with $1 \geq p(R, I(S,R)) \geq 0$

Whereby:

(4) $\frac{\partial p(R, I(S,R))}{\partial I} < 0$

41 As recent assumptions in the Armstrong case suggest, it cannot be ruled out that substantial donations to the UCI have at least created a certain goodwill (Kistner writing in the Süddeutsche Zeitung of Saturday, 7 August). Even the head of the special doping commission in Austria, Andreas Holzer, noted in the Wiener Kurier newspaper that the international doping trade is well organized, the risk in the doping trade is, by contrast, lower than in the doping market, while profits are higher (Kistner, 2010, p. 25).

shall apply, i.e. investments on the part of the suppliers in non-detection of the sale and of the doped athletes definitely lead to a lower probability of being detected themselves. For this reason, the effect of repression on the probability of detection can only be obtained via the derivation of (3):

$$(5)\quad \frac{\partial p}{\partial R} = \frac{\partial p(R, I(S, R))}{\partial I} \cdot \frac{\partial I(S, R)}{\partial R}$$

For the investments, it was assumed that with a growing R they steadily rise (2), so that the sign in front of the second factor is always positive. The sign in front of the first factor, however, depends on the ratio of the effects of the restrictions and the counter-investments on the probability of detection p. If the effect of improved detection methods exceeds that of investments in the avoidance of punishment, the overall probability of detection increases despite counter-investments, and all the suppliers can do is minimize the risk. If on the other hand the effect of the counter-investments exceeds the effect of improved detection methods, an increase in R leads to a lowering of the probability of detection. Government control via increased repression is therefore only possible if we assume that in their effect on the probability of detection the improved detection methods (e.g. efforts by the Federal Criminal Police Office) cannot be fully compensated by counter-investments. The case of repression measures that can be overcompensated by counter-investments ($\frac{\partial p}{\partial R} < 0$) turns out to be trivial in this context, because increasing government investments in the detection of doping offences would always result in rising incomes for suppliers accompanied by a lower probability of detection for dopers.

In the case of potentially effective control ($\frac{\partial p}{\partial R} > 0$), the first derivation of (3) to S produces:

$$(6)\quad \frac{\partial p}{\partial S} = \frac{\partial p(R, I(S, R))}{\partial I} \cdot \frac{\partial I(S, R)}{\partial S} < 0$$

Irrespective of the extent of the perceived level of repressions, the probability of detection p (4) decreases with increasing investment I. If we further assume that the probability of detection is greater than 0, and that at the same time with an increasing level of sanctions individual investments in avoiding detection – in the form of buying expensive, innovative and as yet undetectable products or known products with mimetics – increase, then the probability of detection for athletes and suppliers decreases the higher sanctions are (6).

For consideration of the expected benefit, the following assumptions must be made:

A benefit definitely accrues from the sale of doping substances – we are assuming an actual increase in sales prices and not just a certain rise in reservation prices – and is positive:

(7) $Nv > 0$

The benefit (opportunity costs) from the sanction is negative and decreases the higher the sanction is:

(8) $N(S) < 0$ and $\frac{\partial N(S)}{\partial S} < 0$

In the case of the counter-investments, it follows for the expected benefit of the supplier, who always compensates the negative benefit through counter-investments by means of an actual price mark-up (not just an increase in the reservation price), that:[42]

(9) $EN(S,R) = p(R,I(S,R)) \cdot N(S) + Nv$

If we proceed from the plausible assumption that the expected benefit for suppliers was so far positive (why else would they – give or take the occasional blackmail case – still be on the market), then an increase in the probability of detection is definitely effective if the future expected benefit becomes negative as a result. In this case, there would certainly be a drastic reduction in the number of suppliers. The effectiveness of the increased repression thus primarily depends on the expected probability of detection.

The solution of the inequation $EN < 0$ produces:

(10) $p(R,I(S,R)) > \frac{Nv}{|N(S)|}$

A closer look at this inequation shows that a simultaneous increase in sanctions and in the probability of detection can only be an unreliable means of squeezing the doping market dry and thus of eliminating doping, since for both sides of the inequation the respective term becomes smaller with increasing sanction levels (cf. (6))

The first derivation to R produces:

(11) $\frac{\partial EN(S,R)}{\partial R} = \frac{\partial p(R,I(S,R))}{\partial I} \cdot \frac{\partial I(S,R)}{\partial R} \cdot N(S) < 0$

since given the assumption of reliably effective detection methods (cf. reflections relating to (5)) and the negative benefit of sanctions, increasing repressions thus certainly lower the expected benefit for suppliers.

The first derivation of (9) to S produces:

42 Whether the attainable price goes up is contingent on market conditions. What will certainly increase are the reservation prices (minimum sales price). Since empirical findings currently do not indicate any significant drop in demand – the use of doping substances in amateur and leisure-time sports even appears to increase impartial demand – we not only expect reservation prices to increase, but in fact sales prices too.

$$(12)\quad \frac{\partial EN(S,R)}{\partial S} = \frac{\partial p(R,I(S,R))}{\partial I} \cdot \frac{\partial I(S,R)}{\partial S} \cdot N(S) + p(R,I(S,R)) \cdot \frac{\partial N(S)}{\partial S}$$

A closer look at this derivation does not allow a definitive conclusion to be drawn concerning how the expected benefit varies depending on the level of sanctions, without additional assumptions being made or conditions met.

If we proceed on the assumption that sanctions are effective, the expected benefits should decrease with increasing sanction levels, i.e. $\frac{\partial EN(S,R)}{\partial S} \overset{!}{<} 0$; it should then follow that:

$$(13)\quad p > \frac{\frac{\partial p}{\partial S}}{\frac{\partial N(S)}{\partial S}} \cdot |N(S)|$$ [43]

Since the probability of detection p must (by definition) always lie between 0 and 1 (i.e. between "never occurs" and "always occurs"), at least one of the following conditions must be met: either the change in the benefit of sanctions as a result of the sanction (denominator of the fraction) must be significantly greater than the variability of the probability of detection as a result of the sanction (numerator of the fraction). This condition is symbolically represented in figure 1. The expected benefit of the supplier decreases as a result of this condition only in those areas where the derivation of p to S (solid line) runs below the derivation of N to S (dotted line). This is only the case for low values of S, in other words low sanctions, since with higher values the effect of the counter-investments on the probability of detection overcompensates the decreasing benefit in the event of discovery. The second condition under which the inequation is satisfied is that the costs incurred through sanctions must be significantly lower than 1. The equation is also satisfied if both occur simultaneously. Altogether it becomes clear that the form of the functions of p and N depending on the level of sanctions is decisive for satisfying the condition and there are only a few constellations for satisfying the inequation.

By way of illustration, we compare two types of supplier: Type A supplier earns only a marginal income from the sale of doping substances, is thus a typical chance vendor. Type B supplier earns a high income from the sale of either very expensive or very innovative and/or high quantities of doping substances. If, based on our formalization, both behave rationally, the number of existing suppliers will certainly decrease, because at least for type A suppliers the ex-

---

[43] This inequation can also be resolved with reference to elasticities in economics as follows:

$$\frac{\partial p}{\partial I} \cdot \frac{1}{p} \cdot \frac{\partial I}{\partial S} > -\frac{\partial N}{\partial S} \cdot \frac{1}{N}$$

$$\Rightarrow \frac{\partial p}{\partial I} \cdot \frac{I}{p} \cdot \frac{\partial I}{\partial S} \cdot \frac{S}{I} > -\frac{\partial N}{\partial S} \cdot \frac{S}{N}$$

$$\Rightarrow \varepsilon_{p,I} \cdot \varepsilon_{I,S} > -\varepsilon_{N,S}$$

pected costs arising from the sanctions and the impossibility of factoring the costs of counter-investments into the price of their small quantities of doping substances sold (i.e. passing these on to consumers) would be too high, forcing them to withdraw from the market. Type B suppliers, on the other hand, would remain in the market, since their possibility to make higher counter-investments still provides them with a considerable benefit.

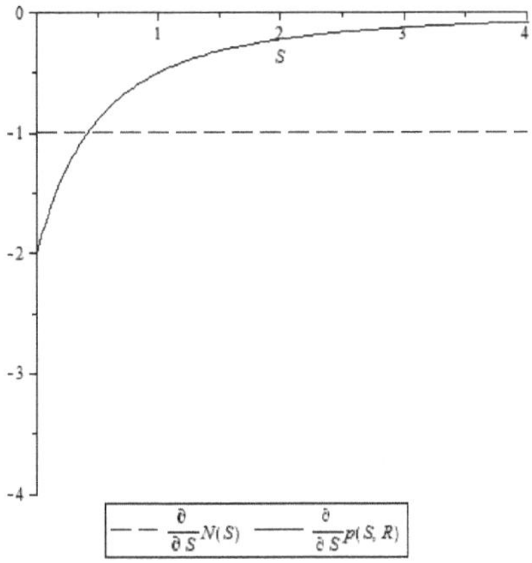

Fig. 1: Graphic representation of the necessary condition for p (see (13))

As an interim conclusion we can therefore note that tightening the penalties for suppliers, i.e. raising the price for violating the norms, leads to concentration effects in the number of suppliers.

4.2 Demand side

Athletes consume doping substances (on the extent cf. Pitsch, Klein & Emrich, 2005, 2007; Pitsch, Maats & Emrich, 2009). This consumption is modelled in the following as demand, and the athlete thus considered as a consuming household. Other aspects, such as demand by the public for peak athletic performances or demand by the media for actual or asserted past doping violations, are not taken into consideration.

By analogy with the supply side, we attempt to model the athlete as a rational actor who makes active counter-investments, believing in their effectiveness and thus having restricted information about the actual impact of counter-measures. The above assumptions (1) and (2), which describe the dependency of the level of investment on the level of sanctions and repression, are adopted for the demand side in the same way as for the supply side, however with the difference that for the athletes the probability of detection is determined above all by the doping tests carried out by the associations. This means that a possible increase in repression has only a minimal influence on the probability of detection and sanctioning. I is a function of R and S and the probability of detection is only indirectly dependent on the level of repression via the effect of R on I. It therefore follows that:

(14) $p = p(I(S,R))$ with $1 > p(I) > 0$

and

(15) $\frac{\partial p(I)}{\partial I} < 0$

i.e. the individual investments in avoiding prosecution definitely lead subjectively to a lower probability of punishment. The first derivation to S and R produces:

(16) $\frac{\partial p}{\partial S} = \frac{\partial p(I(S,R))}{\partial I} \cdot \frac{\partial I(S,R)}{\partial S} < 0$

and

(17) $\frac{\partial p}{\partial R} = \frac{\partial p(I(S,R))}{\partial I} \cdot \frac{\partial I(S,R)}{\partial R} < 0$

With increasing sanction levels, measured in terms of the duration in years of the (future effective) doping-related bans, and increasing repressions on suppliers, which in turn push up prices (cf. (20) below), investments in efforts to escape punishment on the part of athletes also increase (cf. (2)). Depending on the investments, the probability of detection for athletes decreases (15) and thus tougher sanctions for consumers, in the same way as tighter repression measures for suppliers, lead to lower probabilities of detection on the demand side.

Apart from this effect on the probability of detection, the investment in punishment avoidance also has a direct benefit-lowering effect since it incurs costs and therefore reduces income (investments = costs). Since this benefit equals the negative benefit of the investment, in the following we simplify matters by considering the investment directly as a negative benefit in the expected benefit.

The benefit for athletes from the sanction can be formulated in relation to the benefit from the doped practice of sport. If S refers to the number of years of a doping-related ban (currently a maximum of 4) and Nd refers to the (uncertain) average annual income of a doped athlete (due to injuries, fluctuations in performance, etc.) it follows for $N(S)$ that

(18) $N(S) = -S \cdot Nd$

Where counter-investments are made, it therefore follows for the expected benefit of an athlete that:

(19) $EN(S,R) = p(I(S,R)) \cdot (-S \cdot Nd) + (1 - p(I(S,R)) \cdot S \cdot Nd - I(S,R)$

When considering the expected benefit, additional assumptions are made with respect to the functions I and p. Since the counter-investments made by consumers consist on the one hand in repression-induced price increases on the supply side and on the other hand in self-determinable components, the function

$I(S,R)$ can be replaced by the sum of $I(S)+c$. The constant c is determined by the repression on the suppliers and impacts on the maximum investments of the consumers in the form of higher prices (= costs).

Assumption 1: As S increases, I increases in a straight line up to the maximum $\frac{1}{x}(Nd-c)$, whereby $Nd-c$ describes the earnings from sport reduced by the constant c and $\frac{1}{x}$ defines the fraction of this available income that the doper is willing to additionally invest in escaping detection over and above the costs already incurred by doping.

We assume that a consumer will not be prepared to make counter-investments at a level that exceeds his or her expected benefit, and consequently that the maximum fraction ($\frac{1}{x}$) of his or her income is limited by $1<x\leq\infty$.

$$(20)\quad I=\begin{cases} m\cdot S : I<\frac{1}{x}(Nd-c) \\ \frac{1}{x}(Nd-c) : otherwise \end{cases}$$

If we start by taking the current sanctioning practice (four-year maximum ban (S_0)) and the current counter-investments of an athlete (I_0) as a baseline, then it follows for I with a given R that:

$$(21)\quad m=\frac{I_0}{S_0}\Rightarrow I=\frac{I_0}{S_0}\cdot S$$

Based on the definition of I, a distinction can be made between two types. First, depending on the level of sanctions, (individually) increasing counter-investments are made until the "personal pain threshold" $\frac{1}{x}(Nd-c)$ with respect to Nd is reached. From this point on, irrespective of whether the level of sanctions increases, investments are only made up to the threshold amount and it is accepted that beyond this level, the probability of detection cannot be further influenced by investments. An actor who invests a high amount within a short time (m very high), will reach his or her limit (ceteris paribus) faster than an actor who only reacts to a lesser extent to increases in sanctions $(m\rightarrow 0)$. We look initially at the first case, in which increasing counter-investments are made, and then at those actors whose rate of increase with respect to counter-investments is low, since this is the more relevant of the two cases. Given this, as a result of incorporation into (19), it therefore follows for the expected benefit that:

(22) $EN(S) = -2 \cdot Nd \cdot S \cdot p(m \cdot S + c) + S \cdot Nd - (m \cdot S + c)$

This first prompts us to ask under what conditions a doped athlete who makes counter-investments anticipates a negative expected benefit. Based on this, the "doping" strategy would not be an alternative that a rationally acting player would choose. We therefore consider the inequation $EN < 0$:

(23) $-2 \cdot Nd \cdot S \cdot p(m \cdot S + c) + S \cdot Nd - (m \cdot S + c) < 0$

A distinction can be made here between quick-response actors (those who make high investments even in the case of low increases in S) and wait-and-see actors (with low m). The second group is the more interesting to observe in this context, since in the first group the maximum level of investments is quickly reached and thus the second case of (19) applies. Considering the borderline case $m \to 0$ produces the following conditions for a negative expected benefit:

(24) $$\begin{cases} S < \dfrac{c}{Nd(1-2p(c))} & for \quad p < 0.5 \\ S > \dfrac{c}{Nd(1-2p(c))} & for \quad p > 0.5 \end{cases}$$

- If $p > 0.5$, the expected benefit, regardless of the benefit derived from doping and the costs incurred through counter-investments on the part of suppliers, is, whatever the level of sanctions ($S > 0$), always negative. Hence it ought to be possible for the prosecuting authority to increase the probability of detection to over 50% or generate belief in a correspondingly high probability of detection in order to persuade consumers to abandon their "doping" strategy.
- If $p < 0.5$, the expected benefit can only become negative if the costs incurred by the supplier are very low in relation to the benefit derived from doping. In this case, the level of sanctions would have to be very low in order to generate a negative expected benefit.

Assumption 2: As I increases, p decreases. The form of the function p can be approximated to a hyperbolical function in the 1st quadrant and thus takes into account that, relatively, increased investments per employed resource produce decreasing effects. A scaling factor k is needed to meet the conditions that a probability between 0 and 1 is given. Conversely, given the magnitudes of I, a comparatively low investment (for example € 10) would lead to an enormous decrease in p (in the example p would then be 0.1).

(25) $p(m \cdot S + c) = \dfrac{k}{I(m \cdot S + c)} = \dfrac{k}{m \cdot S + c} \text{ with } m \cdot S + c > k$

$$(26)\quad \frac{\partial p}{\partial S} = -\frac{k \cdot m}{(m \cdot S + c)^2}$$

For the further analysis, it would appear relevant in this context to examine the conditions under which the level of sanctions can be drawn on to control (generally: lower) the expected benefit of the consumer. After incorporation of (25) into (22) and derivation to S we obtain:

$$(27)\quad \frac{\partial EN}{\partial S} = -2Nd \cdot p(m \cdot S + c) + 2Nd \cdot S \frac{k \cdot m}{(m \cdot S + c)^2} - Nd - m = Nd(1 - \frac{2k \cdot c}{(m \cdot S + c)^2}) - m$$

In order to bring about a decline in the expected benefit as a result of increased sanctions, $\frac{\partial EN}{\partial S} < 0$ shall apply. It therefore follows for the lowering of EN that:

$$Nd(1 - \frac{2k \cdot c}{(m \cdot S + c)^2}) - m < 0$$

$$(28)\quad \Rightarrow 1 < \frac{m}{Nd} + \frac{2k \cdot c}{(m \cdot S + c)^2}$$

$$\Rightarrow \quad \textit{for } m \to 0 : c < 2k \quad \textit{and from } (24)\ c > k \textit{ applies}$$

$$\Rightarrow \quad c \in (k, 2k)$$

However, against the background of (25), the condition in (28) means that $p \in (\frac{1}{2}, 1)$ must apply. The results of studies conducted by Pitsch et al. (2005, 2007, 2009) reveal, however, that significantly lower probabilities of detection can be expected, so that on the basis of empirical findings it can be assumed that in the case of actors who take a wait-and-see attitude to changes in sanctions a decrease in the expected benefit is all but impossible. It also becomes apparent in this connection that in the sense of adverse selection those who have little regard for social standing and therefore do not overinvest at the threat of doping controls are the ones who remain in the market.

In the second case differentiated in (20), athletes invest all means they are prepared to invest in avoiding detection of their doping activities. This is the case, for example, with those consumers who react very defensively to the threat (m is very high) and for whom the maximum counter-investment limit is reached even where sanctions are low. However, by contrast with a negative expected benefit, these actors stay in the market, because despite non-increasing counter-investments they have a positive expected benefit. In this case it follows for the expected benefit by incorporating the second solution of I into (19) that:

$$(29)\quad EN(S) = -2 \cdot Nd \cdot S \cdot p(\frac{1}{x}(Nd - c) + c) + S \cdot Nd - \frac{1}{x}(Nd - c) - c$$

As in the first case, we consider first of all the conditions under which the expected benefit becomes negative (and thus a decision to engage in doping would be meaningless). We therefore consider $EN < 0$:

$$-2 \cdot Nd \cdot S \cdot p(\frac{1}{x}(Nd-c)+c)+S \cdot Nd-\frac{1}{x}(Nd-c)-c<0$$

$$(30) \Rightarrow \begin{cases} S < \dfrac{\frac{1}{x}(Nd-c)+c}{Nd(1-2p(\frac{1}{x}(Nd-c)+c)} \; for \quad p<0.5 \\ S > \dfrac{\frac{1}{x}(Nd-c)+c}{Nd(1-2p(\frac{1}{x}(Nd-c)+c)} \; for \quad p>0.5 \end{cases}$$

Based on the observations made in the first case, it is sufficient for this condition to consider the first inequation ($p < 0.5$). The expected benefit of an actor would in this case ($p < 0.5$) become negative precisely in cases where S is very small. Let us assume the probability of detection is 10%. If an actor invests 20% of his or her benefit from doping (own investment and the investment that arises through the supplier), then $S < \frac{1}{4}$ would have to be true in order for the expected benefit of this actor to be negative. Thus he or she would have made bad investments precisely in those cases where the first condition in (30) is met. In all other cases, in other words where S is higher, this actor invests his or her entire benefit, even if the threat is minimal. These comparatively high investments are made very quickly and are in turn compensated by the benefit in the event of non-detection. This describes homo sociologicus, who in order to prevent the loss of social standing will keep his or her investments at a consistently high level irrespective of the level of the threat. We thus have the interesting case that homo sociologicus, as the type who has to a high degree internalized values and norms and tends to demonstrate norm-compliant behaviour, is interestingly also to be found among dopers, although even here he will protect himself against discovery by means of high and quick investments with the highest possible feeling of subjective security even if the threats of detection are low, because he wishes to avoid the costs of detection at almost any price. It is conceivable that the logic of the sports system, in which everyone would be better off by not doping, in which, however, a doping rival forces an athlete to engage in doping if they are to have any hope of realizing their competitive and, consequently, earnings opportunities, coerces athletes to dope if they do not want to lose their position in the sports system. In turning to doping, these security-seeking athletes are probably in many cases the "victims" of these structural constraints.

We again turn our attention to the conditions under which the level of sanctions can be drawn on to control (generally: lower) the expected benefit of the consumer, and consider in this context the derivation of EN to S:

$$(31)\quad \frac{\partial EN}{\partial S} = -2 \cdot Nd \cdot p(\frac{1}{x}(Nd-c)+c) + Nd = Nd \cdot (1 - p(\frac{1}{x}(Nd-c)+c))$$

In order to bring about a lowering of the expected benefit through sanctions, $\frac{\partial EN}{\partial S} < 0$ must also apply here. For the second case from (19), this therefore produces the condition:

$$(32)\quad Nd \cdot (1 - p(\frac{1}{x}(Nd-c)+c)) < 0 \quad \Rightarrow \quad p(\frac{1}{x}(Nd-c)+c) > \frac{1}{2}$$

In the event that an actor invests everything he or she is prepared to invest, the only possibility to lower the expected benefit of this actor via changes in the level of sanctions is if the probability of detection p is greater than 50%. However, the observations relating to (27) have already shown that it is currently not possible to achieve such a value for the probability of detection. Control via sanctions thus appears to be unrealistic.

5 Interim conclusion

A government-imposed doping ban that poses a threat to suppliers of doping substances automatically serves to privilege illegal suppliers, since the supplier power of those highly profitable illegal suppliers who remain in the market increases. The tougher the doping ban, the higher the sanctions and the greater the risk of punishment, the stronger the anticipated concentration effect in the market for highly-profitable suppliers could be expected to be, whereby we must anticipate a supranational, at the very least Europe-wide, concentration process in the market. As a non-intended effect, tighter penalties and higher probabilities of being punished would increase the earnings of those doping suppliers who remain undeterred and apply a risk bonus, provided that simultaneously imposed measures do not reduce the number of consumers in the same way.

The probability of punishment is the result of the efforts of the state and suppliers of doping substances who attempt to thwart successful detection efforts. The more illegal doping suppliers are deterred by tighter penalties, the more the police and the special anti-doping prosecutor's office become involuntary aiders and abetters to the doping suppliers by encouraging concentration effects and higher prices, thus generally contributing to higher profits.

This gives rise to the second non-intended effect, namely that the expected benefit of dopers increases, with the extent to which the threat of punishment or an increase in the level of punishment prompts punishment-avoiding investments on the part of suppliers. The higher exogenously-determined penalties are and the greater the probability of them being imposed, the more likely suppliers will be to do everything they can to avoid punishment, thus also reducing the risk of punishment for buyers. This relates not only to distribution channels (risk of discovery) and to efforts to conceal the substances being used by the doper (development and utilization of masking agents), but also to the bribing of laboratory staff, donations for laboratories, etc., although as veiled bribery the latter would even be tax-deductible for high-income professional athletes. The resulting higher prices consequently rule out lower-income buyers as consumers. This could trigger a similar concentration effect on the demand side, which we do not model here.

Added to this is the justified assumption that rational dopers initiate activities of their own in an attempt to lower the probability of being punished. For the demand side it has been shown that neither a negative expected benefit, corresponding to a solution to the "doping" problem, nor a lowering of the expected benefit of athletes through higher sanctions, is plausible.

6 Different European premises

The German anti-doping law is a so-called omnibus act that determines which provisions from various laws should be amended. Its most important cornerstones are punishability of possession, tighter penalties, which have been included in the German Drug Law, as well as a mandatory labelling requirement for doping substances (cf. details in Pitsch & Emrich, 2009). Punishability of possession stipulates that possession of "non-small amounts" of prohibited substances is punishable. This foresees imprisonment and fines for organized and commercial trafficking. Doped athletes are still only subject to the jurisdiction of the respective sports association, provided they do not exceed the limits defined as "non-small amounts".[44]

As mentioned initially, legislation governing doping offences varies within Europe from country to country. Differences are to be found relating to consequences under criminal law with respect to which offences are prosecutable and also with respect to the legal consequences, manifested in the level of punish-

[44] The position put forward for discussion by Bavarian Minister of Justice, Dr. Beate Merk, in the journal Sport und Recht (2010, pp. 104f.; cf. König, 2010, pp. 106f. and Kudlich, 2010, pp. 108f.; cf. also Momsen, 2009) in respect of the pros and cons from the legal point of view does not really change anything from the economy of law perspective. The qualificatory formulations in § 5 Sporting Fraud, Sections 1 and 2, according to which the use of doping substances as well as the use of methods to enhance oxygen transport are not punishable "if the doping substance, the metabolite or the marker stems from the intended administration of a pharmaceutical prescribed to treat a specific medical condition" (ibid., p. 105) or (in Section 2), "if in accordance with medical knowledge application of the method was necessary to treat a specific case of illness" (ibid., p. 105) mean that, despite a higher level of sanctions, the probability of sanctions is fundamentally not influenced. In this respect, tightening the level of penalties for consumers is equally ineffective because of the potentially vast impediments to the likelihood of penalties being imposed created by the above provisions. Moreover, realization is likely to raise interesting problems of balancing legal interests, if, for example, invoking human rights and the right of inviolability of the individual, athletes take legal action against judicially imposed penalties on the grounds that they are entitled to effective treatment, and physicians have ultimately monopolized therapeutic privilege as well as the right to err (cf. Kudlich, 2010, p. 109).

ment. We consider the following nine European countries: Belgium, Denmark, Germany, France, Italy, Austria, Sweden, Switzerland and Spain. Table 1 illustrates legal consequences under criminal law, subdivided according to offence and the consequences imposed by prosecuting authorities.

In addition to these offences, some countries cite the doping regulations of the sports associations or name offences that largely correspond to WADC stipulations (e.g. in Austria, France, Switzerland or Spain). In France, in addition to criminal prosecution for propagating and trafficking doping substances, athletes face the possibility of a 4-year or lifelong ban. Therefore in France possession is an offence that carries unspecified consequences. Spain, too, names other offences. Illegal conduct of coaches, referees, sporting officials or club physicians is a punishable act in the same way as selling or distributing prohibited substances at venues dedicated to the practice of sport.

In some of the countries listed, the organization of controls and subsequent sanctioning proceedings are also partly in the hands of different bodies. In Italy, for example, doping controls are carried out by a "commission for the supervision and control of doping and for health safeguards attached to the Ministry of Health", while sanctioning procedures fall under the responsibility of state jurisdiction. In countries like Spain, controls and sanctioning are in the first instance carried out by the sports associations (state institutions only become implicated after a certain period) and are only dealt with by state authorities at the appeal stage.

It should also not be forgotten that the powers of the authority for prosecuting a (doping) offence present an open question. In Germany, provisions under German law apply provided the offence was committed within Germany (§3 StGB – German Criminal Code). Pursuant to §5 StGB, German criminal law may still apply in the case of some offences perpetrated outside Germany, although these may also fall under the law of the country where the offence was committed. From the consumer/athlete perspective, it must be borne in mind that self-doping is a punishable act only in Italy, and therefore athletes are for the most part ruled out as perpetrators. Other national legislations concentrate first and foremost on possession, trafficking, etc.

Tab. 2: Legal consequences under criminal law (offences and their legal consequences) differentiated according to the various European countries[45]

Austria
1 July 2007: Anti-Doping-Bundesgesetz 2007, 8 August 2008: Änderung des Anti-Doping-Bundesgesetzes 2007, Arzneimittel- und Rezeptpflichtgesetz **Offence:** § 22a: Putting into circulation, use by third parties, possession (with corresponding intention); also applies to gene doping and methods to increase oxygen transfer, § 2a Prescription Drug Act: Prohibition to prescribe illegal substances **Legal consequences:** Up to six months' imprisonment or fine
Belgium
27 March 2001: Décret relatif à la promotion de la santé dans la pratique du sport, à l'interdiction du dopage et à sa prévention en Communauté française (Amended: 26 July 2007 and 12 August 2009) **Offence:** Art. 9 II: Punishability of all participatory actions **Legal consequences:** Six months to five years imprisonment, fine (Art. 13)
Denmark
1 July 1999: Act no. 232 of 21 April 1999, Act on Prohibition of Certain Doping Substances 1 January 2005: Act no. 1438 of 22 December 2004, Act on Promotion of Doping-free Sport 1 January 2007: Executive Order no. 1681 of 12 December 2006, Executive Order on Promotion of Doping-free Sport **Offence:** Production, import and export, dispensing, sale, possession (Art. 3.1) **Legal consequences:** Up to two years' imprisonment, fine (Art. 4.1)
Germany
21 September 2007: Entwurf eines Gesetzes zur Verbesserung der Bekämpfung des Dopings im Sport, Bundesrat document BR-Drs. 223/07 **Offence:** § 6a in conjunction with § 95 subsection 3 of the German Drug Law (AMG): commercial or organized activity; Possession of non-small amounts **Legal consequences:** Up to 10 years' imprisonment
France
Code du Sport (Partie Législative, extraits; Livre II: Acteurs du Sport, Titre III – Santé des Sportifs et Lutte contre le Dopage) – Version dated 4 July 2008; Loi no 2008-650 du 3 juillet 2008 relative à la lutte contre le trafic de produits dopants **Offence:** Trafficking, administering, use by third parties, production, import and export (Art. 2) **Legal consequences:** Up to seven years' imprisonment, fine of up to EUR 150,000 (Art. 7); Occupational ban for physicians

[45] The authors thank Ms Katja Senkel for providing the information listed in the table.

Italy
2 January 2001: Legge n. 376 del 14 dicembre 2000, Disciplina della tutela sanitaria delle attività sportive e della lotta contro il doping **Offence:** Art. 9 para 1 and 2:Ingestion/use; provision, administering; Art. 9 para 7: Illegal trafficking; Drug-legislation regulations: Art. 7: Regulations governing production, import, sale of drugs containing doping substances; warning on packs and package inserts **Legal consequences:** Art. 9 para 1 and 2: 3 months' – 3 years' imprisonment, 5 to 100 million Lire fine, Art. 9 para 7: 2-6 years' imprisonment, 10-150 million Lire fine
Sweden
19 December 1991: Act prohibiting certain doping substances (1991:1969) **Offence:** Import, dispensing, production, mediation, sale, possession and consumption (Section 2) **Legal consequences:** Up to two years' imprisonment (Section 3)
Switzerland
1 January 2002: Ergänzung des Bundesgesetzes über die Förderung von Turnen und Sport (FTSG), Abschnitt: Vb (Maßnahmen gegen Doping) **Offence:** Production, introduction, mediation, distribution, prescription, dispensing or use by third parties, (Art. 11d, f FTSG), where applicable § 19a BetMG (Narcotics Act) **Legal consequences:** Imprisonment or fine
Spain
22 February 2007: Ley Orgánica 7/2006, de 21 de noviembre, de protección de la salud y de lucha contra el dopaje en el deporte **Offence:** Incorporation of Art. 361 into Spanish Criminal Code (Offences against public health): prescription, offering and provision of illegal drugs to athletes taking part in officially organized competitions in Spain (not: possession or consumption by athletes) **Legal consequences:** 6 months' to 2 years' imprisonment

Table 2 illustrates examples of offences from the field of sport and the respective levels of penalties, albeit limited to penalties imposed by sports associations. Nevertheless, it clearly shows that related to the severity of the offence the level of penalties on the one hand differs considerably, and on the other is usually significantly below the maximum penalties defined by WADA.[46]

[46] Cáceres and Catuogno (2010, p. 27) cite the example of swimmer Rafael Munoz to show the scope of fluctuation of the sports associations in dealing with missed doping tests. Despite missing three doping tests in succession, the swimmer was not banned because a psychological assessment attested he was suffering from a "severe crisis".

Tab. 3: Athletes prosecuted for doping with the respective ban for the years 2008 and 2009 (source: http://www.sportgericht.de)

Name	Nation	Sport	Court	Offence	Penalty	Comment
Cases of doping in 2009						
Arbi, Roberto	ITA	Athletics	IAAF	n.s.	lifelong	Repeat offender
Cabreira, João	POR	Cycling	Port. Cycling Federation	Protease	24 mths	n.s.
Draguhn, Sebastian	GER	Hockey	NADA	Doping sample refused	12 mths	n.s.
Grech, Ryan	MAL	Football	Malt. Football Association	n.s.	12 mths	n.s.
Mannini, Daniele	ITA	Football	CAS	Delayed test	12 mths	Violation of anti-doping regulations
Martinaus, Gilbert	MAL	Football	Malt. Football Association	n.s.	12 mths	n.s.
Mattocks, Claude	MAL	Football	Malt. Football Association	n.s.	12 mths	n.s.
Cases of doping in 2008						
Ahlmann, Christian	GER	Riding	FEI	Horse treated with prohibited ointment (Capsaicin)	8 mths/ SFR 3,500 (*16 mths/ SFR 7,000)	CAS doubles ban*
Alifirenko, Sergej	RUS	Shooting	ISSF	Dexamethasone	24 mths	n.s.
Alves, Bernardo	BRA	Riding	FEI	Capsaicin	3 mths	14-week ban
Bastianelli, Marta	ITA	Cycling	Ital. Cycling Federation	Fenfluramine	24 mths	n.s.
Bayer, Nico	GER	Athletics	DLV	Amphetamine	24 mths	Suspended
Beltran, Manuel	ESP	Cycling	AFLD	EPO	24 mths	Suspended, imprisonment and ban pending
Blonska, Ludmilla	UKR	Athletics	Ukrainian Athletics Federation	Steroid	lifelong	Repeat offender
Bond, Chris	USA	Basketball	DBB	Benzoylecgonine	24 mths	Suspended
Chepkemei, Susan	KEN	Athletics	IAAF	Salbutamol	12 mths	Ban reduced from 24 to 12 months on the grounds of illness
Deflorian, Mirko	ITA	Downhill skiing	CONI	Cocaine	18 mths	n.s.

Name	Nation	Sport	Court	Offence	Penalty	Comment
Devi, Kavita	IND	Weight lifting	Indian Weight Lifters' Federation	Anabolic steroid	24 mths	Refusal of B sample
Dunkley, Julien	JAM	Athletics	IAAF	Boldenone	24 mths	n.s.
Ekpukhon, Christy	NIG	Athletics	IAAF	Metenolone	24 mths	n.s.
Fofonov, Dimitri	KAZ	Cycling	FFC	Heptaminol	3 mths	n.s.
Fränkel, Purrel	NED	Football	KNVB	Cannabis	1 mth	Marihuana cigarette, admission
Funck, Annette	GER	Athletics	DLV	Anti-allergenic (asthma drug)	2 mths	NADA belatedly informed
Gaag, Dimitrij	KAZ	Triathlon	ITU	EPO	24 mths	n.s.
Galliker, Martin	CH	Bobsledding	Swiss Olympic	Testosterone	24 mths	Withdrawal
Ghezielle, Bouchra	FRA	Athletics	French Athletics Federation	EPO	42 mths	Appeal against ban
Hansen, Tony Andre	NOR	Riding	FEI	Horse treated with prohibited medication (Capsaicin)	4 mths /€ 2,000	n.s.
Herzog, Tommy	CH	Bobsledding	Swiss Olympic	Testosterone	24 mths	n.s.
Hütthaler, Lisa	AUT	Triathlon	NADA Austria	EPO	18 mths	Accused of bribery, reduced from 24 to 18 months on the grounds of admission
Kohl, Bernhard	AUT	Cycling	NADA Austria	Erythropoetin (Cera)	24 mths	n.s.
Konopka, Mikulas	SVK	Athletics	Slovak Athletics Federation	Methandienone	lifelong	Repeat offender
Kreutzer, Daniel	GER	Ice hockey	NADA	n.s.	3 mths	2 missed samples
Kunpeng, Ouyang	CHN	Swimming	Chinese Swimming Association	Clenbuterol	lifelong	n.s.
Lucas, Ricardo	BRA	Football	CAS	n.s.	24 mths	Initially exonerated by Braz. association, CAS confirms ban
Mazzoleni, Eddy	ITA	Cycling	Ital. Cycling Federation	n.s.	24 mths	"Oil for Drugs" affair, refused to testify
Mourhit, Hassan	BEL	Athletics	Belgian Athletics Federation	Anastrazol	24 mths	n.s.

Name	Nation	Sport	Court	Offence	Penalty	Comment
Naimowa, Tesdschan	BUL	Athletics	Bulgarian Athletics Federation	Accused of manipulating doping samples	24 mths	Ban accepted
O'Neill, Nathan	AUS	Cycling	CAS	Phentermine	15 mths	n.s.
Osmanowa, Ludmila	UKR	Weight lifting	IPC	Anabolic steroid	24 mths	Banned from 2008 Paralympics
Palacios, Noraldo	ESP	Athletics	Columbia Athletics Association	n.s.	6 mths	Banned from the Olympic Games

7 Modelling of differences and derivation of hypotheses

With respect to the level of sanctions, considerable differences exist between various European countries. Based on the model presented above, we consider in the following different manifestations of the sanction level S, to which – depending on the respective situation – the individual European countries can be assigned.

S_s denotes a sanction level on the supply side that shall be considered as a standard value. S_h then describes a level of penalty that lies above and S_n a level below the standard. For the supply side, it shall therefore be established that:

(33) $S_h > S_s > S_n$

From this relation (33) and the assumption (2), it can be derived that a higher sanction also leads to a higher investment and it therefore follows that:

(34) $I(S_h, R) > I(S_s, R) > I(S_n, R)$

i.e. in countries with a higher level of penalties, investments made by a supplier and/or a consumer in escaping punishment are higher than they are in countries where the level of penalties corresponds to the standard. Conversely, actors from countries with a comparatively low level of sanctions invest less in avoiding punishment.

With respect to the impact of different levels of sanctions on the probability of detection – given the same level of repression – it can be concluded from the above reflections relating to (6) that where sanctions are higher, as in Germany or France, the probability of detection is lower than in countries with lower sanctions, i.e.

(35) $p(S_h, R) < p(S_s, R) < p(S_n, R)$

Thus on the supply side, it follows specifically from the reflections relating to the benefit (8) and its impact on the expected benefit of suppliers that initially an increased level of sanctions will reduce the benefit of trafficking doping substances:

(36) $N(S_h) < N(S_s) < N(S_n)$

Reflections concerning the variability of the expected benefit as a result of the level of sanctions show that without additional conditions for the functions p and N no statements can be made. It is revealed that the expected benefit decreases with rising sanction levels provided that the respective condition (13) is met. In condition (13) it was shown that via increasing sanction levels it is only possible to influence the expected benefit of suppliers with a low income (described above as type A). Concerning the difference between European countries this means that in countries where the level of sanctions is higher we ought to find a higher market concentration of a few, high-earning suppliers.

On the demand side, in addition to sanctions relating to the individual European countries it is possible to establish to what extent sanctions exist beyond those stipulated by WADC. It has been found that with the exception of Germany, Switzerland and Spain, consumers (i.e. athletes) can be criminally prosecuted for possession, consumption or importing and exporting illegal substances. In order to classify the occurrences of higher sanctions in cases of doping, we denote a sanction at WADC level (currently in WADC: 4-year ban for dopers) in the following with S_W. If additional sanctions for athletes exist in a given country, this is represented as S_{W+}. Thus we additionally obtain:

(37) $S_{W+} > S_W$, which affects $I(S)$ and $p(I(S))$, therefore:

(38) $I(S_{W+}) > I(S_W)$ and

(39) $p(I(S_{W+})) < p(I(S_W))$

shall apply.

Considerations of the expected benefit on the demand side included giving consideration to different investment strategies. On the one hand there are consumers who react very quickly to tougher sanctions and therefore even in the case of comparatively low sanctions invest everything they are prepared to in investments. On the other hand there are those who take a wait-and-see attitude to increased sanctions and make proportionately low counter-investments $(m \to 0)$. With respect to the relevant conditions, it became apparent that on the one hand the expected benefit and on the other hand the derivation of the expected benefit (i.e. the possibility of control via S) is not possible under real conditions in any of the observed cases (cf. (24), (28), (30) and (32)). Consequently a higher level of sanctions can only produce a negative expected benefit under very restricted conditions and control via S is not possible under any circumstances.

Nevertheless, a change in the level of sanctions results in changes in counter-investments (which are known to increase with higher sanctions), causing a lowering of the probability of detection. Thus consumers in countries with higher sanctions would have to invest more (presumably by consuming more masking agents), therefore lowering the probability of detection. However, based on the observations made, there is no change in the prevalence in these countries.

8 Conclusion

For the supply side it has been shown that the higher exogenously-determined penalties are and the greater the probability of them being imposed, the more likely suppliers will be to do everything they can to avoid punishment, thus also reducing the risk of punishment for buyers. This relates not only to distribution channels (risk of discovery) and to efforts to conceal the substances being used by the doper (development and utilization of masking agents), but also to the bribing of laboratory staff, donations for laboratories, etc., although as veiled bribery the latter would even be tax-deductible for high-income professional athletes. The resulting higher prices consequently rule out lower-income buyers as consumers. In general, we may expect to see a concentration process in the market towards a few, high-earning suppliers.

For the demand side it has been shown that neither a negative expected benefit, corresponding to a solution to the "doping" problem, nor a lowering of the expected benefit of athletes through higher sanctions, is plausible.

For the European comparison it has been shown that different threats of sanctions also tend to produce different investment strategies on the part of consumers. Thus on the one hand we can anticipate consumers who react very quickly to tougher sanctions and in the case of comparatively low sanctions are willing to invest everything they are prepared to in counter-investments. On the other hand there are those who take a wait-and-see attitude to increased sanctions and make proportionately low counter-investments.

The formalization revealed that the conditions for "producing" a negative expected benefit as a precondition for the effectiveness of sanctions were not met under anything approximating real conditions in any of the observed cases. Control via S, i.e. the level of sanctions, on the demand side proved ineffective in the sense of a reduced benefit. However, increasing sanctions produce counter-investments and thus lower the probability of dopers being detected. Consequently, consumers in countries with higher sanctions are likely to invest more (presumably by consuming more masking agents) in order to lower the probability of detection, which in turn simply means that in Europe, despite different sanction levels, a stable market equilibrium is established among those consumers still in the market. However, based on the observations made, there is no change in the prevalence of doping in these countries. It has to be concluded that doping prevalence evades the controlling arm of criminal law and that in light of the existing probabilities of detection and punishment the dilemma of doping cannot be solved via criminal law.

References

Beccaria, C. (1966). *Über Verbrechen und Strafe*. Translated and published by Wilhelm Alff based on the edition of 1766. Frankfurt a. M.: Insel.

Becker, G. S. (1974). Crime and Punishment: An Economic Approach. In: National Bureau of Economic Research, G. S. Becker & W. M. Landes (Eds.), *Essays in the economics of crime and punishment* (pp. 1-54). New York: Columbia University Press.

Bentham, J. (2000 [1781]). *An Introduction to the Principles of Morals and Legislation*. Kitchener (Ontario/Canada): Batoche Books.

Bette, K.-H. & Schimank, U. (1995). *Doping im Hochleistungssport. Anpassung durch Abweichung*. Frankfurt a. M.: Suhrkamp.

Bird, E. J. & Wagner, G. G. (1997). Sport as a Common Property Resource. A Solution to the Dilemma of Doping. *Journal of Conflict Resolution, 41*(6), 749-766.

Buchanan, J. M. (1977). *Freedom in Constitutional Contract, Perspectives of a Political Economist*. College Station: Texas A&M University Press.

Cáceres, J. & Catuogno, C. (2010, August 10). Signal aus dem Wohnwagen. Rafael Munoz entkräftet drei verpasste Dopingtest mit einem psychologischen Gutachten – in Budapest schwimmt er um EM-Gold. *Süddeutsche Zeitung No. 182*, 27.

Digel, H. (1994). Doping als Verbandsproblem. In K.-H. Bette (Ed.), *Doping im Leistungssport. Sozialwissenschaftlich beobachtet* (pp. 131-152). Stuttgart: Nagelschmid.

Höffe, O. (1975). Einleitung. In ibid. (Ed.), *Einführung in die utilitaristische Ethik, Klassische und zeitgenössische Texte* (pp. 7-34). Munich: Beck.

Kistner, T. (2010, August 13). Doping ist wie Frühstück. Teilgeständnis von Sportmanager. *Süddeutsche Zeitung, 185*, 25.

Kistner, T. (2010, August 14/15). Stark ausgebrannt. Landgericht Hamburg weist Jan Ulrichs Unterlassungsklage gegen den Dopingexperten Werner Franke ab. *Süddeutsche Zeitung, 186*, 34.

König, P. (2010). Sportschutzgesetz – Pro und Contra. Pro: Argumente für ein Sportschutzgesetz. *Sport und Recht, 17*, 106-107.

Kudlich, H. (2010). Sportschutzgesetz – Pro und Contra. Contra: Argumente gegen ein Sportschutzgesetz. *Sport und Recht, 17*, 108-109.

Merk, B. (2010). Gesetz zur Bekämpfung des Dopings und der Korruption im Sport (Entwurf). *Sport und Recht, 17*, 104–105.

Mommsen, C. (2009). Strafrechtliche Dopingbekämpfung? In E. Emrich & W. Pitsch (Eds.), *Sport und Doping: Zur Analyse einer antagonistischen Symbiose* (pp. 181-203). Frankfurt a. M.: Peter Lang.

Unattributed (2010). Sportpolitik. Absage für Anti-Doping-Gesetz. Ein Vorgehen gegen Dopingsünder nach italienischem Vorbild wird es in Deutschland nicht geben. Darauf haben sich Sportbund und Politik geeinigt. Trotzdem sollen vor allem Hintermänner der Szene härter bestraft werden. *Spiegel online Sport, accessed on 11.9.2010, http://www.spiegel.de/sport/sonst/0, 1518,434220,00.html.*

Pitsch, W. & Emrich, E. (2009). Aktuelle Änderungen des Dopingrechts - rechtliche Darstellung und ökonomische Würdigung. In E. Emrich & W. Pitsch (Eds.), *Doping und Sport. Zur Analyse einer antagonistischen Symbiose* (pp. 79-94). Frankfurt a. M.: Peter Lang.

Pitsch, W. (in print). Caught Between Mathematics and Ethics. Some Implications of Imperfect Doping Test Procedures. Appearing in M. McNamee & V. Møller (Eds.), *Doping and Legal Rights.* London: Routledge.

Pitsch, W., Emrich, E. & Klein, M. (2007). Doping in elite sports in Germany: results of a www survey. *European Journal of Sport and Society, 4* (2), 89–102.

Pitsch, W., Emrich, E. & Klein, M. (2005). Zur Häufigkeit des Dopings im Leistungssport. Ergebnisse eines www-Surveys. *Leipziger Sportwissenschaftliche Beiträge, 46* (2), 63–77.

Pitsch, W., Maats, P. & Emrich, E. (2009). Zur Häufigkeit des Dopings im deutschen Spitzensport - eine Replikationsstudie. In E. Emrich & W. Pitsch (Eds.), *Doping und Sport. Zur Analyse einer antagonistischen Symbiose* (pp. 19-36). Frankfurt a. M.: Peter Lang.

Pitsch, W. (2009). The science of doping' revisited: Fallacies of the current anti-doping regime. *European Journal of Sport Science, 9*, 87–95.

Rawls, J. (1975). Zwei Regelbegriffe. In O. Höffe (Ed.), *Einführung in die utilitaristische Ethik* (pp. 96-120). Munich: Beck.

Vanberg, V. J. (1982). *Verbrechen, Strafe und Abschreckung. Die Theorie der Generalprävention im Lichte der neueren sozialwissenschaftlichen Diskussion.* Tübingen: Mohr.

Werner Pitsch

Doping controls between test theory and ethics – unintended consequences of in principle imperfect doping tests

1 Introduction

In volume 454 of the journal "Nature", American biostatistician Donald A. Berry (2008) published a commentary on sources of error in doping test practice, in which he pointed out possible grave shortcomings in the current anti-doping strategy due to false positive doping tests. A closer re-analysis of his approach showed, however, that although Berry turned out to be wrong in the discussed Floyd Landis doping case, applying his thoughts to the many doping samples analysed worldwide every year can raise the probability of false positive results to serious levels (Pitsch, 2009). The considerations on which this analysis was based were explained using the example of concrete, single-case assessments of the relevant parameters sensitivity, specificity and the doping prevalence in elite sport. In the following, an attempt will be made to place this argumentation on a broader footing.

The aim of the following considerations and simulation calculations is therefore to illustrate the dependency of the quality of doping test practice on parameters of the test quality as well as on the frequency of doping among elite athletes in general, and on this basis establish possible fundamentally inherent limitations on the fight against doping.

2 The problem of restricted knowledge of required parameters

The quality of biomedical testing methods is typically measured on the basis of the sensitivity and the specificity of the procedure. Sensitivity describes the probability that the test result is positive if the analyzed sample actually contains the substance in question. Specificity on the other hand characterizes the probability that the test result is negative if a clean sample is analyzed. However, these parameters of doing test procedures are not published by WADA. The author was informed by e-mail that this information is considered sensitive as it could be used to optimize doping measures in order to foil or even evade detection.

Although the possibility of false positives is well known at least within WADA's executive committee (WADA foundation board, 2002; WADA executive committee 2006; 2007), there are no minimum thresholds for sensitivity and specificity defined in the international standard for laboratories (WADA, 2004b). The text contains only the following demand: "The ability of the assay to detect only the substance of interest must be determined and documented. The assay must be able to discriminate between compounds of closely related structures" (WADA, 2004b, 32, 33). Furthermore, the international standard for laboratories contains detailed adjustment settings for double blind proficiency testing (WADA, 2004b, 48-53). Thus, data relating to the quality of testing procedures are available in the application phase so that the sensitivity and specificity of the procedures could be estimated; however, the results of the proficiency testing programme are also not published by WADA.

For the following analyses, which due to the restricted information provided by WADA can never be more than simulations of possible occurrences of the phenomenon, the range of sensitivity and specificity values must therefore be narrowed down on the basis of the values stated in the available literature or based on plausibility assessments. We make the conservative assumption that the specificity estimation of the tests is greater than 0.999. This corresponds to one false positive result per 1,000 tests and is a value that comes close to that in many medical laboratory tests. Although it has been proved that considerably higher specificity values can be reached in individual testing procedures (cf. Sphon, 1978, Stein and Heller, 2006), this has not yet been proved, or at least not published, for the many tests on individual substances. This merely leaves us with the possibility of plausible estimation, which must also give consideration to the fact that not all doping test methods have an equally high quality. We must also take into account that in the field of doping, specificity must not be interpreted solely as a parameter characterizing the quality of a biomedical testing procedure, but should be seen as a characteristic of the whole procedure from the moment the sample is taken to the interpretation of the results of the biomedical analysis of the B sample. Hence an average assumed specificity of 0.999, which depicts a nearly perfect analysis procedure, is more or less a conservative estimation.

Regarding the sensitivity of single doping tests, the literature makes various assumptions (Franke & Heid, 2006; Lundby, Achman-Andersen, Thomsen, Norgaard, & Robach 2008; Schmidt, Prommer, Steinacker, & Böning, 2006) that suggest that the test procedures themselves sometimes only identify a small percentage of truly positive samples as being positive. Thus Lundby et al. (2008, 7), even allowing for the partially justified criticism of the study (cf. Schänzer, 2008a; 2008b as well as subsequently published readers' letters, cf. doi: 10.1152/japplphysiol.zdg.8310-comm.2008), found only a maximum of 31 potentially positive EPO tests when they had a total of 100 positive urine samples tested in two different accredited laboratories. Such discussions, however, relate to the quality of the single tests, whereas for the sensitivity of the doping testing strategy in general it is also important whether truly doped athletes are actually tested in the respective time window in which doping is observable. This is illustrated by isolated anecdotal evidence from the coverage of major sporting events (e.g. the "Ricardo Ricco" doping case in the Tour de France 2008, cf. not specified, 2008 as well as Reuters, 2008 and the fact discussed in the media that Marion Jones never once tested positive in the whole of her career). Such reports suggest that the sensitivity threshold tends to be low, at least with respect to the overall doping test procedure including selection of which athletes are to be tested and when in the course of the training year the test is to be carried out. This estimation is supported by the comparison between measurements of doping frequency in elite sport and the percentage of positive doping tests in the annually published WADA statistics. While so-called RRT surveys (cf. Pitsch, Emrich and Klein, 2005; 2007 as well as the article by Pitsch, Maats & Emrich in this volume) have fairly consistently found a rate of approximately 20-35% of doped athletes, WADA statistics also fairly consistently show a rate of approximately 2% of so-called "adverse analytical findings" (cf. WADA, 2004a; 2005; 2006; 2007a; 2008). Since the analyses are intended more to have the character of simulations of possible effects of the fight against doping, we vary the sensitivity in the following between values of 0 and 1. This way, they not only model non-intended effects of a not very effective (not very sensitive) fight against doping, but also those effects that might result if the sensitivity threshold could be raised, for example by imposing a more restrictive duty to report on athletes in future or through satellite-based electronic monitoring systems.

Another important parameter in calculating possible non-intended consequences of the fight against doping is the prevalence of doping, i.e. the percentage of athletes who use illegal drugs or methods to enhance their performance. The importance of doping prevalence for evaluating test results is a well known phenomenon, which above all due to its partly contra-intuitive implications has also found its way into popular scientific literature (cf. Beck-Bornholt & Dubben, 2007; Dubben & Beck-Bornholt, 2006). As far as doping prevalence is concerned, there are a number of more or less reliable sources on which to base estimations, such as WADA statistics on adverse analytical findings (e.g. WADA, 2008), analyses of the results of doping tests (e.g. Bahr & Tjornhom, 1998; Benzi, 1994; Delbeke, 1996), socioscientific surveys using classical instruments (Alaranta et al., 2006; Pedersen, 2005; Petroczi, 2002; Tangen, Bergsgard, Barland, & Breivik, 1997; Yesalis et al., 1988) or based on the randomized response technique (e.g. Pitsch, Emrich and Klein, 2005; 2007 as well as the article by Pitsch, Maats & Emrich in this volume), as well as purely analytical sport sociological (e.g. Bette, 2002; cf. Bette & Schimank, 2006; Bette, Schimank, Wahlig, & Weber, 2002) and sport economic observations (Breivik, 1987; 1992; Daumann, 2003; Eber & Thépot, 1999; Haugen, 2004; Keck & Wagner, 1989; Keck, 1990; Tangen & Breivik, 2001; Wagner, 1993).

Across these sources, the bandwidth of prevalence estimations ranges from almost 0%, for example at the Olympic Games in Beijing in 2008, to almost 100%, as suggested in some studies from the fields of systems theory and games theory. For this reason, in the following we carry out simulation calculations for the entire scale of possible prevalences.

3 The rate of truly positive results of doping tests

Based on the test quality of the single tests, as well as on the prevalence, a first approach to assessing the suitability of a testing procedure for a given frequency of occurrence of a phenomenon establishes the rate of positive tests that is derived from truly positive cases. This so-called "positive predictive value" can thus also be interpreted as the probability with which a positive doping test really shows that an athlete was doped. To obtain this, the Bayesian equation (Bayes 1958) based on knowledge of the prior probability (prevalence), as well as the sensitivity and specificity of doping tests, is drawn on to estimate the posterior probabilities (following a positive test). The probability that a positive doping test really points to a positive specimen (positive predictive value, ppv), can then be calculated as follows:

$$(1) \qquad ppv = \frac{p(d) * Se^2}{p(d) * Se^2 + (1 - p(d)) * (1 - Sp)^2}$$

with p(d)=doping prevalence.

This parameter is highly significant for doping test practice because it expresses how far a conclusion that a positive test result really indicates an incidence of doping is justified. Given that lower standards of evidence apply for doping tests than, for example, is typically the case in criminal law, (cf. e.g. Bowers, 2009, 11) and that evidence, on the grounds of the "strict liability" assumption, can lead directly to sanctioning (cf. the article by Senkel in this volume), finding out what conditions lead to less-than-perfect positive predictive values is crucial both to those active in the anti-doping campaign and to perhaps wrongly blamed innocent athletes.

For doping test practice, equation 1 already took into account that for a doping test to show a positive result, both the A and the B sample must test positive (for a comparative evaluation of the results of A as well as A and B specimens cf. Pitsch, 2009). Based on a specificity of 0.999, we obtain the positive predictive values of single doping tests for one substance respectively as a function of the sensitivity and the prevalence in the range [0.01; 0.1], as shown in Figure 1. It illustrates that even with low prevalence and low sensitivity, the positive predictive value of a single doping test is almost one, i.e. that the positive result of a single test with the assumed specificity of 0.999 indicates fairly reliably that the athlete was actually doped. Figure 2, by contrast, illustrates that specificity is crucial in evaluating a single doping test on one substance. A specificity of 0.99 with an assumed sensitivity of 0.3 and low doping prevalences namely led to false positive results in as many as approximately 10% of all cases.

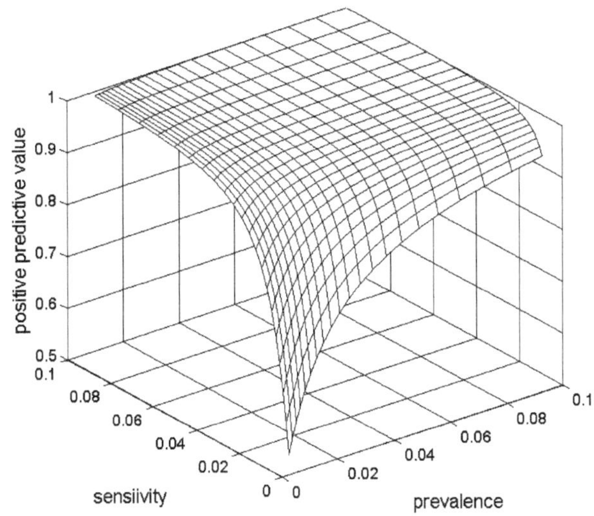

Fig. 1: Positive predictive value of a doping test for one substance as a function of prevalence and sensitivity with a specificity of 0.999

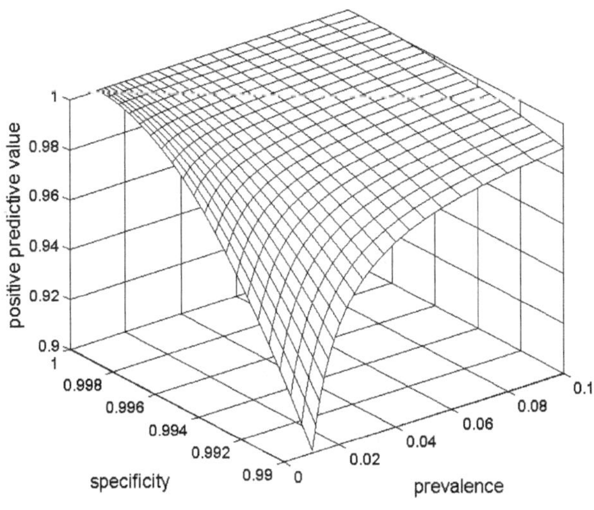

Fig. 2: Positive predictive value of a single doping test for one substance as a function of prevalence and specificity with a sensitivity of 0.3

As shown by Pitsch (2009), however, in testing practice the probability of true and false positive test results depends significantly on the number of substances each of the specimens is tested for as well as on the number of prohibited substances used. Thus if in equation 1 we use the overall sensitivity and the overall specificity for multiple tests or for tests for multiple substances (cf. equations 4 and 6 in the Appendix to Pitsch, 2009), we obtain lower positive predictive values simply because of the higher number of single tests. For this, the number of substances for which each sample is tested is varied in the range from 0 to 200 corresponding to 193 currently prohibited substances and methods (WADA, 2007b). We also assume that each athlete uses 2 different prohibited substances or methods.

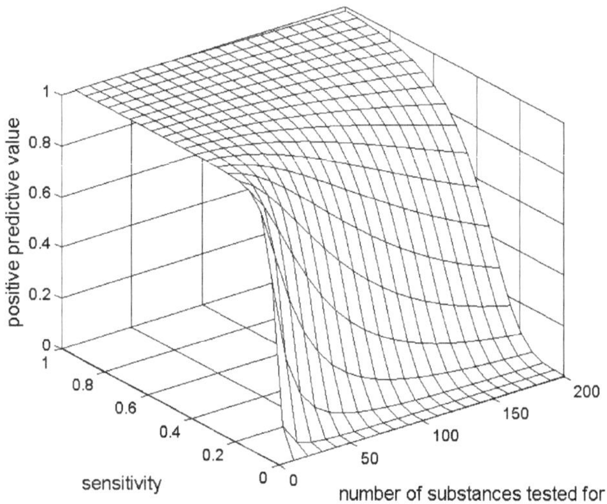

Fig. 3: Positive predictive value of doping tests for multiple substances as a function of the number of substances tested for and sensitivity (Sp=0.999, p(d)=0.5, u=2)

The results of the simulation calculation in Fig. 3 (specificity = 0.999; prevalence = 0.5; number of prohibited substances used = 2) show that it is only justified to conclude that concurring positive results of the A and B specimens really indicate an incidence of doping in the case of an analysis for relatively few prohibited doping substances or significantly higher sensitivity values than currently have to be assumed. Figure 4 (sensitivity = 0.3; prevalence = 0.5; number of prohibited substances used = 2) also makes it clear that for the analysis for multiple substances, the (already very high) specificity assumption of 0.999 still appears to be much too low to justifiably infer an incidence of doping from positive results, even if the samples are only tested for relatively few substances.

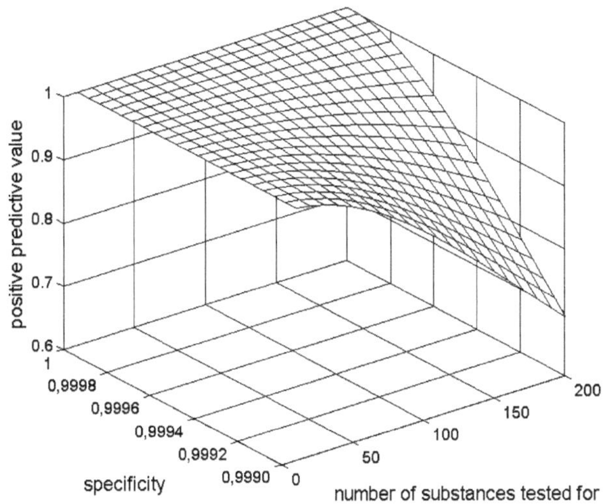

Fig. 4: Positive predictive value of doping tests for multiple substances as a function of the number of substances tested for and specificity (Se=0.3, p(d)=0.5, u=2)

4 The problem with repeated multiple tests

In the following, we shift from focusing on the importance of the issue of test quality with respect to the single case of an accused athlete to focusing on the issue of test quality against the background of the total number of doping samples analyzed every year and the high number of prohibited doping substances. Although lower sensitivity and specificity values have been shown to be high enough to substantiate a suspicion of doping after a positive doping test (see above), even under these very conservative assumptions concerning the quality of the tests for the fight against doping, they lead to a legitimacy problem: out of 200,000 doping tests per year worldwide, even if we assume that almost every athlete uses illegal drugs or methods, there is a probability on average that the doping tests will produce at least one false positive result (cf. Pitsch, 2009, 91). The probabilities presented in Figure 5 for at least one false positive result of the A and B specimen analysis (calculated from the cumulative probability density function of the binomial distribution, prevalence = 0.5, specificity = 0.999) show that whichever scenario of prevalence we choose, the current anti-doping regime and methods used are far from being consistent with the aim of WADA that "it was important not to have any false positives" (Prof. Ljungqvist at the WADA Executive Committee Meeting, 16 September 2006; WADA Executive Committee, 2006, 37). Furthermore, Figure 6 (sensitivity = 0.3, prevalence = 0.5) shows that only with significantly higher specificity values than assumed here can we even begin to lessen the problem of false positive doping tests, let alone actually overcome it. On the other hand, Figure 6 also illustrates that the rate of false positive doping test results increases the more extensive the definition of doping and the greater the number of substances and/or methods for which the samples are tested are.

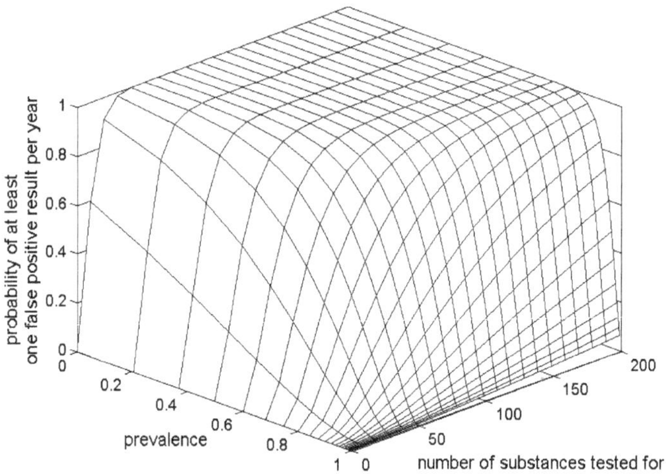

Fig. 5 Probability of at least one concurring false positive result of an A and B specimen analysis as a function of the respective number of substances tested for and the doping prevalence with a specificity of the single tests of 0.999

Thus only if we assume a really severe doping problem in elite sport in the sense that nearly every athlete uses illegal drugs or methods, could the problem arising from the possibility of false negative accusations be neglected. On the other hand, even one falsely accused athlete who maybe loses his or her career and income chances as a result, might serve as a threat to the legitimacy of anti-doping measures. If, however, deviating from this general suspicion we assume a lower doping prevalence on the basis of the rate of annual "adverse analytical findings", the problem of possible false positive results becomes critical. This also means, however, that the better anti-doping strategies work in terms of diminishing the doping prevalence through deterrence, the higher the rise in the false positive rate.

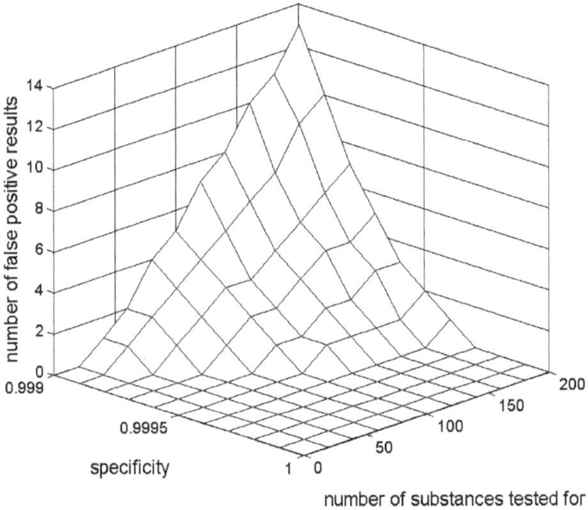

Fig. 6: Minimum number of false positive doping test results per year to be anticipated with a probability of 0.95 as a function of the specificity of the single tests and the respective number of substances tested for

5 Summary and discussion

The presented results of the simulation calculations are on the whole based on rather conservative estimates of the underlying parameters. This approach was taken in order not to falsely accuse the anti-doping movement and its protagonists. Thus, the real extent of the problem of possible false positive results is actually likely to exceed the rates and probabilities calculated. However, the true extent of the problem can only be addressed if WADA or the accredited laboratories publish the information about the test quality and the respective number of substances tested for.

We have shown that biomedical doping tests specifically, as well as doping test practices as a whole, have severe shortcomings that can produce significant negative implications in multiple tests for a high number of prohibited substances. The interpretation of doping test results is far from being trivial with reference to individual athletes and to single or multiple substances tested for, but in the case of a positive result can be considered a fairly dependable indication that the athlete concerned was doped. Nevertheless, this does not save the entire anti-doping test strategy from the problem that as a result of the growing number of doping specimens analyzed every year in the past and a growing number of prohibited substances and methods, there is also a greater probability of apportioning false blame.

A substantiated evaluation of the present anti-doping strategy as well as individual anti-doping accusations requires a broad understanding and evaluation of intended and non-intended effects of anti-doping as a whole. As long as discussions on anti-doping focus on individual athletes' reputation (as well as their income and career chances), the non-intended implications of doping tests applied to multiple substances and multiple doping specimens are lost from sight. It is not enough to develop doping tests based on a high specificity that can stand up in court if these tests have to be passed by thousands of potentially innocent athletes. The protection of potentially innocent athletes against false accusations makes much higher demands on test quality.

However, we are concerned with simulations of possible characteristics of the positive predictive value as well as of the probability of false accusations being made. For this, we had to make various speculations in order to perform the calculations. The parameters were estimated in each case on the basis of plausibility considerations and were exclusively conservative. Nevertheless, the thoughts presented here might still be totally misleading, provided that WADA could show that the estimation of single-test specificity was considerably higher. If the specificity of the single tests were so high, for example, that even with the lowest prevalences the probability of one false positive result occurring in 200,000 doping cases were below 0.01, then the present discussion would be superfluous.

Bearing in mind that the anti-doping test strategies (Kayser & Smith, 2008) lead to severe cuts in athletes' human and civil rights, a personal valuation of the presented results shall be permitted: if an (individual or collective) actor imposes extraordinary charges and restrictions on other actors and legitimizes these with ethical arguments, his or her own position should be morally unquestionable. If such a position cannot be reached, however, the whole undertaking becomes highly precarious. Given the shroud of secrecy surrounding information about test quality and testing practice cultivated by WADA, we might legitimately wonder whether the protagonists of the test procedures are in fact even interested in adopting a morally unquestionable position.

References

Alaranta, A., Alaranta, H., Holmila, J., Palmu, P., Pietilä, K., Helenius, I. (2006). Self-Reported Attitudes of Elite Athletes Towards Doping: Differences Between Type of Sport. *International Journal for Sports Medicine, 27*, 842-846.

Bahr, R., Tjornhom, M. (1998). Prevalence of Doping in Sports: Doping Control in Norway. *Clinical Journal of Sport Medicine, 8*, 32-37.

Bayes, T. (1958). An Essay Towards Solving a Problem in the Doctrine of Chance. *Philosophical Transactions of the Royal Society, 53*, 370-418.

Beck-Bornholt, H.-P., Dubben, H.-H. (2007). *Der Schein der Weisen. Irrtümer und Fehlurteile im täglichen Denken.* 5th edition. Reinbek near Hamburg: Rowohlt.
Benzi, G. (1994). Pharmacoepidemiology of the drugs used in sports as doping agents. *Pharmacological Research, 29* (1), 13-26.
Berry, D. A. (2008). The Science of doping. *nature, 454*, 692-693.
Bette, K.-H. (2002). Biographische Risiken und Doping. In H. Digel, H.-H. Dickhuth (Eds.), *Doping im Sport* (pp. 140-152). Tübingen: Attempo.
Bette, K.-H., Schimank, U. (2006). *Die Dopingfalle. Soziologische Betrachtungen.* Bielefeld: transscript.
Bette, K.-H., Schimank, U., Wahlig, D., Weber, U. (2002). Biographische Dynamiken im Leistungssport. Möglichkeiten der Dopingprävention im Jugendalter. Cologne: Strauß.
Bowers, L. D. (2009). Ensuring quality results in a global testing system. In: J. L. Fourcroy (Ed.), *Pharmacology, Doping and Sports. A scientific guide for athletes, coaches, physicians, scientists and admionistrators* (pp. 9-21). London: Routledge.
Breivik, G. (1987). The Doping Dilemma. Some game theoretical and philosophical considerations. *Sportwissenschaft, 17*, 83-94.
Breivik, G. (1992). Doping games. A game theoretical exploration of doping. *International Review for the Sociology of Sport 27* (3), 235-255.
Daumann, F. (2003). Doping im Hochleistungssport aus sportökonomischer Sicht. *Sportwissenschaft, 33*, 174-190.
Delbeke, F. T. (1996). Doping in Cyclism: Results of Unannounced Controls in Flanders (1987-1994). *International Journal of Sports Medicine, 17*, 434-438.
Dubben, H.-H., Beck-Bornholt, H.-P. (2006). *Mit an Wahrscheinlichkeit grenzender Sicherheit.* 3rd edition. Reinbek near Hamburg: Rowohlt.
Eber, N., Thépot, J. (1999). Doping in Sport and Competition Design. *Récherches Économiques de Louvain - Louvain Economic Review, 65* (4), 435-446.
Franke, W. W., Heid, H. (2006). Pitfalls, errors and risks of false-positive results in urinary EPO drug tests. *Clinica chimica Acta, 373*, 189-190.
Haugen, K. K. (2004). The Performance Enhancing Drug Game. *Journal of Sport Economics, 5* (1), 67-86.
Kayser, B., Smith, A. C. T. (2008). Globalisation of anti-doping: the reverse side of the medal. *British Medical Journal, 337*, 85-87.
Keck, O., Wagner, G. (1990). Asymmetrische Information als Ursache von Doping im Hochleistungssport. *Zeitschrift für Soziologie, 19* (2), 108-116.
Keck, O., Wagner, G. G. (1989). Das Doping-Dilemma im Hochleistungssport Praktische Vorschläge auf Basis der Spieltheorie. Berlin: Institute for Sports Science at the Freie Universität Berlin.
Luhmann, N. (1995). *Social Systems.* Stanford: Stanford University Press.
Lundby, C., Achman-Andersen, N. J., Thomsen, J. J., Norgaard, A. M., Robach , P. (2008). Testing for recombinant human erythropoietin in urine: problems

associated with current anti doping testing. *Journal of Applied Physiology*, 417 - 419.

Not specified (2008). Tour de France: Ricco gibt Doping zu [electronic version]. *Sueddeutsche Zeitung*. Last retrieved under http://www.sueddeutsche.de/sport/315/304291/text/.

Pedersen, I. K. (2005). Doping as a culture-constitutive process: Use of performance-enhancing substances in Danish sports and gyms. In A. R. Hofmann, E. Trangbaek (Eds.), *International Perspectives on Sporting Women in Past and Present* (pp. 381-397). Copenhagen: Institute of Exercise and Sport Sciences.

Petroczi, A. (2002). Exploring the Doping Dilemma in elite Sport: Can Athletes' Attitudes Be Responsible for Doping? Greeley, Colorado: University of Northern Colorado.

Pitsch, W., Emrich, E., Klein, M. (2005). Zur Häufigkeit des Dopings im Leistungssport: Ergebnisse eines www-surveys. *Leipziger Sportwissenschaftliche Beiträge, 46* (2), 63-77.

Pitsch, W., Emrich, E., Klein, M. (2007). Doping in elite sports in Germany: results of a www survey. *European Journal for Sport and Society*. 4 (2), 89-102.

Pitsch, W. (2009). "The science of doping" revisited: Fallacies of the current Anti Doping Regime. *European Journal of Sport Science*. 9, 87-95.

Reuters. (2008). Tour drugs cheat Riccardo Ricco tried to flee testers. Last retrieved on 11.09.2008 under http://www.news.com.au/heraldsun/story/0,21985,24063859-11088,00.html

Schmidt, W., Prommer, N., Steinacker, J., Böning, D. (2006). Sinn und Unsinn von hämatologischen Grenzwerten im Ausdauersport – Folgerungen aus den Dopingskandalen von Turin 2006. *Deutsche Zeitschrift für Sportmedizin, 57* (2), 54-56.

Sphon, J. A. (1978). Use of mass spectrometry for the confirmation of animal drug residues. *Journal of the Association of Official Analytical Chemists* 61, 1247-1252.

Stein, S. E., Heller, D. N. (2006). On the risk of false positive identification using multiple ion monitoring in qualitative mass spectrometry: large scale intercomparisons with a comprehensive mass spectral library. *Journal of the American Society of Mass Spectrometry* 17, 823-835.

Streck, M. V., Volland, B. (11.08.2004). Ben Johnson: "Siegen ist eine Sucht". *Stern.de* Last retrieved on 27.11.2008 under http://www.stern.de/sport-motor/olympia2004/528229. html?eid=527150.

Tangen, J. O., Breivik, G. (2001). Doping Games and Drug Abuse. A study of the relation between preferences, strategies, and behavior in relation to doping in Norwegian sport. *Sportwissenschaft, 31*, 188-198.

Tangen, J. O., Bergsgard, N. A., Barland, B., Breivik, G. (1997). "To Dope or not to Dope". A Study on the Decision to use Drugs in Norwegian Sports. *Corpus,Psyche et Societas, 4* (1), 41-65.

Velonews. (2008). Riccò admits to doping [electronic version]. *Velonews*. Last retrieved on 11.09.2008 under http://tour-de-france.velonews.com/article/81064/.

WADA Executive Committee (2006). Minutes of the WADA Executive Committee Meeting, 16 September 2006, Montreal, Canada [electronic version] Last retrieved on 12.11.2008 under http://www.wada-ama.org/rtecontent/document/ EXCO_Minutes_ 2006_09_16_ en.pdf.

WADA Executive Committee (2007). Minutes of the WADA Executive Committee Meeting, 12 May 2007 Montreal, Canada [electronic version]. Last retrieved on 12.11.2008 under http://www.wada-ama.org/rtecontent/document/EXCO_Minutes_2007_05_12_En.pdf.

WADA foundation board (2002). Minutes of the WADA Foundation Board Meeting, 4 June 2002, Montreal, Canada [electronic version]. Last retrieved on 12.11.2008 under http://www.wada-ama.org/rtecontent/document/040602-ENG.pdf.

WADA (2004a). Wada Statistics 2003. Overview of the results reported by the 31 IOC/WADA accredited Laboratories [electronic version] Last retrieved on 10.09.2008 under http://www.wada-ama.org/rtecontent/document/LABSTATS_2003.pdf.

WADA (2004b). The World Anti-Doping Code. International Standard for Laboratories Version 4.0 [electronic version] Last retrieved on 10.09.2008 under http://www.wada-ama.org/rtecontent/document/ lab_aug_04.pdf.

WADA (2005). 2004 Adverse Analytical Findings Reported by Accredited Laboratories [electronic version] Last retrieved on 10.09.2008 under http://www.wada-ama.org/rtecontent/document/LABSTATS_2004.pdf.

WADA (2006). 2005 Adverse Analytical Findings Reported by Accredited Laboratories [electronic version] Last retrieved on 10.09.2008 under http://www.wada-ama.org/rtecontent/document/LABSTATS_2005.pdf.

WADA (2007a). 2006 Adverse Analytical Findings Reported by Accredited Laboratories [electronic version] Last retrieved on 10.09.2008 under http://www.wada-ama.org/rtecontent/document/LABSTATS_2006.pdf.

WADA (2007b). The 2008 Prohibited List [electronic version]. Last retrieved on 12.11.2008 under http://www.wada-ama.org/rtecontent/document/2008_List_ Format_en.pdf.

WADA (2008). 2007 Adverse Analytical Findings * Reported by Accredited Laboratories [electronic version] Last retrieved on 10.09.2008 under http://www.wada-ama.org/rtecontent/document/LABSTATS_2007.pdf.

Wagner, G. G. (1993). The Triple Doping Dilemma – An Economic Analysis of Anti-Doping Regulations. In G. Gebauer (Ed.), *Die Aktualität der Sportphilosophie / The Relevance of the Philosophy of Sport* (pp. 143-158). Sankt Augustin: Academia.

Yesalis, C. E., Herrick, R. T., Buckley, W. E., Friedl, K. E., Brannon, D., Wright, J. E. (1988). Self-Reported Use of Anabolic-Androgenic Steroids by Elite Power Lifters. *The Physician and Sportmedicine, 16* (12), 91-100.

The doping control market – Are investments into a faked honesty more rewarding than honesty itself?[47]

1 Introduction

According to Messing and Müller (1996, 227, 247; cf. Messing, Müller & Schormann, 2008, 217), in a survey of 475 spectators at the 1992 Olympic Games in Barcelona a total of 90.9% wanted to see peak sporting performances. 75.3% of the respondents saw a threat to the Olympic idea as a result of commercialization and 58.2% through doping (Messing & Müller, 1996, 235). Among those who named more than two and up to six threats to the Olympic Games, 56.3% felt that the Games in Barcelona stood under the motto "win at any price", while 21.8% saw doping and manipulation as the determining factors of Olympic performance in Barcelona (ibid, 237). From the Olympic Games in Sydney in 2000 to Athens in 2004, the percentage of those who see doping practices as jeopardizing the Olympic Games rose from 69.1% to 81.6% (Messing, Müller & Schormann, 2008, 229).

Tröger (2006, 221) asked Olympic experts, athletes, media representatives and sports students in Athens the question: "Is this development [athletes charged for doping, the authors] detrimental to the image of the Olympic Games?" and received an affirmative response from 63.5%. On the one hand Olympic spectators want to see top sporting performances, but on the other hand more than half of those surveyed fear that doping poses a risk.[48] Interestingly, the 12 interviewed media representatives were undecided, with six answering in the affirmative and six disagreeing.

The quality of the consumed sport product is reflected by the consumer and therefore automatically influences demand (on the importance of fair play from a legal perspective cf. also the article by Momsen in this volume).[49] The princi-

[47] The basic formalization of the findings discussed here was presented at the Congress for Sport Economy in Cologne in 2009. It will be published separately after final completion and numerical simulation.

[48] The media, too, must also observe the laws of supply and demand in the media market if they intend to sell sport and survive as a business venture. They find themselves in a kind of antagonistic symbiosis with dopers (on the term cf. Scharpf, 1997). Over the long term, the media are therefore only likely to develop a real interest in fighting deviations from the norm if the overall demand for sports coverage declines as a result, or if it can be empirically shown that as a result of "doping-free" sport the demand rises. However, this is likely to be difficult to establish.

[49] In cycling in the Tour de France, media revelations about widespread doping raised the levels of media attention for cycling in the short term, but over the long term led to reputation losses for cycling. As many as 79% of TV spectators assume that Tour de France cyclists are doped, probably as a consequence of the widespread doping practices from the previous year (Dobbert, Zeit-online dated 11 July 2007, retrieved on 4. 9. 2008).

pal components of the perceived quality consist in the delivered performance and its compliance with the rules, which guarantees the integrity of sporting competition. Creation of the goods sporting performance and compliance[50] takes place in the form of co-products, since both components can only be produced jointly within the production process of sporting competition. These goods are at the same time complementary goods, since they can in general only be demanded together. Peak performance without compliance simply isn't sport. Independently of the production process, compliance is a good that from the consumer perspective may be burdened by costs of trust if there are known violations.

In terms of sporting performance, the consumer can easily observe the quality of the good consumed. In many sports, sporting performances are measured directly, in others indirectly. Performance characteristics can be determined most reliably in sports that are measured in centimetres, grams or seconds. These are above all sports in which record lists are kept, such as track and field, swimming, weight lifting, speed skating, etc. But even in sports in which natural influences and variable conditions make it impossible to establish records (e.g. rowing, canoeing, skiing, etc.), a particular fascination of competition is growing from the decidability of a performance ranking based on physical-technical measurement, even in areas that are not directly perceivable to the human eye. The results of racquet sports and games measured in goals are also relatively clear. In disciplines where record lists are not kept, i.e. the so-called artistic-compositional sports or combat sports, an exceptional display in a performance measured in points – for example a particularly complex free-style move in gymnastics – attracts special attention and is considered to be a quality attribute.

For the organizers of sporting events and for the athletes themselves, this means that they can only uphold or even increase the demand for sport – communicated predominantly via the media – if they continue to produce top performances. As an undetected deviation from the norm, doping enhances peak sporting performance and hence demand; as a detected deviation from the norm it is detrimental to the integrity of competition. Depending on the frequency of its occurrence, detected doping at the same time helps to stabilize faith in the compliance of the performance of athletes who do not test positive (on the positive function of violations of the norm cf. Durkheim, 1999, 181) and like any other exposed deviation from the norm also develops its own entertainment

[50] Simmel (2003) already pointed out in 1908 that competition (against each other) and cooperation (in terms of mutual acknowledgement of the rules) form the basic structure in tournaments. When athletes no longer compete with each other (i.e. adhering to the rules) against each other (in an attempt to reach an uneven outcome), then it is no longer sport. "Competition can be termed "regulated competition" inasmuch as its goals and resources are oriented towards an order" (Weber 1980, 20).

value (on the significance of the number of undetected cases problem cf. Popitz, 1968, 20).[51]

The two complementary co-products performance and compliance each have a different significance with respect to the value of the good in the market. The perceived compliance of the delivered performance is a necessary prerequisite for the performance to achieve a high price in the market. However, an increase in compliance does not increase the value of the complement, which in turn – assuming consumers have confidence in compliance – depends on the level of the sporting performance.

This creates the interesting constellation that athletes produce the collective good "clean sport" for the collective of athletes, which through the marketing of competition performance is turned into a consumer good that is demanded at ever higher prices, the higher the performance is – provided that consumers have confidence in compliance. Confidence in compliance is also produced by those athletes who utilize this collective good as free riders and at the same time enhance their income chances as dopers, as long as they remain undetected. They increase the benefit of the collective good for all – assuming that undetected doping leads to higher performances – which in turn increases their success-dependent personal income as well as the price of the sporting competition product. On the other hand, if detected, their doping activities jeopardize the exploitability of the collective good and hence the benefit for all.

2 Problem definition

If in this context the producer side, which ultimately means the side of the IOC and its member associations, wants the demand-enhancing benefit of undetected deviation from the norm in the form of higher performances, then it must invest in doping controls. At the same time, however, a control structure needs to be established that does not allow too many norm deviators to be detected. For example, within the scope of the most comprehensive doping control programme to date on the occasion of the Beijing Olympics, 4,770 tests were carried out, including 1,462 pre-Games and out-of-competition controls, of which only nine tests had a positive result. By contrast, altogether over 1,000 therapeutic exceptions were confirmed or granted and 61 positive doping test results were not classified as violations of the WADC on the grounds of therapeutic exceptions. Furthermore, the duty to report the whereabouts of athletes was not adequately adhered to by almost half of the National Olympic Committees or the respective athletes, significantly hindering unannounced out-of-competition controls (WADA, 2008).

[51] In this context, Popitz (translated from 1968, 20) says: "Penalties can only keep their social effectiveness as long as the majority "do not get what they deserve". The preventive effect of a penalty also only remains valid as long as the general prevention of the number of unknown cases is preserved."

The question of what sensitivity the entire doping control procedure brings to light, in other words what is the probability that an athlete who is really doped will be found guilty, is not just an issue in the Olympic Games (the problems generated by the principle of strict liability are discussed by Senkel in this volume). If we assume that the rates established for Germany – despite high control standards – of approximately 20-30% of doping athletes across all sporting disciplines (cf. Pitsch, Emrich & Klein 2005; 2007; for a current discussion cf. the articles by Pitsch, Maats & Emrich as well as Pitsch in this volume) are on a similar level internationally, then assuming a rate of 20% of athletes who dope, the approximately 200,000 WADA controls per year (WADA, 2008) should produce 40,000 positive specimens. In fact, according to WADA statistics, only around 2% are detected. This means that 90% of reasonably presumed doping violations go undetected (cf. also the articles by Daumann as well as Pitsch in this volume).

Assuming perfect doping tests in which all positive specimens produce true positive results and no negative specimens produce false positive results, the discrepancy between the rate of doped athletes and the rate of positive specimens can only be explained by the detectability of doping within the scope of doping control practice. Since it is not possible to take samples from all athletes all of the time, the question arises as to how probable it is that a doped athlete is required to give a specimen within the time window in which doping is observable.

The demand for elite sport is at its highest when tests do not catch too many guilty deviators, but at the same time credible investments can be seen to go into control efforts as a means of symbolizing the ethical quality of competition, and additionally peak or if possible even record sporting performances are achieved (cf. Emrich, 2006).[52]

For consumers, this poses the problem that at the moment of consumption (t_0) the quality of the consumed transient good "elite sport" is unknown, since the results of the doping tests are not available until after the end of the respective competition. However, the impression of non-compliance in a competition situation at the moment t_0 can indeed affect the subsequent demand for sport at a moment t_1. If we assume in this context that organizers are aiming to maximize their benefit over long periods of time, then the problem of establishing credibil-

[52] Even those who as individual actors aim to maximize their economic benefit in light of a biologically determined relatively short period of peak performance act as homo oeconomicus in the commercialized sport-related competitive environment (cf. the two articles by Daumann as well as Pitsch & Emrich in this volume). If they dope, they rationally increase their chances of a higher income, provided they are not caught for violating the norm. Within the context of ethics in a capitalist market economy characterized by competition, Götz Briefs (1959, 97; cf. 1957, translated by the authors) coined the term marginal ethics early on: "In competition, it is those with the lowest ethical standards who survive over the long term, because in any conflict maintaining higher ethical standards brings competitive disadvantages." Marginal ethics in this context is the condition that is just about still tolerated.

ity in the quality of the good in the sense of compliance is the same for each individual competition, making it possible to abstract from the time delay between experienced quality and repeat demand.

Table 1 shows a comparison of the four conceivable variants of the correlation of performance characteristics and deviation from the norm in the form of doping. The two diametrically opposed variants a and d are, ceteris paribus, from an analytical point of view the ones with the highest (variant a) and the lowest (variant d) demand.

Tab. 1: Correlation between performance characteristics and compliance

Variant a: Elite sport with a high probability of achieving records low rate of detected dopers	Variant b: Elite sport with a high probability of achieving records high rate of detected dopers
Variant c: Performances falling far short of peak performance levels low rate of detected dopers	Variant d: Performances falling far short of peak performance levels high rate of detected dopers

The central question to be answered in the following is: How do sports associations organize an optimum relation of peak performance characteristics while at the same time maintaining an optimized correlation of detected deviant and compliant behaviour on the part of athletes? To this end, we draw in the following on an institutional economic analysis to examine how institutions resolve this efficiency problem.

3 An institutional economic analysis – corporate and individual actors and their interrelations

The following corporate and individual actors are considered: the International Olympic Committee (IOC), the international member associations in the IOC, the respective host city of the Olympic Games, the athletes, the doping control agencies and the consumers of the Olympic sport product.

3.1 The IOC and its member associations

The IOC offers the rights to Olympic Games in a worldwide market and, in a complex process, grants a "licence" for a limited period of time to organize the Olympic Games contests as a specific sport product for a worldwide market. The so-called host city contract (HCC), which regulates the rights and duties of the IOC as well as of the host city, is signed on the same day as the official nomination of the city by the IOC (cf. Schollmeier, 2001, 71). When it comes to the economic exploitation of rights to the Olympic Games, the international community of states grants the IOC far-reaching exploitation autonomy.[53] Indeed, the IOC strictly reserves "all rights to the Olympic symbols, flag, motto, anthem and Olympic Games" for itself (Olympic Charter, 2001, Rule 17), conducts all negotiations with TV broadcasting companies and top sponsors and checks their activities for image-damaging advertising as well as ambush marketers cashing in on the Games. It monitors the "Olympic" content of sponsors' TV ads and commits the organizers to "public service announcements" and "year around programmes", assumes responsibility for international merchandising, prohibits excessive street sales and leases early on all available advertising space in the candidate city for the duration of the Games (cf. Nieschlag, Dichtl & Hörschgen, 2002, 930 f.). The IOC sees this extreme exploitation autonomy as being clearly legitimate: "By retaining all rights to the organization, marketing, broadcasting and reproduction of the Olympic Games, the IOC ensures the continuity of a unique and universal event" (Olympic Charter, 2001, Rule 17).

The IOC is thus a monopolist that (taking account of summer and winter Games) offers the product Olympic Games every two years and in 2004, for example, received 51% of the revenues from TV rights from the host city (host city 49%), which are in turn distributed between the world sports associations and the IOC.[54] Under Rule 40 of the Olympic Charter, the IOC incidentally assumes no liability for any financial deficits incurred, which naturally increases the incentive for the host city to stage financially successful Games. The rights the IOC as franchisor sells in an almost classic franchise system (on the constitutive characteristics of the franchise system cf. Meffert, 2000, 639) by transferring the entire economic risk to the host city as temporary franchisee, derive from the fact that well known sports providers in the market (winter and summer sports associations [e.g. IAAF, FIFA, ...]) relinquish their decision-making autonomy and combine their product in the Olympic rhythm with the special ethical qualities associated with the Olympic idea of the IOC to create a co-product (peak sporting performance and compliance) and at the same time complement (see above), by transferring the rights to their sport to the IOC for the purposes of organizing the Olympic Games. The transfer occurs formally through membership in the IOC, which necessarily implies acceptance of the conditions of membership in the form of the statutes.

This gives rise to an interesting constellation. On the one hand, corporate actors, namely world sports associations, consolidate their rights of disposal to international sporting disciplines in the IOC, which at the same time is the monopolist in terms of disposal of the rights to the Olympic Games. The IOC coor-

---

[53] Cf. on this the press release of the Federal Ministry of Justice dated 11 December 2003 referring to the Olympic Protection Law that created the legal framework for a possible successful bid of then candidate city Leipzig by granting the exclusive right to utilize the terms Olympics, Olympic and Olympiad to the National and International Olympic Committee. Where this special legal protection does not exist, the IOC does not award the Games.

[54] The revenues are said to be divided roughly equally three ways (cf. Rittberger & Boeckle, 1997, 147).

dinates appropriation of the consolidated resources, i.e. the rights to sporting disciplines and the rights to the Olympics, and for the purpose of utilizing the consolidated rights of disposal, transfers them at regular intervals to an agent in the form of an Olympic Games host against fulfilment of the above-mentioned duties.

As additional agents, the IOC commissions its member associations with the realization of the Olympic contests. The thus generated resources are redistributed in accordance with partly intransparent trust criteria by the in some cases lifetime members of the IOC management. This form of redistribution is stabilized by the extremely high exit costs. Corporate actors wishing to participate in the Olympic Games are not able to relinquish their membership in the IOC. With certain restrictions, the relationship between the IOC and its member associations could also be described as an antagonistic symbiosis in the same way as that between the IOC and the host city.

Between the IOC, the member associations and athletes, there finally also exist specific internal interactions in the sense of a principal-agent relationship. The associations, for example, need willing and able elite athletes who are in a position to deliver Olympic top performances; but on the other hand they must also ensure that these performances are achieved in compliance with the rules, or at least that faith in compliance can be upheld. For their part, athletes wherever possible need successful participation in Olympic Games in order to raise their market value in the many subsequent non-Olympic tournaments in their respective sport. The specific relationships so far discussed can be described within the important context for recent information economics research of asymmetric information, which is inextricably linked to the theory of incomplete contracts (on economics of information cf. Stiglitz, 2000, 1441-1478).

3.2 Some thoughts on asymmetric contracts

The following remarks are oriented towards observations of recent institutional economics research on self-enforcing agreements or self-enforcing implicit contracts (Carmichael, 1989, 81; cf. Richter & Furubotn, 2003, 276 ff). In the case of such contracts, the parties determine themselves whether the implicit or explicit agreement has been violated or not. Characteristic for the economic relations and decisions analyzed within the scope of this theory are the asymmetric distributions of information between the partners concerned, which give the agent an informational advantage over the principal. In this, a distinction is made between three forms of asymmetric information distribution: hidden characteristics, hidden action/hidden information and hidden intention. One way to reduce or even eliminate the action uncertainties resulting from asymmetric information distribution is to design institutional arrangements in the form of incentive-compatible contracts. The costs for overcoming informational asymmetries are generally referred to as agency costs. Attempts are made to minimize these by means of institutional arrangements that contain incentives. The agency costs are made up of signalling costs on the part of the agent and monitoring and control costs on the part of the principal. There is an additional welfare loss brought about by suboptimal exploitation of specialization advantages. All actions of the agent following conclusion of the contract that run counter to the principal's interests are subsumed under the term moral hazard and often incur conventional sanctions (cf. in general on the principal-agent theory Pratt & Zeckhauser, 1985; Laffont & Martimort, 2002; Macho-Stadler & Perez-Castrillo, 2001).

The principal delegates decision-making competences to the agent, who performs tasks on the principal's behalf. In this, it is assumed both parties are personal utility maximizers who act with limited rationality. The actions of both interaction partners mutually influence each other; above all the agent not only influences his own utility level, but also that of the principal. Thus for the principal, the general purpose of the incentive-compatible institutional arrangement is to encourage the agent to utilize his informational advantage to further the principal's interests.

The sale and subsequent consumption of the good Olympic sport typically involves a series of interrelated actions. First, the principal, the IOC, determines what quality standards are to apply to the organization of the Games (sports venues, accommodation, etc.) and then, within the scope of a subsequent bidding procedure, decides which city is to host the Games – whereby the IOC retains the central media and marketing rights. The assigned organizer then determines the prices for the good, after which Olympics-interested buyers around the world decide in favour of consumption or not.

Both sets of exchange parties, i.e. the IOC and the Olympics city as well as the Olympics city and Olympics visitors, are assumed to have different levels of information. In concrete terms this means that at the time of granting the right to host the Games to the bidder, the IOC does not know whether this organizer will fulfil all the conditions, etc. However, it reduces the costs of trust, for example, by regularly inspecting the progress of construction for the Games and like this secures the progress and compliance with the standards. What's more, the financial risk lies exclusively with the Olympics city (partly or mostly with state funding). It can further be assumed that the anticipated damage to the host's reputation if the quality falls short is incentive enough in itself to ensure the quality standards are met.

Future visitors to the Olympics, i.e. the consumers of the product, know neither at the time of ordering and buying admission tickets nor at the time of consumption whether they are buying an inferior-quality (rule-breaking, doping-tainted, unclean sport) or superior-quality good (rule-compliant, untainted, clean sport) or not; all they can judge is the athletes' performance on the day. However, as track and field enthusiasts, for example, they have to pay considerably higher prices for the consumption of the Olympic athletics tournaments than for the world athletics championships.

Indirect spectators who follow the event via the media also do not know at the time of consumption whether they are witnessing rule-compliant, doping-free, clean sport in terms of doping practices or not. Thus consumers buy an admission ticket at a given moment t_0. However, they only know at a subsequent moment t_1, in other words a fairly long time after the doping controls, whether, in terms of compliance, the quality of the consumed product was high or not. The later the final result of the controls becomes known, the less the faith in high quality is probably jeopardized, since the two events are perceived as separate. The current ruling of the IOC during the Olympic Games in Beijing to freeze doping samples and keep them available for a period of eight years for subsequent doping analyses, significantly protracts the length of time until both direct spectators and indirect consumers via the media discover that they have possibly consumed an inferior-quality good at inflated prices.[55]

Thus as a central asymmetry, one significant problem (cf. Richter & Furubotn, 2003, 276 ff.) is that the parties do not know whether the other side is honest or not; in the given case the consumer does not know whether the high-performance athlete is deviating from the norm or not. Honesty is only relevant, however, to the extent that a larger number of individuals can observe that an actor is disciplined for not adhering to the rules. Durkheim (1999, 181) already put forward the idea of the functionality of deviant behaviour, which postulates that the function of the norm and the significance of conformance with the norm can only be inferred through observed violation of the norm and its sanctioning. To this extent, the media and thus publicly sanctioned breach of the norm not only plays a role in increasing costs for the individual who violates the norm; it at the same time has a functional role for the validity of the norm. Only an optimal rate between detected and non-detected norm violators and strictly norm conformists – in our case detected dopers, undetected dopers and strictly non-dopers – can thus support the validity of the norm.

From the perspective of a rationally acting individual, if understood in the sense of bounded rationality (Simon, 1957), it makes sense to follow Telser (1980, 29), who proceeds from the hypothesis "that an individual is only honest if honesty or the appearance of honesty is more rewarding than dishonesty." Thus, if the appearance of honesty, or norm conformance, is to be more rewarding than genuine honesty, or true norm conformance, we can assume that actors will tend to make investments in this appearance of honesty. Keeping up the appearance of a good reputation, as well as keeping up a genuine good reputation, demands investments, which we are only prepared to make if the anticipated rewards are adequate. Once-invested expenses in an apparent or real good

[55] Following the doping confession of former 100-metre sprint world record holder Tim Montgomery, an article in the Süddeutsche Zeitung (No. 275 dated 26 November 2008, 30) stated that the International Olympic Committee called for Montgomery to voluntarily return the Olympic gold medal he won as part of the US sprint relay team. Several years after the Olympic Games in Sydney, with much less media hype, US athletes had already had their wins in the 4x400 and the 4x100 relays voided.

reputation, i.e. in norm conformance, then inevitably give the contracting parties, in this case the consumers, the leverage to demand ever new investments. This is clearly illustrated by the general non-acceptance and public discussions in the media sparked by lacking doping controls or a proposed liberalization of doping.

4 Control costs in view of hidden characteristics and hidden action

How do the IOC and the corporate actors it assigns actually go about securing the probability of top sporting performances as an essential element of the product Olympic sport? First of all, the member associations only allow athletes to compete in the Olympic Games who have signalled that they can produce top performances by meeting the qualification standards. The costs for this signalling lie both with the athlete (time) and with the national association (time and money, for example for organizing qualification tournaments and championships). For the IOC, international member associations and organizers, this considerably reduces the search costs for suitable athletes.

During the Olympic Games, the IOC assigns an agent to carry out doping controls on all medal winners and other randomly selected athletes, which increases consumers' faith in compliance and hence also the quality of the product. As a reputational effect in the sense of a normative self-commitment, the Olympic oath taken by athletes reinforces this effect and demonstrates that athletes can also invest in the real or staged compliance, for example by agreeing to voluntary controls, actively participating in anti-doping campaigns, etc. or, like the German decathlon team in athletics did in the past, carrying out additional voluntary doping controls funded out of their own pocket.

Very different national doping control standards are observed and tolerated, however, when it comes to the much more important out-of-competition testing in the run-up to the Olympic Games. Thus within the scope of national doping controls, it is only the case for some athletes that a high probability of detection resulting from frequent out-of-competition testing leads to a low doping probability. This increases the chances for less frequently tested athletes to perform well in Olympic Games and above all also allows organizers to justify themselves vis-à-vis a not very well informed public by pointing to the implemented controls.

5 The moral hazard problem – empirical findings

The prevalence of dopers in Germany was determined for a representative population according to sporting discipline, squad level and gender using the more advanced Randomized Response Technique, a form of indirect questioning. The results of several studies showed a doping prevalence of around 20% (Pitsch, Emrich & Klein 2007 and with recent findings Pitsch, Maats & Emrich in this volume), which we also assume to be the minimum in the international sphere. Due to the lack of a national anti-doping control system in many countries, this assumption on the international level is, if anything, probably too low, especially in some non-European contexts.

This leads directly to the question of the effectiveness of the monitoring function. Monitoring is carried out on behalf of the IOC by WADA[56] and monitoring agencies instructed by it; a similar system is in place at national level, provided that such an institution as a national anti-doping agency exists in the respective country. An enquiry sent to the NADA and WADA (information via e-mail on 22.1.2009 and on 26.1.2009, cf. document 1 in the Appendix to this article) revealed that these organizations also had no reliable figures relating to the number of qualitatively adequate national anti-doping agencies. According to this information, on 26 January 2009 there were an "estimated 60" functioning national anti-doping agencies. But even within national anti-doping structures distortions can be found. As the NADA 2007anti-doping report valid up to 31 March 2008 for Germany (from: http://www.jensweinreich.de/wp-content/uploads/2008/12/ADB2007.pdf) shows, at this time in Germany the old NADA code valid up to 31.12.2008 was implemented in 8 top Olympic associations to a large extent perfectly, in 13 Olympic associations acceptably with minor shortcomings and in 12 Olympic associations not at all, inadequately or with major shortcomings (cf. document 2 in the Appendix to this article). Weinreich (http://jensweinreich.de/?s=doping, retrieved on 28.1.2009, cf. document 2 in the Appendix to this article) points out that no information is available regarding "whether and how the new NADC valid from 1 January 2009 will be implemented."[57]

The monitoring agencies are also rational actors. For them, stagnating or deteriorating performances point to a high prevalence of doping in the past and

---

[56] The president of the World Handball Association, Hassan Moustafa, for example stated that he does not intend to implement the WADA rules (Koblenzer Rhein-Zeitung online, http://rhein-zeitung.de/on/09/01/22sportsline/handball/news/t/rzo525085.html). Germany's ZDF TV channel reported that the International Handball Federation has in the meantime announced that it will at least partly fulfil its obligations (http://sport.zdf.de/ZDFsport/inhalt/12/0,5676,7505420,00.html; retrieved on 22.01.2009).

[57] According to Weinreich (http://jensweinreich. de/?s=doping, retrieved on 28.1.2009), at a hearing before the Sports Committee of the German Bundestag in 2008 DOSB Director General Michael Vesper affirmed that the NADC would *in principle* be collectively implemented from 1 January 2009, however with transitional rulings. This intention could not be verified until 2010, however, after the associations have submitted their reports, due on 31 March 2010, on measures taken in 2009; these reports then have to be evaluated by NADA and then re-submitted to the BMI/BVA (Federal Ministry of the Interior and Federal Office of Administration).

A further analysis dating from 1999 had shown that a total of 14 Olympic sports associations do not guarantee athletes any procedural rights whatsoever, in 30 associations they even did not have the right to submit evidence, call witnesses or independent experts. Almost half of the regimes laid down the principle of "strict liability" (on further procedural shortcomings cf. Siekmann, 2000, 33 f. and the article by Senkel in this volume).

therefore confirm the deterrent effect of current control procedures. Enhanced performances, by contrast, signal that more controls are needed. These are actors operating in the closed doping control market with personal interests, who are licensed within the sport system. There are as few licensed external candidates able to provide competing monitoring functions as there are government control or monitoring agencies (on the economic analysis of recent legal developments in the fight against doping cf. Pitsch, Frenger & Emrich in this volume).

In the final report of the Anti-Doping Legal Commission of the Sporting Bodies (ReSpoDo) on possible legislative initiatives for more consistent prevention, prosecution and punishment of doping in sport of 15 June 2005, the current situation in anti-doping, relating to NADA, is described as follows: "At the moment, sports associations entrust NADA to varying degrees with conducting out-of-competition doping controls. Doping controls during competitions are carried out by the associations on very different scales" (ibid, 18). Further down under "target situation" (ibid, 18. f.), under the proviso that public funding should only be used for doping-free sport, the report calls for "out-of-competition and competition controls to be foreseen on an appropriate scale and carried out by NADA."

With respect to NADA it reads (translated from ibid, 20 f.): "NADA receives financial and ideological support in particular from the federal government and federal states, Deutsche Sporthilfe (German Sports Aid Foundation), NOC, DSB (German Sports Confederation), the sports associations/state sports federations as well as some business enterprises. The available funds are not sufficient to enable NADA to discharge its extensive and central responsibility in Germany." In this context, the Commission calls for the "legal provision of an appropriate financial framework for NADA on the part of all those involved in the promotion of sport, the organization of sporting events and sport-related advertising"; a demand that has still not been realized.

Since its inception on 10 November 1999, WADA was exclusively financed by the Olympic Movement; since 1 January 2002, the "public authorities" and the "Olympic Movement" have shared the costs. On 31 December 2007, WADA's total income in US$ amounted to 24,408,298 million, expenses were US$ 24,311,061 million, including "testing fees" in the amount of US$ 1,677,543 and "research grants" in the amount of US$ 5,692,853 (World Anti-Doping Agency, Notes to Financial Statements at 31 December 2007, http://www.wada-ama.org/en/dynamic.ch2?pageCategory.id=259, retrieved on 22.01.2009).

The analytical rationale behind why the institution IOC and its member associations indirectly control the probability of attractive peak performances through the resources made available for monitoring also in the run-up to the Olympic Games is clear. If the monitoring agencies charged a high number of potential top performers as a result of out-of-competition controls during the run-up to the Olympic Games, the imposition of bans leading to their disqualification would cause sporting performances, and consequently the demand for sport, to decline; the Olympic Games would be without their stars. If they additionally charge many popular top performers during the Games themselves, this will also cause a drop in demand for sport over the medium term and ultimately also the inflow of resources for controls. If, on the other hand, the monitoring agencies only detect individual athletes, including only very few top performers, consumers' faith in the high quality (compliance with the rules) and the genuineness of peak performances will not be unnecessarily compromised.

It should also be remembered that individual nations that perform effective out-of-competition controls not only reduce their athletes' chances of achieving peak performances, but are at the same time guarantors that the faith in norm conformance is upheld, since athletes who are frequently tested on the national level are less likely to dope. This in turn lowers the risk of detecting deviators in doping controls.

References

Akerlof, G. A. (1970). The Market for "Lemons", *Quarterly Journal of Economics, 89*, 488-500

Andreozzi, L. (2004). Rewarding Policemen Increases Crime. Another Surprising Result from the Inspection Game. *Public Choice, 121*, 69-82.

Briefs, G. (1957). Grenzmoral in der pluralistischen Gesellschaft. In Beckerath, E., Meyer, F. W.; Müller-Armack, A. (Eds.): *Wirtschaftsfragen der freien Welt. Festschrift für Ludwig Erhard* (pp. 97-108). Frankfurt am Main: Knapp.

Briefs, G. (1959). Sozialformen und Sozialgeist der Gegenwart. In A. Vierkandt (Hrsg.). *Handwörterbuch der Soziologie* (pp. 160-173). Unamended reprint. Stuttgart: Enke.

Carmichael, H. L. (1989). Self-Enforcing Contracts, Shirking, and Life Cycle Incentives. *Journal of Economic Perspectives, 3* (4), 65-83.

Bundesministerium der Justiz, press release dated 11 December 2003. Bundestag beschließt Schutz der Olympischen Ringe. www.bmj.de/enid/0,0/58.html?druck=1&presseartikel_id=250 (Retrieved on 14 January 2009).

Durkheim, E. (1988 [1893]). *Über soziale Arbeitsteilung. Studie über die Organisation höherer Gesellschaften.* 2nd edition. Frankfurt am Main: Suhrkamp.

Durkheim, E. (1999 [1895]). *Die Regeln der soziologischen Methode.* 4th edition. Frankfurt am Main: Suhrkamp.

Durkheim, E. (1893). *De la division du travail social.* Paris: Alcan.

Emrich, E. (2006). Zur Kommerzialisierung der olympischen Idee – einige grundlegende Anmerkungen. In F. Kutschke (Ed.): *Ökonomie Olympischer Spiele* (pp. 39-55). Schorndorf: Hofmann.

Laffont, J.-J., Martimort, D. (2002). *The Theory of Incentives. The Principal-Agent Model.* Princeton and Oxford: Princeton University Press.

Macho-Stadler, I., Perez-Castrillo, J. D. (2001). *An Introduction to the Economics of Information. Incentives and Contract*, 2nd edition. Oxford and New York: Oxford University Press.

Meffert, H. (2000). *Marketing. Grundlagenorientierte Unternehmensführung: Konzepte – Instrumente – Praxisbeispiele. Mit neuer Fallstudie VW-Golf.* 9th updated and extended edition. Wiesbaden: Gabler.

Messing, M., Müller, N. (1996). Veranstaltungsbesuch und sportpolitische Polarisation deutscher Olympia-Touristen in Barcelona 1992. In N. Müller, M. Messing (Eds.). *Auf der Suche nach der Olympischen Idee* (pp. 219-249). Kassel: Agon.

Messing, M., Müller, N., Schormann, K. (2008). Zuschauer beim antiken Agon und bei den olympischen Spielen in Athen 2004 – anthropologische Grundmuster und geschichtliche Figurationen. In P. Mauritsch, W. Petermandl, W. R. Rollinger, C. Ulf, with the cooperation of I. Huber (Eds.). *Antike Lebenswelten. Konstanz, Wandel, Wirkungsmacht. Festschrift für Ingomar Weiler zum 70. Geburtstag* (pp. 211-237). Wiesbaden: Harrassowitz.

Nieschlag, R; Dichtl, E., Hörschgen, H. (2002). *Marketing*. 19th updated and extended edition. Berlin: Duncker und Humblodt.

Pitsch, W., Emrich, E., Klein, M. (2007). Doping in elite sports in Germany. *ejss (European Journal for Sport and Society) 4*, 2, 89-102.

Popitz, H. (1968). *Über die Präventivwirkung des Nichtwissens. Dunkelziffer, Norm, Strafe.* Tübingen: Mohr.

Pratt J. W., Zeckhauser R. J. (1985). *Principals and Agents: The Structure of Business*. Boston, Massachusetts. Harvard Business School Press

Richter, R. Furubotn, E. (2003). *Neue Institutionenökonomik. Eine Einführung und kritische Würdigung*. Tübingen: Mohr Siebeck.

Rittberger, V., Boeckle, H. (1997). Das Internationale Olympische Komitee – eine Weltregierung des Sports? In O. Grupe (Ed.). *Olympischer Sport. Rückblick und Perspektiven* (pp. 127-155). Schorndorf: Hofmann.

Scharpf, F. W. (1997). *Demokratische Politik in der internationalisierten Ökonomie.* Max Planck Institut für Gesellschaftsforschung. Working Paper 97/9.

Schollmeier, P. (2001). *Bewerbungen um Olympische Spiele. Von Athen 1896 bis Athen 2004.* Carl und Liselotte Diem Archiv (Eds.). Cologne: Books on Demand.

Siekmann, R. C. (2000): Übersicht über die internationalen Verbandsregelungen zum Verschuldensprinzip, zur Beweislast und zur Sanktionshöhe. In V. Röhricht, K. Vieweg (Eds.). *Doping-Forum. Aktuelle rechtliche und medizinische Aspekte* (pp. 31–34). Stuttgart and others (Recht und Sport; special edition).

Simmel, G. (2003 [orig. 1908]). *Soziologie. Untersuchungen über die Formen der Vergesellschaftung*. Complete edition volume 11. Frankfurt: Suhrkamp.

Simon, H. A. (1957). *Models of Man - Social and Rational*. New York: Wiley and others

Stiglitz, J. (2000).The Contributions of the Economics of Information to Twentieth Century Economics. *The Quarterly Journal of Economics*, *115*, 1441-1478.

Telser, L. G. (1980). A Theory of Self-Enforcing Agreements. *Journal of Business* 53, 27-44.

Tröger, C. (2006). *Olympia – Im Spannungsfeld von Mythos und Marke*. Dissertation. Saarland University.

Wittman, D. (1985). Counter-Intuitive Results in Game Theory. *European Journal of Political Economy 1* (1), 77-89.

Weber, M. (1980 [orig. 1921]). *Wirtschaft und Gesellschaft.* 5th revised edition, provided by Johannes Winckelmann. Tübingen: Mohr.

Document 1: Documentation of the research into the number of national doping agencies worldwide 22.01.09 – 26.01.09

Telephone conversation with Ms Ulrike Spitz (head) Prevention and Communications at NADA
Telephone: +49 (228) 812 92 - 150
Telefax: +49 (228) 812 92 - 269
ulrike.spitz@nada-bonn.de

- No precise up-to-date information possible (current estimate approx. 60) => referred to

Frédéric DONZÉ
Senior Manager, Media Relations and Communications at WADA
Telephone + 1 514 904 8820
Telefax + 1 514 904 8764
frederic.donze@wada-ama.org

- First enquiry by mail on 22.01.09 as to the number of national doping agencies worldwide
- First mail reply on 22.01.09: ...there are indeed around 60 established, functioning and developed national anti-doping agencies... as well as details of a link under which 119 national agencies are listed
- Second enquiry by mail on 26.01.09 regarding the differing figures approx. 60/119
- Second and third reply by mail on 26.01.09: ... there are indeed around 60 actually functioning national anti-doping agencies ... / ...Some countries have less active national agencies, but play an active role in the fight against doping through participation in regional anti-doping organizations.

Document 2: Implementation of the Nada Code valid until 31.12.2008 in the regimes of German top associations

Tab.: German NADA anti-doping reports 2007, from: http://www.jensweinreich.de/wp-content/uploads/2008/12/ADB2007 .pdf, last retrieved on 28.1.2009)

Olympic professional association (German)	Olympic professional association (English translation)	Abbr.	Questionnaire and documentation submitted within deadline?	Implementation of the Nada Code (NADC) in association regime?
Bob- und Schlittenverband für Deutschland	German Bobsleigh, Luge and Skeleton Federation	BSD	yes	for the most part
Bund Deutscher Radfahrer	German Cycling Federation	BDR	yes, after reminder	BDR regime does not correspond to NADC requirements
Bundesverband Deutscher Gewichtheber	German Weightlifting Federation	BVDG	yes	for the most part, dynamic reference, alignment possible via the executive board
Deutsche Eislauf-Union	German Ice Skating Union	DEU	yes	for the most part, dynamic reference
Deutsche Eisschnelllauf-Gemeinschaft	German Speed Skating Association	DESG	yes	in principle
Deutsche Reiterliche Vereinigung	German Equestrian Federation	FN	yes	dynamic reference, with shortcomings
Deutsche Taekwondo Union	German Taekwondo Union	DTU	yes, after reminder	not properly implemented, inadequate AD provisions, no AD officer
Deutsche Triathlon Union	German Triathlon Union	DTrU	yes, within deadline after renewed reminder	statutes for the most part correspond to NADC requirements
Deutscher Badminton-Verband	German Badminton Federation	DBaV	within deadline after reminder	implemented, including prompt amendment possibilities
Deutscher Base- und Softball Verband	German Baseball and Softball Federation	DBSV	yes	work in progress on implementation in the form of a supplementary regime

Olympic professional association (German)	Olympic professional association (English translation)	Abbr.	Questionnaire and documentation submitted within deadline?	Implementation of the Nada Code (NADC) in association regime?
Deutscher Basketball Bund	German Basketball Federation	DBB	no, Nada did not receive information until May 2008; DBB claims to have submitted everything to the DOSB as early as December 2007	inadequate dynamic reference
Deutscher (Amateur-) Boxsportverband	German (Amateur) Boxing Federation	DABV	no, after several reminders not until 17 June 2008	applicable NADC requirements are implemented. But: no doping control agreement with Nada
Deutscher Curling Verband	German Curling Association	DCV	yes	only partly implemented, no doping control agreement with Nada
Deutscher Eishockey Bund	German Ice Hockey Federation	DEB	yes	inadequately implemented
Deutscher Fechter-Bund	German Fencing Federation	DFEB	yes	can only be partly verified due to lack of association documentation
Deutscher Fußball-Bund	German Football Association	DFB	yes	optimally implemented
Deutscher Handball-Bund	German Handball Federation	DHB	no, despite reminders not submitted until 5 June 2008	yes, including prompt amendments
Deutscher Hockey-Bund	German Hockey Federation	DHoB	yes	yes, including prompt amendments
Deutscher Judo-Bund	German Judo Federation	DJB	yes	inadequately implemented
Deutscher Kanu-Verband	German Canoeing Association	DKV	yes	properly implemented
Deutscher Leichtathletik Verband	German Athletics Federation	DLV	yes	excellently implemented
Deutscher Ringer-Bund	German Wrestling Federation	DRB	yes	inadequately implemented
Deutscher Rud-	German Rowing	DRV	yes	not yet fully implemented

Olympic professional association (German)	Olympic professional association (English translation)	Abbr.	Questionnaire and documentation submitted within deadline?	Implementation of the Nada Code (NADC) in association regime?
erverband	Federation			
Deutscher Schützenbund	German Rifle Association	DSüB	yes	properly and fully implemented
Deutscher Schwimm-Verband	German Swimming Federation	DSV	yes	applicable provisions implemented
Deutscher Segler-Verband	German Sailing Federation	DSeV	yes	implemented through dynamic reference
Deutscher Skiverband	German Skiing Federation	DSkiV	within deadline after renewed reminder	main provisions implemented
Deutscher Tennisbund	German Tennis Federation	DTB	yes	applicable provisions correctly implemented
Deutscher Tischtennis-Bund	German Table Tennis Association	DTTB	yes	reference to NADC does not correspond to a dynamic reference
Deutscher Turner Bund	German Gymnastics Federation	DTB	yes	integrated through dynamic reference and also explicitly regulated
Deutscher Verband für Modernen Fünfkampf	German Modern Pentathlon Federation	DVMF	yes	comprehensive implementation cannot be confirmed
Deutscher Volleyball-Verband	German Volleyball Federation	DVV	within deadline after renewed reminder	ensured through dynamic reference
Snowboard Verband Deutschland	Snowboard Federation Germany	SVD	within deadline after renewed reminder	dynamic reference, with shortcomings

Katja Senkel, Eike Emrich, Carsten Momsen

Measures to increase compliance on the part of the international sports federations in the fight against doping – some thoughts on the effectiveness of incorporating the principle of subsidiarity into the WADC

1 Introduction

The World Anti-Doping Code (WADC) was developed within the framework of the World Anti-Doping Program initiated by the World Anti-Doping Agency (WADA). It was adopted by the World Conference against Doping in Sport on 5 March 2003 in Copenhagen and first implemented at the start of the 2004 Olympic Games in Athens. A revised version of the WADC was drafted in autumn 2007 and came into effect on 1 January 2009. It includes a number of regulatory measures to promote doping-free sport. The underlying rationale is seen in the athletes' health as well as the principles of fairness and equality[58], implicitly accompanied by the naturalness argument.[59] The WADC is intended to make a contribution to the preventive and repressive fight against doping within the context of a harmonized, coordinated and effective anti-doping programme. The need for such an approach is justified by the deficits of the (judicial) anti-doping campaign to date, which are principally seen in the (sport-specific) problems arising from competential multidimensionality, such as norm

---

[58] Cf. the introduction to the WADC. Cf. the revised version that came into effect on 1.1.2009: http://www.wada-ama.org/rtecontent/document/code_v2009_En.pdf (retrieved on: 3.6.2008). The *health argument* is not entirely convincing. The rationale behind it is that doping is prohibited because it poses a (potential) risk to the athlete's health. This raises the following problems:

1. There are practices in sport that are permitted and yet also pose a (potential) risk to the athlete's health, e.g. boxing.
2. The Prohibited List also includes substances that probably cannot be proved to have a harmful effect.
3. Forms of doping aimed at preventive performance enhancements, e.g. doping to reduce regeneration time, to prevent overtraining, etc.
4. When setting up standards, the right to self-harm must as a matter of principle be taken into account (arg. § 228 StGB (German Criminal Code) e contrario).

[59] The *naturalness argument*, which claims that the fascination of sport derives from the authenticity of the sporting performance, i.e. outstanding sporting performances are performances that should be achieved through naturally inherent human possibilities (talent and training), is also not entirely convincing. Doping ostensibly represents an unnatural manipulation of an athlete's sporting capacity. But this, too, gives rise to a number of problems (cf. Pitsch, Maats & Emrich, 2008).

1. The borderlines between "natural" and "unnatural" manipulation of the body are fluid (e.g. own blood doping, EPO, creatine phosphate).
2. Not every "unnatural" manipulation is viewed as doping (e.g. vacuum chamber versus training in the Kenyan Highlands).

collisions, overlapping competences, inconsistent adherence to and application of rules, and viewed as being obstacles to the successful prevention of doping (cf. among others Kern, 2007, 150; Senkel, 2005, 99 f.).

The WADA's WADC is seen as the central foundation stone of a new legal instrument in the international anti-doping campaign, although it is openly acknowledged that its effectiveness in fulfilling the objective will first have to prove itself over time (cf. Kern, 2007, 444).[60] In the meantime, one critical problem standing in the way of achieving WADA's harmonization goal has proved to be the lack of compliance on the part of the international sports associations. This is hardly surprising given that although they are members of an umbrella organization, they at the same time compete against each other both internally and in the markets for resources, attention, etc.[61] The effectiveness of the WADC depends largely on how far the sports associations are willing to comply with the transnational regulatory system and thus bring their own existing anti-doping regulations into line with it and apply it. An institutionalized control and enforcement procedure that allows the international and national sports associations to monitor implementation of the WADC regulations and impose respective sanctions in the event of non- or misapplication does not exist.[62]

---

[60] See also with regard to the formation of the WADA Houlihan (1999, 9) and Pound (2002, 53) speaks from an „Experiment in International Law". This kind of ex post effectiveness analysis is frequently encountered in the search for adequate measures to combat doping and suggests that "practical experience" alone can prove the effectiveness of measures, which means measures first have to be implemented before we can determine how they will work (for criticism of this approach cf. Opp, 1975). From an economic perspective, such an approach seems fairly cost-intensive. It could entail the risk not only of possibly not achieving the goals of the fight against doping, but of even hindering it by delaying or even preventing the search for (genuinely) more effective measures. Furthermore, costs are incurred not only for implementing the measures, but also follow-on costs owing to subsequent revisions. A sociological approach ex ante could contribute to avoiding an inefficient legal framework, which according to Schmidtchen (1999, 11) represents "a legal system that is an incentive to waste production factors". From an economic point of view, however, perhaps precisely this approach is rational in the special case of elite sport (cf. the article by Emrich & Pitsch in this volume).

[61] Cf. e.g. dpa press release of 23.9.2003, 19:44 h: "UCI is no longer willing to admit WADA representatives as official observers at cycling races in future"; dpa press release of 5.6.2002: "FIFA adamantly refused to admit WADA observers to the World Cup". The FIFA, UCI and ITF associations had already publicly adopted a frontline position on the signing of the Code, cf. dpa press release of 5.6.2002, 7:15 h: "FIFA wants to remain autonomous", "FIFA does not accept WADA's function as a kind of supervisory body".

[62] This shortcoming is still found even in the revised edition of the WADC. However, stricter implementation requirements were imposed on the international associations inasmuch as they are required to include some provisions verbatim in their subordinate regimes and deviating regulations with respect to minimum and maximum standards are no longer permissible. An overview of the most important changes can be found in Jakob & Berninger (2008, 61 f.).

This means that at least the national sports associations are still forced to cooperate on a trust basis and combat doping, albeit with the risk that other national associations in the same

In the following, we discuss the proposed inclusion of the subsidiarity principle in the WADC from the legal perspective (Kern, 2007).[63] This focuses on reflections on the effectiveness of this measure and the conditions of compliance. First, we describe the proposal and define the problem.[64]

2 Proposal description and problem definition

By formally incorporating the principle of subsidiarity into the WADC, Kern (2007, 443) hopes sports associations would be given incentives to follow the rules more strictly. In this context, he underscores in particular the integrative and regulatory function of the principle and points out that the subsidiarity principle is frequently drawn on for the achievement of harmonization goals (ibid, 303). WADA can only achieve this harmonization goal of general adherence to the rules if the relevant sports associations undertake to apply the WADC regulations (ibid).

Compliance on the part of the international sports federations is especially important because they are the ones responsible for assuring the application of the WADC by their subordinate national sports federations and they therefore control the global application of the anti-doping regulations for the respective sport. The international federations have in fact been the ones in the past to criticize WADA's attempts at harmonization and insist on having a regulatory right

sport fail to cooperate and do not in fact effectively combat doping. Under these conditions, which depend for the most part on morally based voluntariness, the cooperating actor is at a disadvantage. Although this form of altruism is occasionally encountered in isolated cases, it is likely to be rare, since an association that enforces doping controls reduces the international winning chances of its athletes so long as it cannot be certain that others are imposing equally effective controls.

[63] Demands to include the subsidiarity principle in the WADC were already voiced when the WADC was drafted, cf. for example statements issued by the Council of Europe, by IAAF president Lamine Diack or the then French Minister of Sport Jean-Francois Lamour (cf. the reference in Kern, 2007, 302). However, the subsidiarity principle was not written into the revised version of the WADC that with the resolution of autumn 2007 took effect on 1.1.2009. The revised version is accessible under http://www.wada-ama.org/rtecontent/document/code_v2009_En.pdf (retrieved: 3.6.2008).

[64] As part of the theoretical analysis of whether inclusion of the subsidiarity principle in the WADC can help to achieve the harmonization goal, we dedicate a short section to the overriding question of the possibilities and limits of the legal system in regulating the problem of doping. For this discussion, the following assumptions shall be made:

General acceptance of the goal to fight doping using the means provided by the legal system is assumed.

It is assumed on the basis of the sport-specific premise of being bound by uniform rules that a harmonization of (legal) anti-doping measures is necessary, and that the WADC can in principle contribute to this.

Finally, it is assumed that the fight against doping is the more effective, the more the associations make genuine efforts in this direction.

of their own to combat doping.[65] The reasons for this are generally assumed to be sport policy motives and are attributed to the associations' interpretation of autonomy and independence (ibid, 443, economic motives are also conceivable, cf. on this Emrich & Pitsch in this volume).

There is assumed to be a direct connection between acceptance of the WADC and increased compliance on the part of those it targets. It is suggested that strengthening the associations' competences in the WADC leads to its greater acceptance, which in turn produces a corresponding motivation to follow the rules (Kern, 2007, 307).[66] Thus the subsidiarity principle manages to trigger an awareness for the commonality needed to achieve the ultimate goal by creating a system of interdependency between the involved stakeholders and thus increasing the willingness to promote the common goal (ibid, 309). The integrative effect of the subsidiarity principle is supposed to help resolve sport policy and economic conflicts between the organizations concerned (ibid). Consequently, given the sovereignty awareness of the international associations, establishing the subsidiarity principle in the WADC is to be recommended for both political and factual reasons (ibid, 305). However, further details of the proposal and explanations concerning the anticipated cause-effect relationships are not elaborated upon.

Irrespective of the proposal made here, the problem can be formulated as follows: What underlying conditions have to be met to ensure the international sports federations apply the WADC rules?

If we understand institutions as an order or a system of rules, then it is possible to define an institution by a set of rules that restricts actors' behaviour within a given scope of action (cf. on the economics of ethics and on economic framework ethics in general Homann, 1999).[67] In this respect, as a transnational legal framework for the international anti-doping campaign in sport, the WADC represents a supranational institution. The question of how the international sports associations could be motivated to adhere to the rules of this institution has to do with the quality of the foundations for a positive, factual legitimization of WADA and the WADC in the sense of following the system of rules. Whether acceptance or the positive legitimization of institutions enhances the readiness to follow the rules is a question of fact (Vanberg, 1999, 45; Schmidtchen, 1999). If we assume in the sense of the behavioural assumption of eco-

---

[65] Cf. for example FIFA, which rejects any form of interference and UCI, which (for a long time) insisted on its unrestricted controlling and sanctioning competence (cf. Frankfurter Allgemeine Sonntagszeitung dated 18.9.2005, 20; Neue Zürcher Zeitung dated 5.3.2003, 46; sid press release of 4.8.2004, 08:15 h). However, in the run-up to the 2008 European Football Championship, FIFA and WADA stressed their intention to cooperate in future and signed a corresponding agreement (cf. sid press release of 20.5.2008, 13:07 h).

[66] Kern (2007, 443) also stresses, however, that this needs to be underpinned by corresponding control mechanisms to monitor application and implementation processes.

[67] The term institution is not used entirely without ambiguity either in everyday language or in social science literature (cf. Vanberg, 1982, 32. f., with corresponding references).

nomic theory that all stakeholders strive as far as possible to pursue their own interests within the given constraints, in other words to maximize their own benefits, then the decisive possibility to systematically influence the resulting behavioural orders lies in the design of the respective regulatory orders and their reinforcement through sanctions (Vanberg, 1999, 39 f.).[68] Whether in this sense the subsidiarity principle is able to fulfil the hopes vested in it is discussed in the following.

3 Incentive-determining implications of the subsidiarity principle – the anticipated cause-effect relationship

Before discussing the anticipated cause-effect relationships, we must first outline the functions that are in general attributed to the subsidiarity principle. After that, we will attempt to present and evaluate the desired cause-effect prospects within the framework of the international fight against doping.

3.1 General functions and interpretation of the subsidiarity principle

Apart from the general interpretation of the principle, we are interested above all in the integrative and regulatory function pointed out by Kern (2007).[69]

3.1.1 Interpretation of the subsidiarity principle

The principle of subsidiarity is derived from Catholic social teaching and finds its first mention in the Encyclical Quadragesimo Anno, where it was clearly formulated. From there, it found its way into secular political and constitutional theory and is in the meantime considered to be the central principle of organizational and order theory.[70] The precise interpretation of the subsidiarity principle, its limits and its concrete legal applicability remain a topic of controversial debate.[71] Very generally, the principle of subsidiarity states that in relations between two communities, as well as in relations between the individual and all forms of human community, matters ought always to be handled by the lowest

[68] The terms "behavioural and regulatory order" were coined by F. A. von Hayek (1967).

[69] Pieper (1994, 230) points out that within the debate on the European Union, the subsidiarity principle appears to prove "multifunctional". The principle cannot be assigned a unique function because it is associated with a wide variety of different ideas.

[70] Cf. Pirson (2008, 260), Herzog (1998, Column 482). It should be noted, however, that the basic idea behind the principle is already mentioned in the Bible (Exodus 18). But it was clearly formulated in Catholic social teaching and revived for the political theory of the 20th century. Moersch (2001, 82), on the other hand, suggests that the idea was coined in the 19th century by the adherents of the liberal doctrine of the state and state goals on the basis of Kant's personalism. For a more detailed discussion of the social philosophy roots and the development of the subsidiarity principle, see also Utz (1953, 7 ff), Ronge (1998, 137 ff.), Pieper (1994, 45 ff.).

[71] Cf. for example Lecheler (1993, 24 ff), Pieper (1994, 173 ff.). Isensee (2002, 177) points out that the genuinely ethical interpretation of the subsidiarity principle cannot be fully legally defined.

competent authority. In this, it is the task of the higher authority to empower the more immediate or local authority to fulfil its tasks and to support it in doing so (Herzog, 1998, Column 482). It thus assigns the fulfilment of tasks to the next lower authority provided it has the capacity to carry out the specified function (Stein, 1994, 26). The principle of subsidiarity has both a negative and a positive component (Isensee, 1968, 30; Ronge, 1998, 179). The negative component refers to the limitation of the competences of the higher, central authority in relation to the lower, more local forms of organization. The positive component of the subsidiarity principle is expressed in the imperative for the central authority to support the lower forms of organization where they do not have the capacity to adequately or effectively fulfil their tasks independently.

Mieth (1998, 544) points out that precisely these components also give rise to a certain inconsistency in connection with the principle of subsidiarity and that ideologically it appears to be rather weak, because on the one hand it calls for a deferment of assistance and at the same time contains justification for the need to intervene.

The subsidiarity principle is above all widely known as a result of the discussion about the Treaty on the European Union. It has been established as a general rule in the Treaty in Art. 5 II EC. According to Lecheler (1993, 64–69), as well as regulating the exercise of powers and protecting the competences of the member states, it is supposed to reinforce the members' self-administration rights, enhance competition and help to promote integration. This is what Kern (2007, 306) is referring to when he remarks that the subsidiarity principle exhibits fundamental characteristics and functions that also serve the objectives of the WADC. He leaves it open, however, whether he understands the subsidiarity principle as a material or an organizational principle.[72] The contextual dependency of the principle also has to be considered (cf. Van der Ven, 1953, 47; Isensee, 2002, 149; Calliess, 1999, 27).[73] In this respect, it would be wrong to make a direct comparison with the harmonization endeavours of the European Union without giving consideration to the special circumstances and requirements of the anti-doping campaign in the social subsystem of sport.

---

[72] "Irrespective of whether the subsidiarity principle is understood as an imperative of human co-existence anchored in natural law or as an organizational possibility for a task distribution system, WADA's harmonization efforts represent a point of departure that ought to respect the subsidiarity principle" Kern (2007, 305).

[73] Schüller (1997), for example, claims that from a regulatory perspective the scope of the various aspects of subsidiarity (subsidiary assistance, subsidiary competence, subsidiary review) derives from the institutional and functional conditions of the respective overall order, as well as the associated conception of humankind and concept of the state. Depending on the regulatory context, the subsidiary competence and subsidiary assistance could assume a cooperative (performance-enhancing) or defective (performance-damaging) character (ibid, 70).

3.1.2 The regulatory function of the subsidiarity principle

With regard to the regulatory function of the subsidiarity principle, it is understood as a competence allocation principle and exercise of competences rule.[74] In this respect, we can also speak of the subsidiarity principle as a structural and control principle (Moersch, 2001, 80).[75] When it comes to the legally relevant interpretation of the principle, we can assign the competence allocation aspect to the area of legislative enactment and the exercise of competences aspect to the application of the law. Isensee (2002, 147) understands the former as the primary and the latter as the secondary function. According to Höffe (1997, 65), subsidiarity appears to be understood in social ethics primarily as a competence allocation principle. In the Maastricht Treaties, however, the principle of subsidiarity only occurs as an exercise of competences principle.[76]

As a maxim for the exercise of competence, the subsidiarity principle states that the higher authority is not automatically presumed to have the priority to act because it is capable of fulfilling a task more effectively than the lower level, but only if the task is actually beyond the capacities of the lower authority. Thus the central authority does not have the right to seek to retain competences for itself on the grounds of regulatory deficiencies (Pieper, 1994, 235). In its competence allocation function, it is directed at the law creator that allocates the competences to the corresponding levels of action. Apart from its relevance in terms of exercising competence, the subsidiarity principle also has a legitimizing significance inasmuch as it shows the existing competence allocation to be appropriate (Isensee, 2002, 148).

3.1.3 The integrative function of the subsidiarity principle

An incentive with respect to rule following is to be seen especially in the integrative function of the subsidiarity principle (Kern, 2007; cf. also Lecheler,

---

[74] Cf. on this Isensee (2002, 147 f.), Moersch (2001, 79 f.); from a political philosophy perspective cf. Höffe (1997, 54). Schneider (1996, 98) speaks of the "competence recognition principle" rather than the "competence allocation principle", because it (the subsidiarity principle) raises the competence of the individual to the criterion of self-responsible action and thus as a matter of principle takes the allocation competence away from the community (ibid).

[75] Moersch (2001, 79) makes this distinction having first defined the relation between tasks and key competence stakeholders, whereby he sees the tasks as variables and the key competence stakeholders as constants. In the present case, the components would have to be switched, so that the competence stakeholders would be allocated to the tasks, since we are dealing with the framework and acceptance of a newly established authority. Calliess (1999, 27) also speaks of the subsidiarity principle as a relational concept. Nell-Breuning (1962, 832), on the other hand stresses that the subsidiarity principle is not a structural principle.

[76] Höffe (1997, 65), as well as Isensee (2002, 152): "In this respect, it is logical to only ascribe the subsidiarity principle relevance for the exercise of competence, but not for competence allocation." Höffe (1997, 65) explains this with the fact that the member states decide about competences within the EU. These consider the subsidiarity principle not in the sense of surrendering rights, but only via the exercise of the competences vested by them in formal treaties.

1993, 68 f.). We will now attempt to reconstruct what this anticipated cause-effect relationship might look like. References to the origin of the principle of subsidiarity and its integrative effect can, according to Schneider (1996, 18 f.; cf. Isensee 2002, 133 f.), already be found in the Bible. There, Jethro advises his son-in-law Moses to delegate responsibility in order to relieve the burden on himself and at the same time guarantee the satisfaction of the citizens and acceptance by the people.[77] Within the context of the EU, it was also hoped that the introduction of the principle of subsidiarity would result in greater acceptance of the supranational political level (cf. Ronge, 1998, 178; Pieper, 1994, 230). In this respect, the acceptance of the higher authority appears to be an expression of the integrative function of the subsidiarity principle. However, this effect does not happen unconditionally. Rather, allusion is made to the need for a common goal orientation.[78] This is where the solidarity principle comes in.[79]

As a formal principle (Küchenhoff, 1953, 80 f.), the subsidiarity principle finds its material component in the solidarity principle. Solidarity refers to a predetermined commonality, whereby the duty of mutual responsibility derives from the factual interdependency of the people and the elementary awareness of sharing common ground (Baumgartner & Korff, 1999, 231). At the heart of this idea is the common good, the "bonum commune".[80] This is ascribed integrative potential (cf. Moersch, 1999, 209). In terms of the common good, the subsidiarity principle protects the lower authority in the realization of the common good in a system of solidarity-based but also competing responsibilities (Calliess, 1999, 185). In this sense, the subsidiarity principle can pave the way to a unity

---

[77] It reads: "So it will be easier for you, for they will bear the burden with you. If you do this thing and God so commands you, then you will be able to endure, and all this people will also go to their place in peace" (Exodus 18, 18–22).

[78] "Stand before God for the people, so that you may bring the difficulties to God. And you shall teach them the statutes and the laws and show them the way in which they must walk and the work they must do. Moreover you shall select from all the people able men, such as fear God, men of truth, hating covetousness" (Exodus 18, 18–22).

[79] Solidarity is taken in general to mean the willingness to incorporate the concerns of other persons or groups of persons into our own concerns based on common goals and interests. Usually, but not necessarily, this implies the voluntary acceptance of disadvantages – or forgoing advantages – to the benefit of third parties in the interests of common action (Calliess, 1999, 187). He adds: This is done on the assumption that the beneficiary parties would act in a similar way. Solidarity therefore in general develops within a "solidarity framework", in which a network of intersecting current and potential solidarity exists (ibid, 188). Thus solidarity rests on the recognition of commonality and is not just a transaction based on reciprocity (ibid, cf. on solidarity also Münch, 2001, 120 ff.; Hondrich & Koch-Arzberger, 1994, 12–24; Hondrich, 2001, 103–111).

[80] This is generally defined as the goal the community is oriented towards achieving and the members of the community are committed to (Calliess, 1999, 185). By contrast with general language usage, "common good" is sometimes also interpreted as an organizational and organizing service value. In this context, it provides preconditions or prerequisites needed to develop *common property*. According to Nell-Breuning (1990, 32 f.), common property represents the intrinsic value or self-worth we esteem or strive after for its own sake.

in diversity (Baumgartner & Korff, 1999, 236).[81] This, then, is where the intrinsic link to the solidarity principle lies (ibid.). The latter thus becomes the prerequisite for and the counterbalance to the subsidiarity principle by counteracting the purely particularistic representation of individual interests without regard for "the whole" – which the subsidiarity principle can be liable to lead to. In this respect, the solidarity principle acts as a corrective to the subsidiarity principle. It stresses the priority of the integrated whole over the individual parts. The subsidiarity principle is in turn a corrective to the common good by imposing limitations on it and thus empowering the individual authorities with a capacity to function and a justification within the whole (cf. Calliess, 1999, 186).[82]

A similar relationship can be seen between integration and subsidiarity as portrayed in the political discussion on steering and regulation (cf. comments in Moersch, 1999, 39 ff.). Here, conclusions about the relationship between integration and subsidiarity are drawn especially via the corporatism model, which can be viewed as the institutional application or implementation of an integration concept: the two things are both mutually dependent and mutually limit each other. The necessity for communities to integrate is said to follow from the quest to find common ground, which is ultimately the element that creates the identity of any community. On the other side of the coin is subsidiarity as the need of the individual to preserve his or her own identity and sphere of activity vis-à-vis the community as a whole.

It becomes clear that the subsidiarity principle, understood here as a purely formal competence allocation and exercise of competence principle, is not ascribed an integrative effect as such. Rather, this kind of more indirect relationship only develops in connection with the common good and its operationalization in the principle of solidarity. The close relationship between solidarity principle and subsidiarity principle now demands that the subsidiarity principle should only find application if certain formal categories exist (Calliess, 1999, 186).[83] Only then can a connection be established between the subsidiarity principle and the desired effects. In this sense, Isensee (2002, 135) remarks that the creation of acceptance (as an expression of an integrative effect) does not in fact represent the actual goal of the subsidiarity principle, but a desired consequence.

---

[81] Cf. also Durkheim (1977), who points out the connection between division of labour and sense of belonging.

[82] Durkheim (1977, 170 f.) comments on this as follows: "Solidarity, which is based on similarities, achieves its maximum when the collective awareness corresponds precisely to our entire awareness and is identical to it in all points: but at this moment our individuality equals zero. It can only develop if the community consumes less space in us. Thus, we are concerned with two opposing forces, one of which is centrifugal and the other of which is centripetal and which cannot develop at the same time. [...] At the moment when this solidarity takes effect, our personality disappears". Durkheim describes this kind of solidarity as mechanical.

[83] Cf. also Homann & Kirchner (1995, 52), who summarize the ideas of Nell-Breuning. The existence of these prerequisites in the fight against doping is examined later.

3.2 Function of the subsidiarity principle in the harmonization of the anti-doping campaign

In the organizational set-up of sport, the principle of subsidiarity becomes relevant, for example, when describing the relationship between state regulatory entitlements and the autonomous organization of the associations. In this sense it serves in German law to delimit the associations' autonomy on the one hand and the government's reserve to control on the other hand (Vieweg, 1990, 178). At the international level, the subsidiarity principle is written into the Council of Europe Convention against Doping in Sport of 16.11.1989[84] (PHBSportR-Summerer, 2007, 189). The primary responsibility lies with the sports federations and other private anti-doping organizations. The state should only step in where the former lack the capacity to act. Here, we should note that competence allocation is decisive for the sports associations, because outside it the subsidiarity principle is ineffective in the first place. Seen from this perspective, the scope is an important factor for its acceptance, whereby scope can be limited both with respect to extent (what is sport?) and qualitatively or vertically (grievous bodily harm has to be investigated by the state, even if it happens in the context of sport – legality principle).

In the following, we take a more detailed look at how the principle of subsidiarity should and can develop its full potential in the context of the WADC.

3.2.1 Allocation and exercise of competences in the WADC

The allocation and exercise of competences in the WADC is to be based on the regulatory function of the subsidiarity principle. WADA is incorporated into the organization of sport, which is structured according to the one-place principle, by means of a rule recognition contract. Through this, the respective sports association is bound by contract to the WADC and recognizes WADA as the central authority in the fight against doping within the organizational structure of sport. WADA acquires its legal capacity to act through a corresponding allocation of competences.[85]

a) Competence allocation: powers to enact and amend regulations

The original version of the WADC goes back to the initiative of WADA and was drawn up under its supervision.[86] Other organizations officially involved in the anti-doping campaign were incorporated insofar as they were asked to comment and were kept informed of the status of its development process.[87] Drafting the WADC did not grant WADA any intrinsic regulatory powers (Kern, 2007,

---

[84] BGBl. II (Federal Law Gazette) 1994 334, published in: HBSportR, Vol. 1, C.I.1. (in effect since 1.6.1994).

[85] Cf. Art. 20. 7, 23, in connection with the revision and amendment of the Code.

[86] WADA is composed of a wider Foundation Board and a narrower Executive Committee.

[87] WADA's first draft of the WADC received comments and amendment proposals from over 120 different organizations and individuals, cf. Kern (2007, 155).

275). WADA is thus just one of many signatories to the WADC that can be described as its creators. The regulatory competence of the original version of the WADC is thus vested in all of these jointly.

This has to be distinguished from the competence to modify the regulations. This lies with WADA (Art. 23.6 WADC), which is first of all responsible for overseeing the evolution of the Code and, where appropriate, drawing up proposals for its improvement. These must be presented to the signatories, athletes and governments for review and feedback. Within the scope of this mutual consultation process, the signatories, athletes and governments have the possibility to submit amendment recommendations of their own (Art. 23.6.2 WADC).[88] By contrast, the WADC does not accord the athletes, signatories and governments a right of co-decision. Amendments to the regulations are approved by the Foundation Board with a two-thirds majority.[89]

The implementing regulations of the anti-doping program (international standards, models of best practice) are also drawn up by WADA. There are no provisions for observing a particular procedure in setting these rules. However, in practice a consultation process has become established in which the proposals are submitted to the signatory organizations. WADA thus also has a guideline competence which allows it to exert influence over how the signatory organizations exercise their competences (Kern, 2007, 276). These primarily procedural guidelines are intended to guarantee the consistency and reliability of the executive measures (ibid).

In this respect, the subsidiarity principle is meant to act as a limitation on the exercise of competence and thus necessitates preventive control (cf. Kern, 2007, 312 f.).[90] WADA would thus be obliged to involve the national and international sport organizations in the formulation of the regulations by way of a consultation and notification procedure. Through this, WADA and the sport organiza-

[88] In this respect the responsibilities are not intended to be exclusive, but as a matter of principle competitive, although the WADC does not contain any information about how the cooperation process should work in detail, cf. Kern (2007, 310).

[89] Pursuant to Art. 6 of the foundation statutes, the Foundation Board is supposed to initially be composed of ten members, which are nominated by the IOC as founder. There may be a maximum of 35 members. A maximum of 16 members are to be appointed by the Olympic Movement and by inter-governmental organizations or governments. The remaining members are appointed upon the joint proposal of the Olympic Movement and the public authorities. The Foundation Board is currently composed of 38 members, 16 of which are IOC members and six presidents of international sports federations. These include FIFA president Josef Blatter, who was (for a long time) critical of WADA. Cf. http://www.wada-ama.org/en/dynamic.ch2 ?pageCategory.id=289 (retrieved: 2.6.2008).

[90] According to Kern (2007, 312), the "classic form" of the subsidiarity principle as a presumption of responsibility in favour of the lower authority tends to be rather counterproductive when it comes to achieving the goal (consistent regulations). According to this, powers are only vested in WADA if it can manage the tasks in question better and more efficiently than other sport organizations. The goals of the WADC serve as the benchmark for this (ibid, 313).

tions are supposed to monitor the expediency of the envisaged measures for achieving the goals. It is hoped applying the subsidiarity principle will reinforce the sport organizations' willingness to endorse the WADC (ibid).

b) Exercise of competence: executive powers and powers of jurisdiction

Application of the WADC is not carried out exclusively by an organization, but by various authorities with parallel or competing competences. Art. 15 WADC determines who is responsible for performing doping tests, the procedure for test results, holding hearings, the procedure for positive doping samples and the imposition of sanctions within the doping control system. When it comes to conducting competition testing, the WADC specifies that at international events international sport organizations and at national competitions corresponding national sport organizations should be responsible in the sense of an overlapping competence (Art. 15.1 WADC). Out-of-competition testing should be initiated and directed by national and international sport organizations. The Code does not foresee an explicit distribution of responsibilities. Rather, this should be coordinated through WADA (Art. 5 and 15.2 WADC).[91] Responsibility during legal proceedings after an anti-doping rule violation is committed is in principle based on who is responsible for conducting the doping tests, in the sense of implied competence.[92]

The WADC rules are implemented in the first instance by the various international and national sport organizations, which can draw on their own implementation and administrative organization for this. The international sports federations in particular have always had regulatory and sanctioning powers by virtue of membership or membership-similar relationships.

The powers of jurisdiction are distributed in parallel to the executive competences. Jurisdiction over the decision of the executive bodies follows the rules set up by those bodies, whereby the fundamental principles of the rule of law laid down in the WADC must be respected (Art. 13.1 in conjunction with Art. 13.2.2). Thus all doping disputes are initially decided internally by the respective organization. Subsequently, the parties have the possibility to appeal before a court of arbitration.[93] The fundamental appeal body for decisions relating to the WADC is the Court of Arbitration for Sport (CAS).[94]

---

[91] To this end, WADA has drawn up binding "International Standards for Testing" for the sport organizations. These include rules for planning and conducting doping tests. Art. 5 WADC contains the task distribution with respect to the pool of athletes to be tested.

[92] This is understood as the logical-consistent inclusion of themes in a described competence object which can be implicitly allocated to an assigned subject, cf. Stettner (2006), in: Dreier (Ed.). Basic Law commentary, Art. 70, Marginal Number. 60; Stern (1980, 610 f.)

[93] Details of arbitration provisions are provided by Haas (2001, 325 ff.).

[94] An exception to this are the rights of appeal of national athletes, where the decision is appealed to an independent and impartial body in accordance with rules established by the respective NADO (Art. 13.2.2 WADC). In Germany, since 1.1.2008 this has been the national Court of Arbitration in Sport.

Establishing different areas of competence for the application and the enforcement of the regulations is intended to support the goal of an effective, harmonized anti-doping policy (Kern, 2007, 297). However, this can also give rise to conflicts of responsibility.[95] Such conflicts can only be resolved through corresponding priority and cooperation rules. This is where the subsidiarity principle is supposed to come in. It shall – in line with the "classic" interpretation of the principle of subsidiarity – be refutably[96] presumed that the lower authority is responsible (Kern, 2007, 318).[97] In this respect, scope is also given to the integrative and solidarity-generating effect of the subsidiarity principle (ibid).

The component of subsidiary assistance (positive aspect) is already apparent in the WADC, which stipulates that international associations should be responsible for international events. Competence is allocated to the international sports associations on the assumption that the lower authorities do not have the capacity to adequately fulfil the task (ibid). The negative aspect of subsidiary competence manifests itself in the responsibility of national organizations for national events. Kern (2007, 315) concludes from this that with respect to executive powers, the founders of the WADC took the capacities and possibilities of the individual sports associations into consideration in the distribution of competences and thus endorsed a decentralized organization of the anti-doping campaign.

This presupposes that the suitability of the various authorities can also be verified on a case-by-case basis. In order to establish responsibility, i.e. the most capable authority, in a particular case, WADA must establish and evaluate the capacities of the individual sport and anti-doping organizations. To this end, Kern (2007, 315) proposes a two-step verification system that must at all times be oriented towards the goals of the WADC: first, the (negatively formulated) question has to be answered of whether the respective lower level is not capable of achieving the desired goals. The next question would be whether the higher authority is in a better position to achieve the goals.[98] In this respect WADA is

---

[95] These are particularly virulent in the case of in-competition and out-of-competition testing. No systematic separation possibilities exist, cf. Kern (2007, 297 ff.).

[96] This onus of presentation falls to WADA. It must substantiate the need for the tasks to be carried out centrally and in doing so eliminate the presumption that the lower authority is more familiar with the facts (Kern, 2007, 316).

[97] Application and enforcement of the WADC rules do not necessarily have to be carried out by a central authority. It is without prejudice to the harmonization success if consistently established rules are applied by different authorities, in that they are united by the common goal and the will to combat doping. The fact that this is the case for all sport organizations is according to Kern already apparent in their statutes, in which they have committed themselves to the goal of removing doping from sport (Kern, 2007, 314 f.). Furthermore, it remains open how the competences should be distributed where various similarly regulated organizations exist, such as on the national level the respective national sports federations and the national anti-doping organization.

[98] Kern (2007) refers among others to Calliess (1999, 92 ff.) and Merten (1994, 82 f.).

obliged to justify itself if it wants to expand its field of activity at the expense (among others) of the sports associations.

Kern (2007, 318 f.) is also of the opinion that the subsidiarity principle in this classic interpretation should be drawn on with respect to jurisdiction, so that responsibility of the lower (national) level should be presumed. This is supported in his view by the fact that many sport organizations have their own functioning judicial system (ibid, 319). The WADC also stipulates that any post-decision rules provided in the sport organization's rules must be exhausted before an appeal to the CAS is commenced (Art. 13 WADC).[99]

3.2.2 Application prerequisites for the subsidiarity principle

From the above remarks it is clear that the regulatory function of the subsidiarity principle is hoped to have an integrative effect. It has already been established that such an integrative effect can only possibly develop via the correlation between the formal subsidiarity principle and the solidarity principle. Therefore, application of the subsidiarity principle must fulfil three formal criteria. According to Isensee (1968, 71)[100] these are:

- a hierarchically structured superordinate/subordinate relationship,
- a common field of activity and
- pursuit of a common goal.

When it comes to incorporating the subsidiarity principle into the WADC, Kern (2007, 305) is happy to accept these prerequisites as given. In the following, we take a closer look at the individual components as a fundamental prerequisite for considering the effectiveness of the measure.

a) Hierarchically structured superordinate/subordinate relationship

The subsidiarity principle makes reference to vertically structured levels of action in the sense of a hierarchy. What is needed is a hierarchically structured superordinate/subordinate relationship, whereby the term hierarchy is to be understood in its formal-organizational meaning, in the sense of a superordination by virtue of rules of legal precedence or superior real power (Isensee, 2002, 146; Höffe, 1997, 55).[101]

Within the organization of sport, this precedence is vested in the IOC as the central authority of the Olympic Movement and in the international sports federations for the respective sports disciplines. Together with the subordinate au-

[99] As a role model for establishing the subsidiarity principle in the WADC, Kern (2007, 321) refers to the Subsidiarity protocol of the EC Treaty. With respect to the WADC, corresponding principles could be developed in the form of the so-called "international standards" (ibid).

[100] All studies concerning the subsidiarity principle are based on these prerequisites, cf. for example Calliess (1999, 186).

[101] Caplow (1964), for example, believes that provided the organizations pursue the same goals a prestige order emerges that confirms and reinforces itself since it among other things determines the distribution of resources.

thorities, they were also responsible for organizing the anti-doping campaign. Upon establishment of WADA, this took over as the harmonization and coordination authority in the fight against doping. To this end, WADA is vested with corresponding roles and responsibilities (cf. Art. 20.7; 23 WADC). Their integration into the hierarchical structure[102] of the organization of sport does not take place via the creation of an umbrella organization to which the subordinate authorities belong as members, but contractually. By signing the Code, the signatories of the WADC and other anti-doping organizations recognize the competences of WADA. The precedence of WADA in the fight against doping results from the contractual relationship the respective sport organizations enter into on signing.

In this sense, the international sport organizations are in a position of some power, as with their private-autonomous declaratory act they decide about the effectiveness of the WADC and WADA's capacity to act.[103] Thus a superordinate/subordinate relationship only comes into being after the international sports federations have contractually accepted the WADC (rule recognition contract) and thus grant WADA corresponding executive powers.

According to Nell-Breuning (1962), the subsidiarity principle only applies when a smaller and a larger social authority have a part-whole relationship (cf. also Homann & Kirchner, 1995, 49 f.). This rules out the situation where the various authorities end up competing with each other and distinguishing themselves from each other in their independence. (cf. Höffe, 1994). For the anti-doping effort, the idea is that as the harmonizing authority, WADA should have the role of "supervisor or coordinator" in the fight against doping. The international sports associations are responsible as necessary elements for the practical implementation of anti-doping measures, so that in this sense a part-whole structure can be assumed. With a view to the interest of the international sports associations in taking action[104], competition-similar structures could nevertheless possibly occur; for example when it comes to privileged interests, attention, etc.[105]

---

[102] Although umbrella organizations are not essentially superordinate authorities, but rather functional structures that are assigned certain tasks bottom-up by their founders. For the purpose of fulfilling these tasks, resources are coordinated, which are then redistributed by a coordinating authority according to defined criteria. "Depending on the perceived distributive justice, individual members are given a wide spectrum of decision possibilities" (Emrich, 2008b).

[103] Currently no binding obligation on the addressees of the standards exists under international law. A detailed description of the legal nature of the WADC can be found in Kern (2007, 159 ff.).

[104] For details about this and the common goal as a prerequisite for applying the subsidiarity principle, see below in Section 3.2.2, c).

[105] Thus, for example, a transfer of supervisory powers to WADA could be seen as a public admission on the part of the international sports associations that they do not wish or are not able to exercise the powers themselves, cf. Bette & Schimank (2006, 342).

b) Common field of activity: overlapping competences

As a directive for exercising competence, the subsidiarity principle presumes common responsibilities of the different levels in the sense of overlapping competences. Overlapping competences occur when the responsibilities are distributed equally to different authorities, but one of these authorities has the power to limit the responsibilities of the other authority by exercising its competence.[106] A common field of activity understood like this exists with respect to the anti-doping measures initiated by WADA and the international sports federations.[107] The common field of activity necessarily points to a collective goal towards which the task distribution is oriented.

c) Pursuit of a common goal

(1) Dependency of the subsidiarity principle on the common goal

As an elementary prerequisite for a functional application and effectiveness of the subsidiarity principle, the literature highlights pursuit of a common goal by the authorities concerned (Isensee, 1968, 71; 2002, 145; Moersch, 2001, 69).[108] This is said to be particularly important for achieving the identity-building effect of the subsidiarity principle. Thus, the not uncontroversial[109], but in legal practice[110] widespread final-teleological action theory assumes that the orientation function underlying the direction of the various authorities' actions towards a common goal secures the identity of the community. Structural-functional systems theory also points to an orientation and benchmark function of goals.[111] Thus Moersch (2001, 71) points out that the reason for the dependency of the subsidiarity principle on the goals of the respective community does not lie in the respective objectives as such, i.e. in their concrete contents, but in a specific

[106] Cf. Stettner (2006), in: Dreier (Ed.). Basic Law commentary, Art. 72, Marginal Number 10 f.; Kunig (2003), in: Münch & Kunig (Eds.). Basic Law commentary, Art. 72, Marginal Number 1, Art. 74, Marginal Number 1.

[107] Cf. Section 3.2.1, b). It should be noted that in principle an overlapping competitive relationship only exists if both acting authorities are capable of fulfilling the function in question (with no better/worse evaluation).

[108] On the goal level, too, differentiation according to collective and individual goals, which may be convergent or divergent, is recommended. While the development and maintenance of the popularity of a sport is shared by all, actors compete with the other association members for a share in the success or a share in the redistribution of the association's resources. According to Etzioni (1961) a goal is to be generally understood as the concept of a future state which the organization is attempting to create or maintain.

[109] For criticism of the final-teleological action concept see the evidence presented by Luhmann (1968, 18 ff.). Against the theoretical model of objectives cf. Tönnies (1923, 235 ff.).

[110] For example in the Law of Association and Company Law (§§ 21, 22 BGB (German Civil Code, etc.) and the recognized teleological interpretation method.

[111] However, the final-teleological action theory above all views objectives as goals of human actions, whereas functional systems theory draws on the system-building aspects of objectives.

function generally inherent in objectives. Accordingly, the subsidiarity principle is linked in a number of ways to a community's objectives. On the one hand the common goal serves as a criterion for determining which is the more appropriate authority in each case. Furthermore, specifying defined objectives also helps to formulate tasks. As normative imperatives, these tasks in turn represent goals (ibid, 70 f.).[112]

The prerequisite "common goal" is on the one hand understood – very generally – to mean the common good, which derives quasi from the "nature of the matter" and consequently takes on more concrete shape within the context of the needs of the respective community. On the other hand, it can result from an organization's statutes. In this respect, they represent the collective goals of a community.

As already suggested (Section 3.1.3 "Integrative function"), a thus-understood common accomplishment of goals does not always give rise to an integrative effect. In this context, Durkheim (1977, 169), points out that only positive solidarity that is explicitly based on mutual cooperation in the sense of the distribution of labour can produce integration.[113] In this sense, negative solidarity may prevent the overlapping of actions by recognizing the respective other party's freedom to act, however, it does not (yet) give rise to cooperation and support.[114] Thus above all the "density of the division of labour"[115] – which is also produced by allocating competences to the respective lower authority – is claimed to represent the prerequisite for the development of a sense of belonging, which in turn functions as the "integration medium" for positive solidarity(cf. for example Preyer, 2005, 61; Mayntz & Ziegler, 1969, 471). In this sense, alongside the existence of a common or collective goal, for cooperation and the willingness to cooperate in the sense of an "organic contractual solidarity" a division of labour in the form of a reinforcing mutual interdependence is above all important (Durkheim, 1977, 423). This, in turn, is dependent on how important the collective goal to eliminate doping is for the respective organization and above all on its being anchored in regimes reinforced by incentives and sanctions. Above all in the competitive societies based on a high division of labour outlined by Durkheim, in which due to the concatenation of action the individual can no longer foresee the consequences of his or her action and in which the individual actor is forced to react to exploitation attempts of others, a framework reinforced by sanctions is essential.

---

112 The orientation function of goal and objective definitions depends to a large degree on how clearly specified they are, Moersch (2001, 77 f.).

113 It has already been discussed above that the integrative function of the subsidiarity principle is above all also a consequence of the interaction of this principle with the solidarity principle.

114 Negative solidarity according to Durkheim (1977) relates (only) to the mutual recognition of proprietary rights.

115 Preyer (2005, 61) sees other factors in political consensus, a common sense of belonging to a group, as well as the level of the social budget.

(2) Goals of WADA and the international sports federations

The common goal to "combat doping" shared by WADA and the international sports federations does not derive from the "nature of the matter", but – as indeed is typical for elected socializations (Tönnies) – results from their statutes. In this respect it refers to a collective goal of the organization. This has to be distinguished from the respective individual goals, which can deviate from the collective goals.[116]

It does not constitute an obstacle to the prerequisite of a common goal – as a criterion for determining which is the more appropriate authority in each case – that the individual associations may pursue different interests, provided that these fall within the scope of the common goal (Isensee, 2002, 148). It is therefore necessary to consider whether in addition to the collective goal laid down in the statutes to eliminate doping, WADA and the international sports federations pursue different interests and whether these, insofar as they exist, exceed the scope of the common goal or not.

This scope is determined by the criteria of fairness and effectiveness (Kern 2007), which demand that the individual goals do not depart from the fundamental ethical decision underlying the collective goal to combat doping. The imperative for the sport organizations to effectively implement the anti-doping measures results from the concept of fair play also as the main guiding principle of the sport organizations (ibid, 269).

The traditional interpretation of fair play is based on the ethical behaviour of the individual. The competitive situation associations are forced into by commercialization, however, favours a degradation of the socially binding ethos, which Briefs (1980) describes as declining marginal ethics.[117] In modern competitively organized and growth-oriented economies, individual actions are so interwoven with each other in long interdependency chains that frequently cause and effect of the action are no longer directly correlated and that non-intended effects are no longer noticeable. By virtue of the emergent competition, actors intentionally work to achieve individual goals and their own advantage, whereby the individual goal is in this case personal gain and no longer that of a community.[118] As homo oeconomicus, actors are forced by the expanding competitive system to react to the exploitation attempts of others, which favours an individual who thinks exclusively in terms of profit and self-interest. The tendency

---

[116] Cf. also Mayntz & Ziegler (1969, 468). Only in the case of a (maximum) mechanical solidarity in the sense of Durkheim (1977) do individual goals correspond completely to collective goals. Vogt (1999, 275) points out that striving for personal advancement does not, however, necessarily have to harm the collective goal enshrined in the statutes, but can in fact also be advantageous to it. On the logic of collective action cf. Olson (1968), on the logic of collective action in the case of delegation cf. Schmidt-Trenz (1996).

[117] Cf. Emrich (2008b) on the following remarks.

[118] On the failure of moral accountability cf. Bohnstedt & Senkel (2007, 207) against the background of minors in elite sport.

seems to be that morally ethical behaviour is nowadays influenced by others and is thus motivated and determined by incentives.

The implemented actions of the selfish individual are controlled by incentives which stabilize ethically desirable behaviour within an action framework made up of rules and a more or less comprehensive formal control apparatus. Action is controlled by virtue of the economic framework or other social subsystems and rules reinforced by sanctions, through which the egoistic interests of the individual can be channelled as a motive. However, this presupposes consistent monitoring of standards and rules, as well as sanctioning. In this sense, the systematic seat of ethics shifts to the regime, the quality of which becomes a decisive characteristic for balancing out individual and collective interests. In an economic or sport system dominated by market and competition, ultimately only two basic demands can be derived on the individual level:

- "The individual must not exploit their capacity [...] to undermine the rules for competition by assuming the attractive outsider position; they must compete – even keenly – according to the rules.
- Faced with the risk of economic ruin, they as an individual cannot realize the framework alone, but they can be expected to publicly support and respect the framework under the sole condition "that others are prepared to do the same", and they can be expected to engage politically in establishing this framework (in parties, associations, trade unions, etc.)" (Homann, 2002, 34; cf. Hobbes, 1980, 119).

Following Homann's (2002, 35 ff.) line of argument, individual ethics is therefore not dispensable. It is stabilized in this case by the contractually established framework and plays a role alternatively and temporarily where market and competition fail to function, whether this is because a framework has not yet been formulated and taken effect, whether because despite the framework the competitive processes are not yet functioning or whether because the framework is insufficiently reinforced by sanctions. Marginal ethics is in this context the lowest, socially just tolerated ethical behaviour; the borderline to ethically still generally accepted and practised behaviour, and points to the threat to the "common good" (Briefs, 1963). Against this background, hope of establishing a mutual interdependence based on individual ethical demands – in the sense of positive solidarity for achieving the collective goal to combat doping – appears to fade. Competition for the spectators' attention, media attention and the recruitment of monetary resources makes it indispensable from an economic perspective to pursue personal goals in this regard – albeit to the neglect of the collective goal to combat doping – up to the point where the limit of the existing norms is reached, but (apparently) not yet exceeded.

From this perspective, the international associations are not per se going to view the phenomenon of doping as negative if it can be turned to advantage to satisfy expected individual benefit calculations. Sensational top sporting performances and records have an attention-enhancing effect. For the international sports associations it is therefore at first immaterial whether doping substances and methods were involved in achieving these performances, provided their use goes undetected. Furthermore, positive doping controls are tantamount to self-defamation, which is why it cannot be ruled out that the associations' sovereignty over testing could lead to complicity jurisprudence. The suspicion seems likely that the sports associations are not really seriously interested in the realization of the goal to combat doping (cf. also Bette & Schimank, 2006 and the article by Pitsch & Emrich in this volume).

However, it apparently also cannot be taken for granted that WADA's interests in taking action are oriented exclusively towards the goal to combat doping.[119] A look at how WADA is composed at least leaves room to doubt.[120] Furthermore, WADA also struggles for recognition as the harmonization and coordination authority in the fight against doping. Thus it is not surprising that WADA should contemplate making concessions towards the established (power-aware) sport organizations at the expense of the effectiveness and possibly also the sincerity of the anti-doping effort.[121] The proposed inclusion of the subsidiarity principle in the WADC could also point in this direction.

In light of this, it would be wrong to uncritically assume that the action of the organizations is guided by the collective goal to combat doping as laid down in their statutes.[122] Rather – above all as far as the international sport organizations are concerned – it appears to be heeded merely for the sake of (marginal) ethics and accordingly serves the organizations' external image cultivation; for the legitimization and mobilization of resources.[123] The fight against doping therefore only proves to be a collective and individual goal for association actors to the extent and for as long as this is in the interests of the spectators. Given the considerable deviations from the "common goal", strengthening the self-interests of the international sport organizations by including the subsidiarity principle in the WADC would actually appear to be detrimental to achieving that goal. The motivating force of self-interest would in such a case run against the collective goal.

3.2.3 Evaluation of the anticipated cause-effect relationship

We shall now attempt against the background of the above analysis to evaluate the anticipated cause-effect relationship that would result from the inclusion of the subsidiarity principle in the WADC.

---

[119] As evidence of this, we refer for example to the analysis results presented by Emrich & Pitsch in the present volume.

[120] Cf. also footnote 97 for the composition of the Foundation Board.

[121] Thus the WADC does not provide for any sanctions against sporting bodies.

[122] Added to this is the aspect of the separation of talk and action, Brunsson (2002); in the context of the Olympics cf. Emrich (2006).

[123] To obtain an insightful indication of the really targeted goals, according to Mayntz & Ziegler (1969), it would be meaningful to analyze the desired information feedback, i.e. the information the actor attempts to obtain.

a) With respect to the prerequisites and justiciability of the subsidiarity principle

As the above discussion shows, it can only conditionally be presumed that the formal prerequisites for application of the subsidiarity principle are given. Above all the existing "common goal" (and with it in this sense a division of labour) appears to be no more than a chimera.[124] Superficially, this may not necessarily appear to be an obstacle to achieving the anticipated higher acceptance of the WADC as a result of introducing the subsidiarity principle.[125] Indeed, on the contrary, the granting of concessions in the form of privileged interests appears to be an adequate means to this end. It is another matter, of course, whether this serves the goal of a harmonized fight against doping.

Insight is provided by the justiciability of the subsidiarity principle on the one hand and the existence of sanctioning possibilities against the international sporting bodies on the other. The latter were in the past only rudimentarily covered by the WADC, and this remains the case in the new version of the Code.[126] The Code contains a corresponding provision (Art. 12 WADC), without implying independent sanctioning powers. The provision merely states that the signatories or governments have the possibility to enforce their own rules for the purpose of imposing sanctions on another sporting body and declares this to be permissible. Kern (2007) therefore advocates – in the same breath as the introduction of the subsidiarity principle – establishing infringement proceedings. He points out that the WADC in principle allows for the possibility in Art. 13.4 to monitor the sport organizations in the implementation of the measures incumbent upon them and, where appropriate, sanction them (Kern, 2007, 295). What remains doubtful is whether the chances of establishing such a procedure increase if, through the inclusion of the subsidiarity principle, the international sport organizations are to be granted competences that go beyond mere co-determination rights in legislative enactment; it is hardly possible to be the one who makes the regulations and the one who controls them at the same time.

The justiciability of the subsidiarity principle is supported by Kern (2007, 308).[127] This relates to (judiciary) control (here: where appropriate through the CAS) of whether the responsible authorities exercise their competence in the fields of legislative and executive action in compliance with the subsidiarity principle. This is possible if in cases of dispute the subsidiarity principle is able to provide the tribunal with criteria for making decisions about the responsibility of the respective authority, i.e. for the execution of competence (Zuleeg, 1997,

---

[124] Brunner (1994, 11) speaks of the "fiction of common government goals".

[125] In fact what is missing is the "positive solidarity" that is so essential for the integrative effect (Durkheim, 1977).

[126] Cf. the revised version that took effect on 1.1.2009: http://www.wada-ama.org/rtecontent/document/code_v2009_En.pdf (retrieved on: 3.6.2008).

[127] However with a questionable argumentation: "The justiciability of the subsidiarity principle is not evaluated uniformly. The dispute between those who reject justiciability and those who advocate it cannot be decided here, nor is a decision necessary if we assume with the overriding majority of opinions that [...]." (Kern, 2007, 308).

201 f.; Kern, 2007, 308). For this, the subsidiarity principle must be incorporated into the rules and regulations in a sufficiently concrete and legally determined form (Kern, 2007, 308 with further evidence). Whether this is to be expected is – given the background outlined here – open to question. Furthermore, such judicial control is not exercised continuously, but only in the case of a current dispute. It is WADA's job to continuously oversee the process. Ultimately WADA is also under an obligation to justify and prove that the "lower level" has failed in or is incapable of adequately fulfilling the task (cf. Isensee, 2002, 147). Given the personnel and organizational costs this would involve – not to forget the need to rely on an intensive willingness on the part of the associations to communicate and cooperate when it comes to executing their anti-doping measures – and taking account of the desire for recognition (also) by the international sports federations, these controls would appear to be beyond WADA's capabilities.

The principal-agent theory makes a fundamental distinction with respect to opportunistic behaviour of the actors between "moral hazard" and "hold-up" (cf. Erlei, Leschke & Sauerland, 2007, 103 ff.). By contrast to the open infringement of the principal's interests through "hold up", in the case of "moral hazard" the opportunism occurs covertly, i.e. by exploiting the existing informational asymmetry. For the international sports federations as WADA agents, it would be easy given the largely sanction-free scope of action described here to conceal behaviour that contravenes their assignment.[128] Due to the asymmetrical organization of the responsibilities in the form described here (section 3.2.1) combined with the lack of corresponding control and sanctioning mechanisms for assuring that the competences are properly exercised, the international sports associations could even derive a considerable utility benefit: they could on the one hand continue as before – only with more far-reaching competences – and on the other hand by publicly committing to WADA and the WADC, and hence to a "ruthless" fight against doping, they could benefit their image. In this respect, the effects associated with the introduction of the subsidiarity principle appear to be of a more preserving nature.

b) With respect to the fundamentally promised correlation

Inadequate rule compliance can be compensated by creating sufficient interest in following the rules (Vanberg, 1999). The degree of acceptance of the regulatory order, however, is not a suitable indicator for this. Acceptance and compliance are not necessarily congruent, so that increased acceptance does not directly indicate higher compliance with the rules. According to Vanberg (1999, 45), it is rather a *question of fact*, whether acceptance of an institution can positively influence the readiness to follow the rules. Against the background of the dis-

[128] Attention should be paid in this context to the "external control authority" exercised by the sports consumers; cf. in general in this context the article by Pitsch & Emrich in this volume.

tinction between regulatory and behavioural orders in the meaning of Hayek (1967), in the case of the WADC the rule applicability and rule following interest (Vanberg, 1999) should be viewed independently of one another. The international sports associations make the pursuit of both interests dependent on a benefit-cost calculation in each case.[129] The results of this consideration can lead to a differentiated weighting of rule applicability and rule following interest.

The interest of the international sports federations as rational actors in the applicability of the WADC depends on their economic calculation and how, among other things, they assess the public value judgement in the fight against doping, the existence of control mechanisms and in this context also the possibility of being able to derive benefits from violating the rules.[130] As a result, a rule applicability interest will be the case if the actors stand to gain more from applicability of the WADC – taking into consideration the costs incurred – than without the WADC. In light of the fact that doping currently (still) generates considerable outrage among the general public and that the participation of the sports associations in an effective anti-doping campaign is seen and expected as a given, recognition of the WADC by the associations appears inevitable, in the sense of cost avoidance. The possible benefit derived from a rule violation as a result of the only fragmentary control mechanism can, however, positively influence the interest in applicability of the rules. Given this constellation, it stands to reason that the associations will declare a regulatory or constitutional interest. Thus, however, acceptance of the WADC in the sense of the interest in rule applicability rests on shaky foundations. While a consensus on the regulatory order is usually achieved[131], there are, however, a fairly large number of associations that only accept it because under the given circumstances – public demand for stringent anti-doping measures – they have no choice; a situation that Rawls (1993, 133 ff.) describes as *modus vivendi*.[132] The WADC is thus based on an initial consensus, but this consensus is barely resistant to changes in the relevant circumstances, and is therefore unstable. As soon as the disadvantageous initial conditions for the international sports federations no longer apply, those that had initially only reluctantly agreed will urge for the rules to be changed or abolished (cf. Vanberg, 1999, 46). Thus under the present circumstances an interest in rule applicability can be assumed, even though this is likely to prove fragile.

---

[129] In the meaning of modern economics, "benefits" is understood as everything the actors themselves consider to be benefits (Homann, 1999, 59).

[130] The sports associations do not (necessarily) have a primary interest of their own in eliminating doping. See Section 3.2.2, c), (2).

[131] Cf. the impressive list (Code Acceptance) of signatories on the WADA website: http://www.wada-ama.org/en/dynamic.ch2?pageCategory.id=270 (retrieved on: 18.6.2008)

[132] By contrast, he describes a situation where a regulatory order finds firm general acceptance that is largely impervious to changes in external circumstances as "overlapping consensus", Rawls (1993). Weber (1980, 16) also stresses the instability of an order adhered to out of purely instrumental-rational motives.

The interest in rule applicability or in taking action is linked to the respective preferences in terms of action alternatives. These derive – as we have seen – from the rational personal interests of the individual actors. For the latter it appears useful to derive competitive advantages through undetected bypassing of the rules. The interest in rule following is, for example, also expressed via a willingness – beyond a mere statement of intent – to establish a procedure that guarantees compliance. This is currently not apparent and was not an object of the modification catalogue relating to the new version of the WADC, so that a lack of interest in rule following can be assumed.

It is inappropriate in the present case to draw conclusions from the sports associations' acceptance of the WADC to their compliance; it is a big step from talking to acting. This would not be changed by the inclusion of the subsidiarity principle in the WADC. Although the assurance of freedom – through the subsidiarity principle – can serve as a performance, innovation and disciplinary incentive (Vogt, 1999, 282), personal interests in assuming responsibility and co-determination, however, do not seem to be developed in such a way that they can as far as possible be used constructively for the collective goal.[133] In this respect, while inclusion of the subsidiarity principle in the WADC can be expected to lead to higher acceptance, this is not likely, however, to be accompanied by a more intensive interest in rule following.

4 Conclusion and outlook: conditions for effectively laying the foundation stone

If one takes Kern's (2007) view of the WADC as a foundation stone for a new legal instrument in the international anti-doping campaign, this is necessarily subject to specific requirements to ensure that the construction built on it is not lopsided from the outset and therefore in danger of collapsing. Faults when laying the foundation stone have a cumulative effect. The alignment and correlations with the other required elements are therefore particularly important. If the laying of the foundation stone is not checked until after completion of the project, the action alternatives with respect to optimal goal realization are limited. If no faults are ascertained, construction is successfully completed, whereby its success can most likely be put down to chance. In the opposite case, it is no longer possible to access the source of the fault, so that – depending on the nature of repairs – sooner or later the construction has to be knocked down; however, when this happens, the desired result can no longer be optimally achieved.

In this respect, special attention must be given to the organization, implementation and further adaptation of the WADC. This above all makes it necessary to bring forward the evaluation of corresponding measures.[134] This has been done

[133] Above all there is a lack of a sanctioning mechanism against the international sports federations. Only introducing such a mechanism subsequent to the subsidiarity principle in the form of infringement proceedings does not – as already described – appear likely.

[134] Cf. the criticism of "ex-post effectiveness tests" mentioned above (fn. 62).

here. The criteria on which the evaluation is based are also important. The few institutional economic studies have suggested that proposals can by all means fulfil all the necessary legal prerequisites for a possible application without necessarily judging the effectiveness of the respective measure in each case.

To ensure the successful laying of the foundation stone, it has to be aligned with the foundation. This has proved problematic since the coming into effect of the WADC, since (above all) the international sports federations only adhere to its guidelines to a limited extent. In this respect the idea to introduce the subsidiarity principle does not appear unattractive. The allocation of competences would satisfy the privileged interests of the associations. Consequently, the WADC would enjoy a higher level of acceptance and, as a result, befitting stability. But the stability is only specious. In fact, despite its formally documented acceptance, the WADC is built on sand in the sense of Rawls' *modus vivendi.* The reasons for this have been sufficiently explained above. Under these circumstances, the hope that the subsidiarity principle would increase compliance on the part of the international sports federations is also unlikely to materialize. On the contrary, the proposal could even have negative consequences. The inadequate cohesion between foundation stone and foundation in the absence of a corresponding control and sanctioning mechanism seems especially tenuous, so that the subsidiarity principle entails the risk of a factual competence-competence of the international sports federations (cf. Böttger, 2004, 61). It does not seem realistic to contemplate making subsequent repairs.

The foundation stone therefore has to be stable in itself and must not crack. What counts, then, is the effectiveness of the WADC, which, for the reasons described above, cannot be inferred from its level of acceptance. Rather, it is the result of the interaction between the action restrictions imposed by the regulatory order and the efforts of the actors concerned to pursue their own interests as effectively as possible under the given constraints (Vanberg, 1999, 39). Within the meaning of the collective goal pursued with the WADC, personal preferences should be promoted through a framework in such a way that they reward desirable behaviour through corresponding incentives and prevent undesirable behaviour through cost-causing sanctions. A general panacea for creating such an interest in rule following does not, however, exist, as this depends in each case on the type of rules in question and the respective particular circumstances (ibid, 48). In the present case, it is imperative to detect and sanction rule violations on the part of the international sports federations (on the treatment of the doping sanctions problem under commercial law cf. Momsen in this volume). Without going into any greater detail about the organization, the establishment of corresponding infringement proceedings is a prerequisite to even starting to think about further measures if these are not to be totally lacking in seriousness. It also seems worthwhile taking a look at corporate governance concepts for business enterprises. In principle, these aim "as far as possible to create an ideal framework for efficient corporate decisions", so that diverging personal goals of individual interest groups can be given consideration in a way that serves both the personal and the contractual goals (Grundmann & Mülbert, 2001, 215).

References

Baumgartner, A., Korff, W. (1999). Sozialprinzipien als ethische Baugesetzlichkeiten moderner Gesellschaft: Personalität, Solidarität und Subsidiarität. In W. Korff et al. (Eds.). *Handbuch der Wirtschaftsethik. Band 1: Verhältnisbestimmung von Wirtschaft und Ethik* (pp. 225-237). Gütersloh: Gütersloher Verlagshaus.

Bette, K.-H., Schimank, U. (2006). *Doping im Hochleistungssport. Anpassung durch Abweichung*. 2nd extended edition, Frankfurt a. M.: Suhrkamp.

Bohnstedt, K., Senkel, K. (2007). Minderjährige im Hochleistungssport. Anmerkungen zum Begriff der Verantwortung. In N. Müller, D. Voigt (Eds.). *Gesellschaft und Sport als Feld wissenschaftlichen Handelns. Festschrift für Manfred Messing*. (pp. 191-231) Niedernhausen/Ts.: Schors.

Böttger, U. (2004): *Ansätze für eine ökonomische Analyse des Subsidiaritätsprinzips des EG Art. 5 Abs. 2*. (Schriften zur wirtschaftswissenschaftlichen Analyse des Rechts; Vol. 50) Berlin: Duncker & Humblot.

Briefs, G. (1980 [orig. 1963]). Zum Problem der Grenzmoral. In H. B. Streithofen, R. von Voss (Eds.). *Götz Briefs. Ausgewählte Schriften. Volume 1: Mensch und Gesellschaft* (pp. 51-61). Berlin: Duncker & Humblot.

Brunner, M. (1994). Das Subsidiaritätsprinzip als europäisches Prinzip. In D. Merten (Ed.). *Die Subsidiarität Europas* (pp. 9-22) (Schriften zum Europäischen Recht; Vol. 16). Berlin: Duncker & Humblot.

Brunsson, N. (2002). The Organization of Hypocrisy. Talk, Decisions and Actions in Organisations. Copenhagen: Abstrakt forlag.

Buchanan, J. (1991). Möglichkeiten für eine europäische Verfassung. Eine amerikanische Sicht. In H. O. Lenel et al. (Eds.). ORDO. *Jahrbuch für die Ordnung von Wirtschaft und Gesellschaft*. Vol. 42. (pp. 127-137) Stuttgart, New York: Fischer.

Calliess, C. (1999). *Subsidiaritäts- und Solidaritätsprinzip in der Europäischen Union. Vorgaben für die Anwendung von Art. 5 (ex-Art. 3b) EGV nach dem Vertrag von Amsterdam*. 2nd updated and revised edition. (Schriften des Europa-Instituts der Universität des Saarlandes – Rechtswissenschaften; Vol. 10). Baden-Baden: Nomos.

Caplow, T. (1964). *Principles of Organization*. New York and others: Hartcourt, Brace and World.

Dreier, H. (Ed.) (2006). *Basic Law Commentary*. Vol. II: Art. 20-82, 2nd edition. Tübingen: Mohr Siebeck.

Durkheim, E. (1977 [orig. 1893]). *Über die Teilung der sozialen Arbeit*. Introduction by Niklas Luhmann, translated by Ludwig Schmidts. Frankfurt a. M.: Suhrkamp.

Emrich, E. (2006): Zur Kommerzialisierung der olympischen Idee – einige grundlegende Anmerkungen. In Kutschke, F. (Ed.): *Ökonomie Olympischer Spiele* (pp. 39-55). Schorndorf: Hofmann.
Emrich, E. (2008a). Markt oder Tempel? Zwischen Moral und Eigennutz: Was können wir von der Bienenfabel für die Ökonomie der Olympischen Spiele lernen? In Wacker, C., Marxen, R. (Eds.). *Olympia – zwischen Ideal und Wirklichkeit. Festschrift für Norbert Müller zum 60. Geburtstag* (pp. 103-132). Berlin: LIT.
Emrich, E. (2008b). Sportverbände. In Weis, K., Gugutzer, R. (Eds.). *Handbuch Sportsoziologie* (pp. 122-132). Schorndorf: Hofmann.
Erlei, M., Leschke, M., Sauerland, D. (2007): *Neue Institutionenökonomik.* 2nd revised edition. Stuttgart: Schäffer-Poeschel.
Etzioni, A. (1961): *A Comparative Analysis of Complex Organizations, On Power, Involvement, and their Correlates.* New York: Free Press.
Fritzweiler, J., Pfister, B., Summerer, T. (Eds.) (2007): *Praxishandbuch Sportrecht* (2nd edition). Munich: Beck. [quoted: PHBSportR-*editor*]
Grundmann, S., Mülbert, P. O. (2001). ECLR. Corporate Governance – Europäische Perspektiven. Symposium zum 60. Geburtstag von Klaus J. Hopt am 1./2. September 2000 in Mainz. *ZGR* (2), 215–223.
Haas, U. (2001). Zur Einführung von Schiedsklauseln durch Satzungsänderungen in Vereinen. Besprechung des Urteils BGH WM 2000, 957. *ZGR* (2), 325–349.
Hayek, F. A. von (1967). Rechtsordnung und Handelnsordnung. In E. Streißler (Ed.). *Zur Einheit der Rechts- und Staatswissenschaften* (Freiburger Rechts- und Staatswissenschaftliche Abhandlungen; Vol. 27) (pp. 195-230). Karlsruhe: C. F. Müller.
Herzog, R. (1998): Art. Subsidiaritätsprinzip. In J. Ritter, K. Gründer (Eds.). *Historisches Wörterbuch der Philosophie* (pp. 482-486). Volume 10. St – T. Basel: Schwabe.
Hobbes, T. (1980 [orig. 1651): Leviathan, Erster und zweiter Teil, translated by Jacob P. Mayer. Stuttgart: Reclam.
Höffe, O. (1994). Subsidiarität als staatsphilosophisches Prinzip? In A. Riklin, G. Batliner (Eds.). *Subsidiaritätsprinzip. Ein interdisziplinäres Symposium* (pp. 19-46). Baden-Baden: Nomos.
Höffe, O. (1997). Subsidiarität als staatsphilosophisches Prinzip. In K. W. Nörr, T. Oppermann (Eds.). *Subsidiarität: Idee und Wirklichkeit. Zur Reichweite eines Prinzips in Deutschland und Europa* (pp. 49-67). Tübingen: Mohr Siebeck.
Hondrich, K. O. (2001). *Der neue Mensch.* Frankfurt a. M.: Suhrkamp.
Hondrich, K. O., Koch-Arzberger, C. (1994). *Solidarität in der modernen Gesellschaft.* Frankfurt a. M.: Fischer.
Homann, K. (1999). Die Legitimation von Institutionen. In W. Korff et al. (Eds.). *Handbuch der Wirtschaftsethik. Volume 2: Ethik wirtschaftlicher Ordnungen* (pp. 50-95). Gütersloh: Gütersloher Verlagshaus.

Homann, K. (2002). *Vorteile und Anreize. Zur Grundlegung einer Ethik der Zukunft*. Edited by Christoph Lütge. Tübingen: Mohr Siebeck.
Homann, K., Kirchner, C. (1995). Das Subsidiaritätsprinzip in der Katholischen Soziallehre und in der Ökonomik. In L. Gerken (Ed.). *Europa zwischen Ordnungswettbewerb und Harmonisierung. Europäische Ordnungspolitik im Zeichen der Subsidiarität.* (pp. 45-69) Berlin, Heidelberg: Springer.
Houlihan, B. (1999). The International Anti-Doping Agency. Prospects for success. *Sports Law Administration & Practive 6 (1)*, 8-9.
Isensee, J. (1968). *Subsidiaritätsprinzip und Verfassungsrecht. Eine Studie über das Regulativ des Verhältnisses von Staat und Gesellschaft* (Schriften zum Öffentlichen Recht, Vol. 80). Berlin: Duncker & Humblot.
Isensee, J. (2002). Subsidiarität – Das Prinzip und seine Prämissen. In P. Blickle et al. (Eds.). *Subsidiarität als rechtliches und politisches Ordnungsprinzip in Kirche, Staat und Gesellschaft. Genese, Geltungsgrundlagen und Perspektiven an der Schwelle des dritten Jahrtausends* (pp. 129-177). (Rechtstheorie Beiheft 20). Berlin: Duncker & Humblot.
Jakob, A., Berninger, A. (2008). Die wichtigsten Änderungen des WADA-Codes. *SpuRt 15,* 61–62.
Kern, B. (2007). Internationale Dopingbekämpfung – Der World Anti-Doping Code der World Anti-Doping Agency. Hamburg: Kovac.
Küchenhoff, G. (1953). Staatsverfassung und Subsidiarität. In A. F. Utz (Ed.). *Das Subsidiaritätsprinzip* (pp. 65-99). Heidelberg: Kerle.
Lecheler, H. (1993). *Das Subsidiaritätsprinzip. Strukturprinzip einer europäischen Union* (Soziale Orientierung; Vol. 8). Berlin: Duncker & Humblot.
Luhmann, N. (1968). *Zweckbegriff und Systemrationalität. Über die Funktion von Zwecken in sozialen Systemen*. Tübingen: Mohr Siebeck.
Mayntz, R., Ziegler, R. (1969). Soziologie der Organisation. In R. König (Ed.). *Handbuch der empirischen Sozialforschung* (pp. 444-513). Vol. II: Ausgewählte Gebiete der empirischen Soziologie. Stuttgart: DTV.
Merten, D. (1994). Subsidiarität als Verfassungsprinzip. In ibid. (Ed.). *Die Subsidiarität Europas* (pp. 77-96) (Schriften zum Europäischen Recht; Vol. 16). Berlin: Duncker & Humblot.
Moersch, W. (2001). *Leistungsfähigkeit und Grenzen des Subsidiaritätsprinzips. Eine rechtsdogmatische und rechtspolitische Studie* (Schriften zum europäischen Recht; Vol. 73). Berlin: Duncker & Humblot.
Mieth, D. (1998). Artikel Subsidiarität. In D. Mieth, O. Grupe (Eds.). *Lexikon der Ethik im Sport* (pp. 534-545). 2nd edition, Schorndorf: Hofmann.
Münch, I. von, Kunig, P. (2003) (Eds.). Basic Law Commentary. Volume 3. Art. 70–146, 4th/5th revised edition. Munich: Beck.
Münch, R. (2001). *Offene Räume. Soziale Integration diesseits und jenseits des Nationalstaats*. Frankfurt a. M.: Suhrkamp.
Nell-Breuning, O. von (1962): Art. Subsidiaritätsprinzip. In Görres-Gesellschaft (Eds.).: *Schwurgericht bis Venezuela* (pp. 826-833) (Staatslexikon. Recht,

Wirtschaft, Gesellschaft Volume 7) 6th completely revised and extended edition. Freiburg i. Br.: Herder.
Nell-Breuning, O. von (1990 [orig. 1968]). *Baugesetze der Gesellschaft. Solidarität und Subsidiarität.* Freiburg i. Br.: Herder.
Olson, M. (1968): *Die Logik des kollektiven Handelns. Kollektivgüter und die Theorie der Gruppen.* Tübingen: Mohr Siebeck.
Opp, K.-D. (1975). *Soziologie der Wirtschaftskriminalität.* München: Beck.
Pitsch, W., Maats, P., Emrich, E.: Skizzen zu einer Ökonomik des Dopings. In: Müller, N., Messing. M. (Eds.). *Olympismus – Erbe und Verantwortung* (pp. 381-418). Kassel: Agon.
Pieper, U. S. (1994). *Subsidiarität. Ein Beitrag zur Begrenzung der Gemeinschaftskompetenzen* (Völkerrecht – Europarecht – Staatsrecht; Vol. 6). Cologne and others: Heymanns.
Pirson, D. (2008). *Gesammelte Beiträge zum Kirchenrecht und Staatskirchenrecht.* 1st sub-volume. Tübingen: Mohr Siebeck.
Pound, R. W. (2002). The World Anti-Doping Agency: An Experiment in International Law. *International Sports Law Review*, 53-59.
Preyer, G. (2005): Luhmanns Theorie der sozialen Differenzierung – Das Ende der Inklusionslogik. *Rechtstheorie* (2), 49–67.
Rauscher, A., Hollerbach, A. (1995). Artikel Subsidiarität. In Görres-Gesellschaft (Eds.). *Staatslexikon. Recht, Wirtschaft, Gesellschaft* (pp. 386-390). 5th volume, 7th completely revised edition, Freiburg and others: Herder.
Rawls, J. (1993). *Political Liberalism.* New York: Columbia University Press.
Ronge, F. (1998). *Legitimität durch Subsidiarität. Der Beitrag des Subsidiaritätsprinzips zur Legitimation einer überstaatlichen politischen Ordnung in Europa* (Schriften des Zentrum für Europäische Integrationsforschung; Vol. 1). Baden-Baden: Nomos.
Schmidtchen, D. (1999). Die ökonomische Analyse des Rechts. In D. Schmidtchen, S. Weth (Eds.). *Der Effizienz auf der Spur. Die Funktionsfähigkeit der Justiz im Lichte der ökonomischen Analyse des Rechts* (pp. 9-34). Baden-Baden: Nomos.
Schmidt-Trenz, H.-J. (1996). *Die Logik kollektiven Handelns bei Delegation. Das Organisationsdilemma der Verbände am Beispiel des Beitragszwangs bei den Industrie- und Handelskammern* (Die Einheit der Gesellschaftswissenschaften; Vol. 94). Tübingen: Mohr-Siebeck.
Schneider, L. (1996). *Subsidiäre Gesellschaft – Erfolgreiche Gesellschaft. Implikative und analoge Aspekte eines Sozialprinzips.* 4th extended edition, Paderborn and others: Schöningh.
Schüller, A. (1997). Subsidiarität im Spannungsfeld zwischen Wettbewerb und Harmonisierung. Interpretationsversuche aus ordnungspolitischer Sicht. In K. W. Nörr, T. Oppermann (Eds.). *Subsidiarität: Idee und Wirklichkeit. Zur Reichweite eines Prinzips in Deutschland und Europa* (pp. 69-104). Tübingen: Mohr Siebeck.

Senkel, K. (2005). *Play True. Die Dopingproblematik zwischen sportethischen Anforderungen und allgemeinem Rechtsanspruch.* Kassel: Agon (Olympische Studien; Vol. 7).

Stein, T. (1994): Subsidiarität als Rechtsprinzip. In D. Merten (Ed.). *Die Subsidiarität Europas* (pp. 23-40) (Schriften zum Europäischen Recht; Vol. 16). Berlin: Duncker & Humblot.

Stern, K. (1980). *Das Staatsrecht der Bundesrepublik Deutschland.* Volume II: Staatsorgane, Staatsfunktionen, Finanz- und Haushaltsverfassung, Notstandsverfassung. Munich: Beck.

Tönnies, F. (1923). Zweck und Mittel im sozialen Leben. In P. Melchior (Ed.). *Hauptprobleme der Soziologie. Erinnerungsgabe für Max Weber* (pp. 235-270). Vol. 1. Munich: von Duncker.

Utz, A. F. (1953). Die geistesgeschichtlichen Grundlagen des Subsidiaritätsprinzips. In ibid. (Ed.). *Das Subsidiaritätsprinzip* (pp. 7-17). Heidelberg: Kerle.

Vanberg, V. J. (1982). *Markt und Organisation. Individualistische Sozialtheorie und das Problem korporativen Handelns.* Tübingen: Mohr Siebeck.

Vanberg, V. J. (1999). Die Akzeptanz von Institutionen. In W. Korff et al. (Eds.). *Handbuch der Wirtschaftsethik. Volume 2: Ethik wirtschaftlicher Ordnungen* (pp. 38-50). Gütersloh: Gütersloher Verlagshaus.

Van der Ven, J. J. M. (1953). Organisation, Ordnung und Gerechtigkeit. In A. F. Utz (Ed.). *Das Subsidiaritätsprinzip* (pp. 45-65). Heidelberg: Kerle.

Vieweg, K. (1990). *Normsetzung und -anwendung deutscher und internationaler Verbände. Eine rechtstatsächliche und rechtliche Untersuchung unter besonderer Berücksichtigung der Sportverbände* (Schriften zum Bürgerlichen Recht: Volume 132). Berlin: Duncker & Humblodt.

Vogt, M. (1999). Institutionen als Organisationsformen menschlichen Handelns. In W. Korff et al. (Eds.). *Handbuch der Wirtschaftsethik. Volume 1: Verhältnisbestimmung von Wirtschaft und Ethik* (pp. 268-284). Gütersloh: Gütersloher Verlagshaus.

Weber, M. (1980). *Wirtschaft und Gesellschaft. Grundriss der verstehenden Soziologie.* 5th revised edition, obtained by Johannes Winckelmann. Tübingen: Mohr.

Zuleeg, M. (1997). Justiziabilität des Subsidiaritätsprinzips. In K. W. Nörr, T. Oppermann (Eds.). *Subsidiarität: Idee und Wirklichkeit. Zur Reichweite eines Prinzips in Deutschland und Europa* (pp. 185-204). Tübingen: Mohr Siebeck.

World Anti-Doping Code:

Old version: http://www.wada-ama.org/rtecontent/document/code_v3.pdf (last retrieved on: 3.6.2008)

New version: http://www.wada-ama.org/rtecontent/document/code_v2009_En.pdf (last retrieved on: 3.6.2008)

Composition of the WADA Foundation Board: http://www.wada-ama.org/en/dynamic.ch2?pageCategory.id=289 (last retrieved on: 2.6.2008)

dpa press release dated 5.6.2002, 7:15 h

dpa press release dated 23.9.2003, 19:44 h
sid press release dated 4.8.2004, 08:15 h
sid press release dated 20.5.2008, 13:07 h
Frankfurter Allgemeine Sonntagszeitung dated 18.9.2005, 20
Neue Zürcher Zeitung dated 5.3.2003, 46

Katja Senkel

"Strict liability", presumption of guilt and reciprocity in anti-doping measures initiated by sports associations

1 Protagonist and/or victim: the athlete as the "central figure in the doping scene"

In the discussion by Adolphsen (2008) on the new German anti-doping law, the athlete is highlighted as the "central figure in the doping scene". Adolphsen criticizes that the new anti-doping law paints a false picture of the athlete by wrongfully placing the focus on existing networks of supervisors, physicians and coaches and largely ignoring the athlete. Although he mentions the "sometimes immense pressure imposed by the sport system" (Adolphsen, 2008, 88), he at the same time points out that as empowered sportsmen and women, athletes are protagonists and not victims. Recent empirical studies also suggest that doping athletes are more likely to be found in the role of protagonist (Pitsch, Maats & Emrich, 2008).

Adolphsen (2008, 88) draws two conclusions from this. On the one hand he asserts that athletes should be criminalized. On the other hand he points out that the anti-doping discussion is too focused on the role of criminal law and that this cannot be a cure-all. He feels attention should be more intensively directed at prevention, and athletes must be encouraged to "rediscover a personal code of ethics towards the use of prohibited substances".

The way in which these two approaches correlate with respect to anti-doping measures initiated by sports associations stands in need of further discussion. Athletes are indeed acknowledged as the "central figures in the doping scene", and they are confronted with drastic sanctions. Their basic rights are severely restricted.[135] The consideration given to the weight of athletes' rights in the anti-doping balance so far justifies the question of whether athletes are "victims".

In the following the demands made on athletes and the consequences they entail, shall be considered, referring to the current discussion in Germany. Nonetheless the arising questions also concern the principles of law of all countries taking part in the fight against doping. The extent to which the procedural embodiment of anti-doping measures actually achieves the stated objectives and helps athletes to rediscover a "personal code of ethics" appears doubtful, especially in light of the principle of reciprocity.

---

[135] An analysis dating from 1999 had shown that a total of 14 Olympic sports associations do not guarantee athletes any procedural rights whatsoever, in 30 associations they even did not have the right to submit evidence, call witnesses or independent experts. Almost 50% of the regimes laid down the principle of "strict liability". On further procedural shortcomings (overview) cf. Siekmann (2000, 33 f.)

2 On "rediscovering a personal code of ethics": obstacles posed by legal mechanisms of the associations

Reciprocity directs the attention towards the influence of expectations on individual behaviour (Ockenfels, 1999, 19). Social action generally presupposes the subjective expectation that a given action is reflected either in the present or the future by a corresponding counteraction. Thus in sociology and ethnology the importance of reciprocity norms is frequently highlighted (Malinowski, 1960; Mauss, 1968; Gouldner, 1960).

The principle of reciprocity is in general described as a mechanism that promotes cooperation; its effect being based on establishing direct interaction between one's own cooperative behaviour and the cooperative behaviour of others (Vanberg, 1975, 15 ff.; 1987, 265; cf. Emrich, 2006).[136] Reciprocity can thus be seen as a form of mutual exchange (cf. Homans, 1972). It comes in two versions, positive reciprocity and negative reciprocity. While positive reciprocity can lead per se to cooperation, as a response in kind to friendly behaviour, negative reciprocity refers to a kind of "quid pro quo" type of response to negative action in the form of retaliation (Diekmann & Voss, 2008, 90), whereby indirect experiences can also determine personal actions (Vanberg, 1987). The comment by Court (1994, 348), who remarks that the idea of fairness is only harmed if it is undermined by undemocratic practices also has to be understood in this context.

The effectiveness of legal mechanisms is determined multi-dimensionally and reciprocity considerations play more than just a subordinate role. This is also substantiated by numerous experimental economics research studies (comments in Diekmann & Voss, 2008). These show that individuals' behaviour is not only driven by the desire to increase material benefit, but is also oriented towards the norms of fairness. "Homo reciprocans" (Adloff & Mau, 2005) in general rewards positive cooperative behaviour, while he is more likely to react to negative cooperative behaviour with retaliation, even if this means accepting costs (Fehr & Gächter, 2000). Neuroscientific studies suggest that reciprocal behaviour is an inherent part of our biological make-up and that retaliation tendencies can be attributed to deep-rooted emotions that lead us to demand retribution (Cory, 1999; Rilling et. al., 2002).

Given this, it appears inadequate to simply make general preventive presumptions about the level of penalty or the degree of probability of being disciplined as the determining factor behind athletes' decisions, and to ignore the aspect of reciprocity.[137] This is reflected in the model of absolute criminal theory, which

[136] According to Vanberg (1987, 278), it should be noted in this context that the mechanism of reciprocity plays a different role in cooperative regimes of the type "market" and the type "order".

[137] A statement by the chairman of the Sports Committee in the Bundestag, Peter Danckert suggests that this is the practice in the current anti-doping discussion and that considerations regarding a proposed anti-doping law for example point in such a functionalist direction: "The

builds on the principle of retaliation, while also drawing on the principle of talion to limit the punishment (Hof, 1996, 342). Accordingly, the retribution against the offender should not be higher than the crime committed against the victim (ibid). The consideration of guilt plays an important role in this, without which the punishment could not be matched to the offence.

2.1 The question of guilt: strict liability

The principle of strict liability is anchored both in the World Anti-Doping Code (WADC) and in the National Anti-Doping Code (NADC).[138] A violation against the anti-doping rules is given when a specimen taken from an athlete tests positive for a prohibited substance, its metabolites or markers (Art. 2.1 NADC/WADC). Thus, an athlete is liable if he or she is found to have used a banned substance or method, irrespective of whether due to wilful intent, culpability, negligence or deliberate use (Art. 2.1.1 NADC/WADC). These means if an athlete meets the objective criteria for a doping offence, he or she is liable to sanctions pursuant to Art. 10 WADC/NADC. In terms of legal consequences, the strict liability rule literally means that sanctions are imposed on principle, whether the athlete is guilty or not.

To answer the question of the culpability requirement, a distinction must be made between the types of legal sanctions imposed by the associations. In the case of "minor penalties", prevailing law in Germany raises no objections to associations imposing disciplinary procedures without proving the guilt of the accused (BGHZ (Federal Court of Justice, Civil Law), 29, 352, 359; OLG München (Munich Higher Regional Court), SpuRt 1997, 134). If "minor penalties" are understood as being purely preventive measures aimed solely at protecting competition, then a disqualification pronounced within the context of a doping violation can also be subsumed under this category. It is intended exclusively to restore equality of opportunity and does not imply any imputation of guilt, nor is it aimed at personally punishing the athlete. The same can be argued in the case of a suspension: this serves merely to re-establish equal opportunity and does not constitute an accusation of blame. Hence – so the rationale goes – here too, the question of culpability can be ignored. Given that a suspension already has grave consequences for the athlete and the tournaments cannot be repeated, however, such a waiver is highly questionable and therefore also not without controversy. A suspension, for example, contains elements of both a disqualification and a ban. However, we cannot consider this problem in any

idea is not that hundreds should be punished, but that the measure should shake up the scene." (FAZ dated 7 March 2007, p. 31). Reciprocity considerations play hardly any role in the general prevention theory, so that negative reciprocity – as a response to this practice by the athletes affected and observing this practice – could contradict the effectiveness of the mechanisms.

[138] Opie (2004, 275) speaks from „absolute liability".

more detail here.[139] The discounting of the guilt question becomes extremely problematic when it comes to doping bans. These represent real disciplinary action affecting the athletes' basic rights and serve both as a punishment with an impact on the athlete's future and as a deterrent to other athletes. A ban both points the finger of blame and at the same time enforces punishment (cf. also Soek, 2006, 398 f.). Advocates of the strict liability approach argue that this is the only way to win the fight against doping.[140] They reason that the necessity to prove the athlete's guilt arising from the consideration of culpability constitutes a decisive weakness in the anti-doping campaign and is ultimately also responsible for its failure (Adolphsen, 2003, 334). Thus the conflict over the legitimacy of the strict liability rule hovers somewhere on the borderline between an effective fight against doping on the part of the sports associations and the necessary protection of the athletes against the associations' power (Adolphsen, 2003, 340). The discussion ignores the possibility that these two intended purposes do not necessarily have to mutually exclude each other, but on the contrary, can mutually influence each other. Voices such as Petri (2004, 212) or Opie (2004, 275), which expressly view the waiver of the principle of culpability as being irreconcilable with the aims of the anti-doping campaign, are obviously seldom heard.[141] Nevertheless, the strict liability rule contradicts the demands for a reciprocal punishment that fits the offence, which, however, is indispensable in light of the (sport ethics) principle of fair play that (not only) athletes need to remember.[142] This includes, among other things, the aspect of equal opportunity and thus specifically constitutes a generally recognized protective function of the doping ban. Punishing innocent athletes is irreconcilable with guaranteeing and upholding equality of opportunity and hence also with the protective function of the doping ban.[143] Against this background, it seems more than questionable to hope that ignoring the question of fault will make the fight against doping more effective, since the means contradict the ends.

The principle of strict liability applied to the doping ban is also incompatible with applicable national law (cf. also Adolphsen, 2003, 339 f.; Lob, 1999, 272;

---

[139] One particular problem is the so-called protective ban, cf. on this Adolphsen (2007, 259), who in this context correctly speaks of "indirect anti-doping measures".

[140] In the focus stands the so-called „floodgate"-argument, cf. Gardiner et.al. (2006, 275).

[141] Opie (2004, 275): „this rule offends universal notions of fairness, justice, and personal responsibility".

[142] Cf. on this the "case Baxter", Baxter v. IOC, CAS 2002/A/376 para.3.33, Lausanne, Oct. 15, 2002. Opie (2004, 276) commentates this as follows: „This is not consistent with the notion of fair play and such outcomes present a threat to the moral authority of the anti-doping cause." To this case see also McLaren & Clement (2004, 52).

[143] Consideration should also be given here to the problem of opposing rules of procedure, inasmuch as it is not intended to replace criminal law, or, conversely, incorporate the strict liability rule into criminal law. This again gives rise to the (standard) question of the autonomy of the associations. For this and other references, I thank Prof. Dr. Momsen.

Wise, 1997, 20).[144] Although the doping ban is a penalty imposed by the associations based on private autonomy, the badge of shame and the devastating consequences for the athlete's professional situation it brings with it – the doping ban has the same effect as an occupational ban – the application of criminal principles cannot be avoided altogether (for this purpose also Soek, 2006, 399). German criminal law as well as common law (Soek, 2006, 133) is based on the overriding principle that guilt must be proved beyond doubt. Being held responsible for wrongdoing is therefore the prerequisite for imposing sanctions. Procedural principles, such as the right to be heard, are also limited, since strict liability would make a disciplinary hearing of the athlete unnecessary (cf. also Gardiner et.al., 2006, 274 f.). Furthermore, the principle of strict liability applied to the doping ban is also incompatible with the norms of German civil law. Pursuant to § 138 BGB (German Civil Code) it is unethical and pursuant to § 307 I BGB inappropriate. The general provisions of §§ 138, 307 BGB help to justify (third-party) effect of constitutional rights in relations between the association and the athlete (Petri, 2005, 113). This affects the athlete's personal rights (Art. 2 I in conjunction with 1 I GG (German Basic Law), as well as their occupational freedom (Art. 12 I GG). A doping ban imposed by the respective sports association court without any consideration of culpability, would therefore be null and void at least before German national courts.[145] Furthermore the "strict liability"-principle is considered to be incompatible with article 6 of the European Convention of Human Rights (Soek, 2006, 401).[146]

For these reasons among others, the strict liability principle as contained in the World Anti-Doping Code and in the National Anti-Doping Code is not "strictly" applied. In this context, Haas (in: HBSportR, 2005, 63) refers to the different application of this rule beyond the abstract concept and Adolphsen (2007, 240) claims that we should not allow ourselves to be fooled by the frequent inaccurate use of the term, as it is not (any longer) used in the meaning of imposing sanctions irrespective of fault. Rather, a shift is taking place to the legal consequences level, where the issue is imposing sanctions that are commensurate with the offence. This means that an anti-doping violation should be investigated even if the athlete is not at fault (alone the objective corpus delicti suffices), but that on the grounds of their innocence the athlete should not be

---

[144] Wise (1997, 20 f.): „Les fondements juridiques pour de telles décisions varieront sans doute d´un cas à un autre, d´un pays à un autre. En bref, la règle de «responsabilité stricte» a [...] un concept incompatible avec les principies juridiques fondamentaux des sociétés civilisées."

[145] Even the Court of Arbitration for Sport (CAS) considers that the strict liability-rule contradicts to the conception of legality in Continental Europe as well as to the athletes' personal rights concerning the law in Switzerland (CAS 2000/A/317, 9-7-2001, F. Aanes v. FILA, ground V.2.3.), vgl. Soek (2006, 165).

[146] Soek (2006) arrives at the conclusion that the sport federations are bound to article 6 ECHR (European Convention of Human Rights), because „the disciplinary law concerning doping as essentially punitive law should be regarded as pseudo-criminal law." (ibid, 401).

punished. This does not really represent an improvement in the athlete's (legal) position at all, since it is by no means only a dogmatic difference as, however, Adolphsen (2007, 240) would have us believe. Rather, it cannot simply be dismissed that there is a considerable difference between a milder punishment and no punishment at all (cf. also Petri, 2004, 213).[147] Here, we need only think of the consequences of a repeated doping violation. The shift of focus towards the procedural demands on athletes to prove their innocence also points to a simply "disguised act of grace" (ibid).

2.2 Proof of guilt

The rules of evidence in doping procedures not only appear intransparent and inconsistent to legal laypersons. Neither can they give the athlete concerned any feeling of legal certainty. Even within a given association, the procedures for introducing evidence are understood and interpreted in quite different ways, as a glance at the decisions of the IAAF court of arbitration makes clear. Here, Rule 32 (formerly Rule 55: "strict liability")[148] is applied in three variants:

1. In the case of German javelin thrower Carolin Soboll (2001), the rule appears to have been applied in accordance with the letter, i.e. regardless of fault, as the presented mitigating evidence was not considered. The evidence consisted of statements by the food inspection agencies, which the athlete had commissioned prior to taking the food supplement, confirming its harmlessness.
2. In the case of Italian high-jumper Antonella Bevilacqua (1996) and Australian sprinter Dean Capobianco (1997) by contrast, the court of arbitration acted on a presumption of guilt and placed the burden of proof on the athletes, which led to sanctions being imposed.
3. Finally, in the case of Nigerian hurdler Ime Akpan (1995) the burden of proof rested on the association (cf. on the cases in the written opinion of the OLG (Higher Regional Court) Frankfurt a. M., decision of 18.5.2000 – 13 W 29/2000; to the case Capobianco see also Opie 2004, 272).

Given such arbitrary treatment of the claim to truth in doping proceedings, the question of how effective these legal mechanisms really are should be evident, bearing in mind the reciprocity principle. Despite this, on the grounds of their autonomy Adolphsen (2007, 247) assigns the sports associations the right to create their own evidential rules, which do not even have to approximate the government's rules of procedure and evidence. The granting of such a power of

[147] Against this background, a comparison with the practice under criminal law relating to dropping proceedings pursuant to § 153 StPO (German Code of Criminal Procedure) (Non-Prosecution of Petty Offences) and § 153a StPO (Germany Code of Criminal Procedure) (Provisional Dispensing with Court Action; Provisional Termination of Proceedings) would be interesting.

[148] To other rules of the sport federations see Soek (2006, 140 f.).

definition effectively means that athletes' fate is sometimes already decided, if not sealed, in advance on simple evidence of the objective doping offence, i.e. in general a positive test result. We raise the question merely in passing as to whether the sports associations are in fact the right place to deal with doping prosecution.[149] The sports associations' "right to define norms", which according to Adolphsen (2007, 247) "has to be respected", hinders proceedings especially when it comes to interpreting the "serious possibility" as a criterion for alleviating athletes' counter-evidence (cf. Petri, 2004, 288) and can largely stand in the way of "rediscovering a personal code of ethics".

In order to make the problem somewhat easier to understand, in the following we present some pitfalls of the considered evidential reasoning approaches against the background of the burden of proof and the standard of evidence laid down in the World Anti-Doping Code and the National Anti-Doping Code. In this respect, we must additionally point out the less-than-adequate implementation of the transnational and national anti-doping regime by the sports organizations (cf. for example the final report of the Special Doping Testing Project Group (Sonderprüfung Doping) of the Federal Ministry of the Interior dated 19.12.2007, 16). This is just one reason why it is difficult to shed light on the evidential jungle.

For the outcome of the proceedings, the allocation of the burden of proof, the standard of evidence and the consideration of evidence are of decisive importance. Although these instruments for establishing the truth are universal, the process of establishing the truth differs depending on the respective legal culture and the type of proceedings (Walter, 2004, 602). Difficulties when it comes to understanding, interpreting and implementing the WADC – based as it is on Anglo-American legal principles – seem inevitable against the background of the principles of continental European law.

The *allocation of the burden of proof* has a central decision-relevant influence on the outcome of the doping proceedings. However, the concept of the burden of proof can have different interpretations. When it refers to deciding who is responsible for producing certain evidence at the outset or during the trial it is known as the subjective burden of proof or burden of producing evidence. If a single doping prerequisite cannot be proved in a legal dispute or if the presented evidence fails to convince the judge, it must be decided which party has the disadvantage. In this kind of non liquet situation, the objective or material burden of proof is applied. In civil proceedings, the risk of unprovability of a claim to evidence in principle lies with the party that lays charges. In criminal proceedings, the burden of proof for the case and the charges brought lies with the court.

[149] Moreover, (at least in Germany) the considerable costs of legal proceedings pose an obstacle to athletes being able to appeal to the independent court of arbitration (cf. on the cost aspect Eimer 2008, retrievable under: http://www.sportgericht.de/premium/EIMER_Richard_Deutsches_Sportschiedsgericht.pdf (retrieved on: 21.12.2008).

An excursion into *proof of an objective doping offence* shows that the first significant problems with providing evidence can already arise here. The onus is always on the responsible sports organizations to provide proof of an objective doping violation (Art. 3.1 p. 1 NADC/WADC). To this end, they usually have to present one or more positive doping specimens from the athlete concerned, whereby the test results have to be determined according to certain procedural criteria. The evidence rules of the WADA code and the NADA code stipulate that compliance with laboratory standards is to be assumed (Art. 3.2.1, cf. also the article by Pitsch in this volume). Proof of an objective doping offence also implies the onus of providing evidence of endogenously produced substances (cf. Adolphsen, 2007, 254 ff.), whereby it is also the responsibility of the sports organizations to prove that a substance has been exogenously introduced (Adolphsen 2007, 254; Eufe, 2005, 61). According to this rationale, it should then be possible to assume a doping violation when a certain threshold value is exceeded. The scientific validation of such a threshold value in turn has to be verified within the scope of the objective facts of the case (Adolphsen, 2007, 255). The international Court of Arbitration for Sport (CAS) sees this differently – with far-reaching consequences for the athletes. The CAS passes the problem of endogenously produced substances on to the athletes by stipulating that the question of the reliability of the threshold value has to be taken into consideration in providing evidence of culpability (cf. CAS, 2000/A/310, Leipold/IOC, award of 22.10.2001, marginal number 64 ff.). According to this, the onus is on the athletes to prove that the threshold value is unsuitable for separating endogenous and exogenous production, which is even in contradiction to the WADA Code, which clearly lays the burden of proof for an objective doping offence at the door of the sports organizations. The objective burden of proof must lie with the sports organizations. The fact that this is treated differently in sports practice presents a further obstacle to the athlete in his or her pursuit of a "personal code of ethics".

Just as problematic is the question of *evidence of culpability* of the athlete. The burden of proof rules relating to proof of fault are sometimes interpreted differently. This also applies to the WADC, which does not state unequivocally whether the burden of proof for the evidence of culpability lies with the respective responsible sports organization or the athlete concerned. There is contention over how the WADA stipulations are to be interpreted, whereby the ones to suffer as a result of this dispute are again the athletes, who because of the lack of certainty and foreseeability are given the feeling that they are "victims". We draw on two interpretation variants of the burden of proof rule here that are explained by way of illustration in the context of the German or continental European legal system.

The first of these proceeds from the presumption of guilt, whereby the athlete can exculpate him- or herself. This is also referred to as presumption of guilt with the possibility of exculpation. This variant represents a reversal of the burden of proof. In the case of non liquet, the athlete bears the burden of proof, meaning the court decides he or she is at fault. The second variant is based on the presumption of innocence. In this case, the decision if the violation cannot be proved is taken against the sports association, which bears the burden of proof. In this context, the association charged with the burden of proof has the possibility to draw on prima facie evidence ("Anscheinsbeweis") to alleviate the standard of evidence, which is intended to avoid any situation of non liquet.

The applicability of these concepts depends in particular on how the influence of principles of criminal law on situations in civil law is evaluated. The presumption of innocence is a principle of criminal proceedings. It states that a person accused of committing a crime is innocent until proved otherwise. The person must be proved guilty, and in case of doubt they are to be acquitted ("in dubio pro reo"). Those who reject application of the presumption of innocence in anti-doping charges brought by the sports associations (Adolphsen, 2000; Haas & Adolphsen, 1996) stress the civil law basis of the power to impose sanctions vested in the associations as well as the insufficient possibilities of the associations to furnish proof of fault, as they have no government sanctions to fall back on.[150] The first argument lacks conviction quite simply because the basis in civil law does not necessarily constitute an obstacle to introducing criminal law principles. On the contrary, these also find application in civil law via § 242 BGB (German Civil Code) in conjunction with the principle of proportionality (Fenn & Petri, 2000, 233; Petri, 2000, 275 ff.). Furthermore, the parallels in the relationship between the club/association and athlete and the relationship between the state and its citizens also speak in favour of an application of criminal law principles (PHBSportR-Summerer, 2007, 205).[151] What is more, the doping ban has the same effect as a genuine penalty (see above). The difficulties of the associations in providing proof of the athlete's fault are the only real reason that speaks against applying the presumption of innocence. They lack the government sanctions that are possibly necessary for the provision of proof (cf. Adolphsen, 2000, 100). However, here the sports organization may be granted an alleviation of the standard of proof. Regardless of what this alleviation is called, whether – as in Germany – "Anscheinsbeweis", prima facie evidence, presumptive evidence, factual presumptions or natural presumptions, it can in principle represent a suitable means of reaching an appropriate solution without a reversal of the burden of proof, while interfering as little as possible in the rights of the athletes. In the case of typical sequences of events, prima facie evidence makes it possible to provide proof of culpable behaviour with the help of empirical judgements, although it may be necessary to differentiate between

---

[150] However, the plaintiff in a civil action must also provide evidence for a claim, whereby in this respect the associations rely on the A sample. In this regard, according to civil law criteria, requirements in terms of proof of causation would need to be questioned and the terms "liability-founding" and "liability-extending" causation explained. These constitute the basis of fault under civil law.

[151] In favour of it also Soek (2006, 391).

intentional and negligent culpability.[152] The prerequisite for this is a situation which, drawing on general life experiences, permits conclusions to be drawn about certain causes or a certain sequence of events as being decisive for the occurrence of a certain success. A positive doping test is typically expected to point to the culpable use of banned substances by the athlete (initially Walker, 1998, 144). From this, we infer the empirical judgement that someone who tests positive for doping substances also bears responsibility for using them.

The athlete can in turn shatter the prima facie evidence-based reasoning by proving the "*serious possibility*" of an atypical sequence of events for the case in question. This is the neuralgic point already suggested at the beginning of this section at which the practice-oriented problems of prima facie evidence become apparent and on which the judgement of prima facie evidence as a (currently) really "worthwhile" alternative to the presumption of guilt in terms of athletes' rights depends.

Practice has shown that this is in fact not a question of less onerous counter-evidence. Even the demands on the nature of the facts athletes must produce to meet the criterion of "serious possibility" are still unclear. As long as associations are permitted to determine their own threshold from which the serious possibility of a different sequence of events exists, there is unlikely to be any clarification in the foreseeable future. We remind ourselves here of the already mentioned right of sports associations "to define norms, which has to be respected" (Adolphsen, 2007, 247), which also encompasses defining their own evidential rules. This is not least one reason why some authors conclude that there is no difference between the concepts of the presumption of guilt with the possibility of exculpation and the presumption of innocence applying prima facie evidence as an alleviation of the standard of proof, since they ultimately lead to the same result: the onus is always on the athlete to prove his or her innocence (cf. Kern, 2007, 369 f.). It is only mentioned as an appendage that different results "only occur if the standard of evidence [...] differs" (Kern, 2007, 370). It should do precisely this, so that prima facie evidence does not violate the presumption of innocence (BVerfG (Federal Constitutional Court of 23.4.1991 – Court Ruling 1 BvR 1443/87, BVerfGE (Decision of the Federal Constitutional Court) 84, 82, 87 f.), and precisely this is the intention for the application of prima facie evidence in doping proceedings. The associations' power of definition thus obscures the fact that the criterion of "serious possibility" represents precisely the borderline between still reasonable alleviation of the standard of evidence for the association and unreasonable reversal of the burden of proof (Petri, 2004, 288). From the application of prima facie evidence, it thus follows that the athlete does not have to prove his or her lacking culpability, but (only) the existence of an atypical causal process (Walker, 1998, 144). To en-

[152] Cf. to the prima facie evidence Soek (2006, 160 ff.). He points out that the prima facie evidence also has been applied by the European Court of Human Rights in the case "John Murray v. United Kingdom" (ECHR 8-2-1996, 41/1994/488/570, 22 EHRR 29), (ibid, 163).

sure the athlete's struggle no longer resembles that of Don Quixote and prevents him or her from "rediscovering a personal code of ethics", the discussion surrounding the application of prima facie evidence should not simply be discontinued at this point on the grounds of presumed "similarity", but rather broadened and deepened with a view to the possibilities of a transparent definition of the criterion of seriousness.

This is above all also a discussion about the *standard of evidence*. The standard of evidence is the measuring stick used to decide to what degree the evidence has succeeded. It assigns certain content to judicial conviction by determining what the judge must be convinced of when considering the evidence.[153] Both the WADC and the NADC contain different demands on the standard of evidence, depending on whether the burden of proof lies with the responsible sports organization or the athlete. Such a regulation exists also in the common law criminal procedure. In practice this use of the standard of evidence seems to be difficult and leads to the question: „How [...] is this concept to be elucidated?" (Gardiner et.al., 2006, 278).

The required standard of evidence for the sports organizations is paraphrased in Art. 3 of the WADC as "greater than a mere balance of probability but less than proof beyond a reasonable doubt". The judge must have reached the "firm conviction" that the argument presented should be considered to be true. These guidelines are legal concepts of the common law. The difficulties in the implementation of these instructions are especially caused by the combination of terms referring to criminal and civil law (Walter, 2004, 602). Not least there are deviations from this wording in the official (German) translation of the WADC by the National Anti-Doping Agency (as pointed out by Petri, 2005, 117) and partly in the literature (cf. Adolphsen, 2007, 244, 254). This gives rise to "subtle shifts of meaning" (translated from Petri, 2005, 117) by "stripping the doubt of reasonable grounds and reinterpreting the probability as something unspecific" (ibid). The current NADC, however, also states that the required standard of evidence is greater than the equally high probability but less than proof beyond a reasonable doubt. In any case, the standard of evidence is lower than the general standard of evidence provided for in § 286 I ZPO (Code of Civil Procedure), which stipulates "a degree of probability beyond any reasonable doubt" and thus requires the judge to be "fully convinced" of the truth of a proposition.

Art. 3 WADC/NADC indicates that a lower standard of evidence is required of athletes, which is seen as a corrective to the strict liability rule. Thus the standard of evidence requirement is equally high, i.e. 50% probability. Walter (2004, 615) points out the fact that this measuring stick is not consistently applied in the WADC when he asks about the evaluation criteria for the situation in Art.

[153] While in Continental Europe the judge's personal conviction about the truth of a claimed issue stands in the first place in the estimation of evidence, the decision in the legal sphere of the common law is taken according to the higher probability, i.e. the decision does not depend on the conveying of the conviction for the judge (cf. Habscheid, 1990, 117 f.).

10.1.1 WADC which states that if the athlete to be disqualified establishes that he or she bears no fault or negligence for the anti-doping rule violation, the athlete's individual results in competitions other than the competition in which the anti-doping rule occurs shall not be disqualified unless they were "likely to have been affected by the athlete's anti-doping rule violation." Furthermore, a look at the jurisdiction of CAS shows that the standard of evidence appears in principle to be much higher. For example, no athlete has ever succeeded in proving his or her innocence (cf. Pfister, 2008, 93). This is probably justified through the argument that in the WADC and NADC the standard of evidence requirements can also be made dependent on the severity of the allegation and that the applicable standard of evidence is placed at the discretion of the law enforcement agency. Against the background that CAS proceeds from the presumption of guilt and rejects the application of evidence prima facie (cf. Pfister, 2008, 93), and given the correlation that the earlier a burden of proof decision is taken, the higher the standard of evidence is set, the athlete appears to be in a hopeless situation. In any case, this treatment of the standard of evidence can in no way be considered a corrective. Under these circumstances, the argument that the question of the burden of proof becomes less important the lower the standard of evidence thus also loses its validity as a confirmation of the legitimacy of the presumption of guilt.

3 Conclusion

The attempt to materially and procedurally simplify the detection of a doping violation as undertaken in the WADC at times fails to consider that the fight against doping is above all also aimed at protecting non-dopers. This also stressed by Petri, when he identifies the following goals of the anti-doping campaign and urges that they be kept separate from each other in the resolution of the conflict: "Firstly those who do not dope need to be protected. Secondly those who could dope need to be deterred. Thirdly, those who have doped need to be disciplined" (translated from Petri, 2004, 365 f.).

A "zero tolerance policy" does not meet these requirements. This pushes the first (and for the effectiveness of the other two goals partially decisive) goal into the background by waiving the existence of voluntative elements for practical reasons. Such ideas hardly reflect a consideration of consequences motivated and oriented by responsibility.

It seems much more pertinent to ask how the interest in adhering to rules and the interest in the application of rules are affected when cooperative behaviour is not reciprocated. Although a certain tolerance towards temporary unbalanced conditions in the performance record and the willingness to effect prior performance in the form of personal cooperative contributions are characteristic for reciprocity relations (Vanberg, 1987, 275), here excessive demands sometimes seem to be made on this tolerance. This appears to be the case for the simple reason that the willingness to invest in cooperative prior performance depends on trust in the other party's willingness to cooperate, whereby this trust "has a retrospective and a foresighted component" (Vanberg, 1987, 275; Adloff & Mau, 2005, 35). The measures introduced by associations to combat doping discussed here are totally lacking in legal certainty, so that under these conditions it is extremely difficult to build trust in these mechanisms and hence the acceptance that is so important for compliance.

Added to this is the already mentioned aspect of retaliation against uncooperative behaviour in the sense of negative reciprocity. According to this, athletes who comply with the sporting rules and the principle of fair play expect others to treat them with corresponding fairness in return. If this expectation is not met, for example if an athlete who has tested positive is sanctioned despite not being culpable, or observes such a procedure, this can stand in the way of achieving the set objectives. In this respect, Pitsch, Maats & Emrich (2008, 400) also point out that changes in the expected benefit arising from compliant behaviour are reflected in changed activity patterns. Against the background of the correlations outlined here, the policy deemed as reasonable by the CAS of simply ignoring such a "negligible injustice" (Soek, 2000, 45) has to be viewed extremely critically. Admittedly, criminal proceedings – if considered as an alternative – also involve considerable constraints. Such criminal proceedings, even in the case of a relatively minor suspicion, generally take considerably longer, especially if followed by a formal appeal procedure. If the evidence is clear, various far-reaching sanctions, for example a period of remand, can be imposed. These correspond at least de facto to a temporary occupational ban. The required "strong suspicion" could by all means be justified through a positive A sample or the unexcused failure to participate in controls.[154] In this respect, the intention to orient association proceedings towards the interests of a speedy and efficient settlement of the case is understandable. Nevertheless, this pushes all other interests too far into the background, leading to the problems outlined here.

The question of the influence of reciprocity expectations on the effectiveness of legal instruments in achieving the anti-doping objective so far remains unanswered, if not even unasked. This issue needs to be subsequently addressed in the interest of a consideration of consequences oriented by responsibility and is attributable to appeals to athletes that are (still) based on an ethics of conviction. To what extent the legal mechanisms of anti-doping measures can build on reciprocity expectations or give consideration to these remains to be analyzed.[155]

---

[154] Cf. Momsen, e-mail correspondence of 10 February 2009.

[155] This is among other things given consideration in the Federal Institute of Sports Science (BISP) research project no. 20070300144, in which the effectiveness chances of legal mechanisms for conflict resolution in sport are analyzed using the example of the doping problem.

References

Adloff, F., Mau, S. (2005). Zur Theorie der Gabe und Reziprozität. In: F. Adloff, S. Mau (Eds.). *Vom Geben und Nehmen. Zur Soziologie der Reziprozität* (pp. 9-57). Frankfurt a. M., New York: Campus Verlag.

Adolphsen, J. (2000). Anforderungen an Dopingstrafen nationaler Sportverbände – am Beispiel des Falles Dieter Baumann. *SpuRt 7,* 97–101.

Adolphsen, J. (2003). *Internationale Dopingstrafen.* Tübingen (Jus Privatum; Vol. 78).

Adolphsen, J. (2007). Aktuelle beweisrechtliche Fragen im Dopingverfahren. In: O. Arter, M. Baddeley (Eds.). *Sport und Recht. 4th conference volume* (pp. 239-261). Bern: Stämpfli.

Adolphsen, J. (2008). Der Staat im Dopingkampf. *Sportwissenschaft 38*, 82–88.

Cory, G. A. (1999). The Reciprocal Modular Brain in Economics and Politics. New York: Kluwer.

Court, J. (1994). Kritik ethischer Modelle des Leistungssports. St. Augustin: Academia.

Diekmann, A., Voss, T. (2008). Soziale Normen und Reziprozität. Die Bedeutung „sozialer" Motive für die Rational-Choice-Erklärung sozialer Normen. In A. Diekmann, K. Eichner, P. Schmidt, T. Voss (Eds.). *Rational Choice: Theoretische Analysen und empirische Resultate. Festschrift für Karl-Dieter Opp zum 70. Geburtstag* (pp. 84-100). Wiesbaden: VS Verlag.

Emrich, E. (2006). „Ars Corrumpendi". Zur Interaktions- und Beziehungsdynamik bei Bestechungen. *sozialersinn* 7 (2), 327-343.

Eufe, T. (2005). Die Unschuldsvermutung im Dopingverfahren. Gleichzeitig eine Analyse der Sportrechtsprechung des Deutschen Fußball-Bundes und des Deutschen Leichtathletik-Verbandes (Schriften zum Sportrecht; Vol. 1). Baden-Baden: Nomos.

Fehr, E., Gächter, S. (2000). Cooperation and Punishment in Public Goods Experiments. *The American Economic Review* (4). 980–994.

Fenn, H., Petri, G. (2000). Unschuldsvermutung und Anscheinsbeweis im Verbandsstrafverfahren – Anmerkungen zu OLG Frankfurt/M. dated 18.5.2000 – 13 W 29/00 –. *SpuRt 7,* 232–235.

Fritzweiler, J., Pfister, B., Summerer, T. (Eds.) (2007). *Praxishandbuch Sportrecht* (2nd edition). München: Beck. [quoted from: PHBSportR *editor*]

Gardiner, S., James, M., O`Leary, J., Welch, R., Blackshaw, I., Boyes, S., Caiger, A. (2006). Sports Law. Third Edition, Sydney, London: Cavendish Publishing.

Gouldner, A. W. (1960). The Norm of Reciprocity. A Preliminary Statement. *American Sociological Review* (25), 161–178.

Haas, U., Haug, T., Reschke, E. (Eds.). *Handbuch des Sportrechts. Dokumentation mit Erläuterungen.* (53rd updated version). Munich: Luchterhand. [quoted from: HBSportR editor 2005].

Haas, U., Adolphsen, J. (1996). Sanktionen der Sportverbände vor ordentlichen Gerichten. *NJW (36)*, 2351–2353.

Habscheid, W. J. (1990). Beweislast und Beweismaß. Ein kontinentaleuropäisch-angelsächsischer Rechtsvergleich. In: H. Prütting (Eds.). *Festschrift für Gottfried Baumgärtel zum 70. Geburtstag* (pp. 105-119). Köln u.a.: Carl Heymanns.

Hof, H. (1996). Rechtsethologie. Recht im Kontext von Verhalten und außerrechtlicher Verhaltensregelung. Heidelberg: Decker.

Homans, G. C. (1972). *Elementarformen sozialen Verhaltens.* 2nd edition. Opladen: Leske und Budrich.

Kern, B. (2007). Internationale Dopingbekämpfung. Der World Anti-Doping Code der World Anti-Doping Agency (Studien zur Rechtswissenschaft; Vol. 198). Hamburg: Kovac.

Lob, J. (1999). Dopage, responsabilité objective („strict liability") et de quelques autres questions. *SJZ* (12), 270–272.

Malinowski, B. (1960 [orig. 1926]). *Sitte und Verbrechen bei den Naturvölkern.* Vienna: Humboldt.

Mauss, M. (1968 [orig. 1923/24]). *Die Gabe. Form und Funktion des Austauschs in archaischen Gesellschaften.* Frankfurt a. M.: Suhrkamp.

McLaren, Richard H., Clement, P. (2004). Court of Arbitration for Sport: The ad hoc Division at the Salt Lake City Olympic Games. *International Sports Law Review*, 44-60.

Ockenfels, A. (1999). *Fairneß, Reziprozität und Eigennutz. Ökonomische Theorie und experimentelle Evidenz* (Die Einheit der Gesellschaftswissenschaften; Vol. 108). Tübingen: Mohr Siebeck.

Opie, Hayden (2004). Drugs in Sports and the Law – Moral Authority, Diversity and the Pursuit of Excellence. *Marquette Sports Law Review* 14 (2), 267-281.

Petri, G. (2000). Die Unschuldsvermutung im Verbandsstrafverfahren. In K. Bepler (Ed.). *Sportler, Arbeit und Statuten. Herbert Fenn zum 65. Geburtstag* (pp. 239-287) (Beiträge zum Sportrecht; Vol. 7). Berlin: Duncker & Humblodt.

Petri, G. (2004). *Die Dopingsanktion. Zur Anwendung strafrechtlicher Grundsätze im Dopingverfahren der Sportverbände* (Beiträge zum Sportrecht; Vol. 16). Berlin: Duncker & Humblodt.

Petri, G. (2005). Zur AGB-rechtlichen Inhaltskontrolle des World Anti-Doping Codes und des NADA-Codes. In K. Vieweg (Ed.). *Perspektiven des Sports. Referate der Vierten und Fünften Interuniversitären Tagung Sportrecht* (pp. 105-125) (Beiträge zum Sportrecht; Vol. 19). Berlin: Duncker & Humblodt.

Pfister, B. (2008). Die Rechtsprechung des Tribunal Arbitral du Sport (TAS) 2001-2003. *SpuRt 15,* 93–97.

Pitsch, W., Maats, P., Emrich, E. (2008). Skizzen zu einer Ökonomik des Dopings. In: N. Müller, M. Messing (Eds.). *Olympismus – Erbe und Verantwortung* (pp. 381-418) (Olympische Studien; Vol. 10). Kassel: Agon.

Rilling, J. K., Gutman, D. A., Zeh, T. R., Pagnoni, G., Berns, G. S. Kilts, C. D. (2002). A Neural Basis for Social Cooperation. *Neuron* (35), 395-405.
Siekmann, C. R. (2000). Übersicht über die internationalen Verbandsregelungen zum Verschuldensprinzip, zur Beweislast und zur Sanktionshöhe. In V. Röhricht, K. Vieweg (Eds.). *Doping-Forum. Aktuelle rechtliche und medizinische Aspekte* (pp. 31-34) (Recht und Sport; special volume). Stuttgart and others: Boorberg.
Soek, J. (2000). Die prozessualen Garantien des Athleten in einem Dopingverfahren. In V. Röhricht, K. Vieweg (Eds.). *Doping-Forum. Aktuelle rechtliche und medizinische Aspekte* (pp. 35-52) (Recht und Sport; special volume). Stuttgart and others: Boorberg.
Soek, J. (2006). *The Strict Liability Principle and the Human Rights of Athletes in Doping Cases*. The Hague: T.M.C. Asser Press.
Vanberg, V. (1975). *Die Zwei Soziologien – Individualismus und Kollektivismus in der Sozialtheorie.* Tübingen: Mohr.
Vanberg, V. (1987). Markt, Organisation und Reziprozität. In K. Heinemann (Ed.), *Soziologie wirtschaftlichen Handelns* (Kölner Zeitschrift für Soziologie und Sozialpsychologie; special issue 28) (pp. 263-279). Opladen: Westdeutscher Verlag.
Walker, W.-D. (1998). Beweisrechtliche und arbeitsrechtliche Probleme des Dopings. In K. Vieweg (Ed.), *Doping – Realität und Recht. Internationales Symposium am 4. und 5.7.1997 in Erlangen* (pp. 135-175). Berlin: Duncker & Humblodt (Beiträge zum Sportrecht; Vol. 1).
Walter, G. (2004). Zur Umsetzung von Art. 3 WADA-Code in das Schweizer Recht. In Bernd Heinrich and others (Eds.). *Festschrift für Ulrich Weber zum 70. Geburtstag. 18. September 2004* (pp. 601-621). Bielefeld: Gieseking.
Weber, M. (1980 [1921]). *Wirtschaft und Gesellschaft. Grundriß der verstehenden Soziologie.* 5th revised edition, obtained by Johannes Winckelmann. Tübingen: Mohr.
Wise, N. (1997). De la Légalité des Règles Anti-Dopage et du Système de la « Responsabilité Stricte ». *Revue juridique et économique du sport*, 5-22.

Carsten Momsen

Criminal penalties in the fight against doping?[156]

1 Introduction

Whereas in the past the run up to the Olympic Games was all about the individual athletes, their outstanding performances, possibly also the medals table and award ceremonies, before the start, during and after the summer Olympics in Beijing in 2008 many were more interested in unannounced controls, disqualifications and the sporting value of the performances on show – or asking about the most effective and surprising testing methods (cf. the article by Emrich & Pitsch in this volume). What has happened? As far as the value of the sporting achievements is concerned, we are tempted – no doubt with a touch of irony – to answer: nothing actually!

I would like to investigate the question "What has happened to sport?" with a double focus.

On the one hand I am interested purely in the criminal law aspects, and on the other purely in the judgement of doping as the problem that – at least in certain areas – has been mainly responsible for the negative development of the image of elite sport. Many countries have in the meantime recognized doping as a problem whose direct and indirect consequences lead to undesirable effects that impact far beyond the scope of competitive and elite sport – in fact far beyond the scope of sport in general.

1.1 Classification of an "anti-doping offence"

Thus in Germany, the legislator also passed a so-called "anti-doping law" at the end of 2007: this law also contains criminal prohibitions, in particular regarding the possession and sale of doping substances. In my opinion – to be substantiated in the following – this has unfortunately been incorporated into the German Drug Law (Arzneimittelgesetz, AMG). However, pursuant to § 1, the purpose of this law is to ensure the "quality and efficacy of drugs". Conducting the fight against doping in sport under this heading represents a particularly fine form of irony that is perhaps still not evident to all stakeholders.

Before looking at this law in more detail, I would first like to address a couple of general questions:

---

[156] This text is a slightly revised version of a paper held within the scope of the "Wissenschaftsmatinée und Ringvorlesung: Doping im Spitzensport" ("Scientific matinée and lecture series: Doping in elite sport") at Saarland University, Saarbrücken in summer semester 2008.

1.2 Criminal law as an instrument in the anti-doping battle

First we need to clarify what effect applying criminal law is intended to have in the fight against doping. On the one hand this means: "Which interests are to be protected, what interests justify application of criminal law?" and on the other: "What advantages does the criminalization of doping promise in the fight against its undesired consequences?"

Let us start with the second aspect: What can criminal law achieve in the fight against doping? Before going any further, I would like to admit that I have to qualify the very optimistic view I used to hold regarding the "creating" power that criminal law has on moral.[157] This meanwhile occurred state of disillusion is not only based on the fact that the discussion about a doping criminal law apparently leaves doping participants vastly unimpressed and maybe even encouraging them because of its hesitancy. Rather, it is triggered by a comparative look at other "fronts" where criminal law is applied: doping in sport is just one of many, complex social problems where representatives of every political stripe have been all too quick to call on the criminal-law legislator to resolve in recent years. Added to this is the growing suspicion that they are more interested in high-impact and – even more important – low-cost solutions. On the other hand the focus rarely appears to be on the sustainability of the problem's solution. This phenomenon – which to all intents and purposes can be described as an "abuse of criminal law" – became particularly apparent in the unspeakable discussion about criminal law relating to young offenders in the Hessian state election campaign. And that was just one particularly crude example of such an aberration.

This kind of symbol-oriented approach is not only of no use for solving the problems, but can above all significantly damage the credibility, constitutional legality and functionality of the criminal law system itself. Especially when it comes to doping, creating criminal penalties arouses hopes that cannot – and indeed must not – be met with constitutional criminal law or law of criminal proceedings!

Basically, I believe many protagonists of a criminal law solution to the doping problem would like to see the postulated negative general preventive effects of the threat of criminal penalties combined with "lean" procedural rules on the part of the associations, which, despite many improvements over the past few years, still fail to generally feature essential guarantees, such as a consistent presumption of innocence and a corresponding right to introduce evidence (cf. the articles by Pitsch & Emrich as well as Senkel in this volume). A comparison of both types of proceedings quickly shows that disciplinary proceedings initiated by the sports associations open up more far-reaching possibilities of gathering evidence. Moreover, for the aggrieved party the allocation of the burden of

[157] Cherkeh & Momsen (2001, 1745 ff.) – This also applies in relation to the lacking operationalizability – resulting from too high moral charging – of "sport ethos" as a potential legally protected interest already mentioned elsewhere.

proof in many cases has proved less favourable than in public criminal proceedings.

This appears to offer the opportunity to single out from both types of proceedings – prosecution by the associations and state-initiated criminal proceedings – the most efficient segments for an effective fight against doping, almost in the sense of a joint venture. However, this kind of "cherry picking" is leaving a lasting damage on the character of criminal proceedings based on the rule of law. It would thus be unacceptable for public criminal prosecution authorities to obtain proof required for a prosecution – which they are not authorized to obtain themselves – from the associations within the framework of proceedings based on the principles of strict liability and reversal of the burden of proof brought by the associations (cf. on strict liability the article by Senkel in this volume). Of course, this gives rise to the question of whether, as in the case of a store detective who extorts information with improper means, such proof obtained via third parties may be used as evidence – even if it has to be conceded that the associations are bound by fundamental rights and as such are not "private".

Quite apart from issues relating to the admissibility of evidence and the associations' commitment to fundamental rights, the element of constitutional legality is inherently affected, in the same way as if the police were to ask a third party to extort an admission from suspects through torture because they are prohibited from doing so themselves, or – a little less dramatically – as in the case of Liechtenstein, where criminal prosecution authorities obtain data records illegally acquired by a third party, which they would not have had access to themselves, and use this evidence to initiate criminal proceedings. Although, even in individual cases, the results may trigger rapid enthusiasm – perhaps too rapid sometimes – each individual case constitutes the highly detrimental derogation to the principle vis-à-vis as a whole.

If, in contrast, criminal proceedings are brought in the normal way against suspected dopers, the limitations of criminal law soon become apparent, as it does not permit a flexible response, but requires equal treatment of all suspects and proof beyond reasonable doubt in order to be able to arrive at a conviction. Not only in the case of Jan Ullrich, but in almost all doping allegations, the plausibility of every single explanation given by a suspected athlete – however transparent – as to how the detected substance might have entered his or her body has to be checked before a sentence can be pronounced. This can sometimes take years or even never be refutable.

If, in addition to this, the presumption of innocence was also universally applied, in my opinion there would also be no legal basis for suspending the athlete until such time as he or she is proven guilty. Since nobody who advocates more effective anti-doping measures has this in mind, ultimately the aim has to be to find the most effective combination possible of the public criminal law system and the sanctioning system of the sports associations on a national and international level. If such a combination of both systems is to be admissible, again two premises have to be set:

Firstly, the principle of legality on which criminal law is based, the so-called obligation to take action in relation to all prosecutable criminal offences, must not be relativized. In other words, where an initial suspicion exists, that a crime has been committed through behaviour linked to doping practices, criminal proceedings must be initiated alone on the grounds of equality before the law. Suspected dopers are in this sense treated in the same way as ordinary suspected criminals.

Secondly, the charges and consequences of proceedings brought by the associations must be given consideration when ruling on subsequent criminal sanctions, in order to prevent athletes from receiving more severe penalties than "normal" offenders of the same crimes.

Furthermore, application of criminal law can only be meaningful where effective protection of interests is not given otherwise . Criminal law is ultima ratio!

With respect to fully responsible doping athletes, one might in principle be inclined to think that sanctions imposed by the associations, specifically long-term suspensions, stripping of titles, possibly also prize money; to put it in a nutshell: the threat of a ruined career, in many cases the athlete's purpose in life, has a significantly higher deterrent effect than the threat of a fine or a suspended prison sentence. This would, however, presuppose that the sports associations implement their sanctioning possibilities with the same consistency and objectivity as it is happening (at least generally) in public criminal proceedings.

However, precisely this still appears to be the weak point on the part of the sports associations, both on the national and international level (cf. the article by Senkel, Emrich & Momsen in this volume). The interdependent interests between association and elite athlete appear to be too strong in many cases, or more precisely so strong that there exists a convergence of interests in not sanctioning athletes and instead allowing them to continue to compete. The association as a whole, as well as individual officers in particular, are to a greater or lesser degree dependent on their athletes' successes. This is increasingly giving rise to a form of almost schizophrenic behaviour. On the one hand, the association needs to give the outside world the impression it is taking active measures to fight doping in order to preserve the general esteem in this regard. On the other hand, they are under pressure to keep a sufficiently large pool of elite athletes free of all reproach over the long term, in order to similarly preserve funding, advertising revenue and the appreciation and esteem associated with sporting success (cf. in this context the article by Emrich & Pitsch in this volume).

In respect to this, criminal law would appear to be an absolutely necessary instrument, namely in order to discipline the associations and commit their representatives to the primary goal of fighting against doping. This – it shouldn't be perceived along the way – implies that the management level of an association also has joint responsibility to monitor and prosecute. When it comes to criminal liability, the association management as a monitoring guarantor has the obligation to prevent members of the association from becoming offenders. This structure's proximity to criminal business law, especially the responsibility of the management for offences committed by their employees, is not merely coincidental. Criminal law in the field of elite sport is to no small extent a manifestation of criminal business law!

Apart from cutting off access, i.e. persons outside the association who assist the athlete in procuring and administering substances or in using prohibited methods, personal criminal liability of the athlete for self-responsible doping would therefore appear imperative, also and especially in light of the increased risk for the management echelons of the associations. This brings us back to the deferred question of interests that are worthy of protection and are violated through doping.

1.3 Classification of anti-doping offences in the AMG (German Drug Law)

So far, attempts to establish anti-doping legislation based on criminal law have mainly been derived from parallel reflections relating to the German Drug Law (Arzneimittelgesetz, AMG) or the German Narcotics Act (Betäubungsmittelgesetz, BtMG). The rationality of criminal law protection thus lies in preventing persons getting in contact with, possessing or trafficking substances subject to authorization and posing a potential health risk and in this way creating risks, namely of addiction, for third parties. However, when it comes to effectively fighting doping, this is evidently the wrong way, as it gives no consideration whatsoever to the of the actor's goals. This is clearly shown in the most recent studies by Adolphsen (2008) and Grotz (2008, 243 ff.) on the possession of doping drugs as a prosecutable offence pursuant to §§ 6a, 95 AMG.

Yet it is in principle almost insignificant whether one considers the implemented or rather envisaged regulations unsuccessful because they are based on the totally unsuitable type of "national health" as a legally protected interest, whether like Grotz (2008, 243 ff.) – arguably not completely convincingly – one considers them being a contravention of fundamental rights referring to proprietary possession they constitute an unequal treatment of athletes compared to other drug users, or whether one basically approves of the implemented measures but considers them as inadequate. Although in total opposition to Grotz, in my opinion, Adolphsen's (2008, 84 ff.) criticism of the restriction of prosecutability to "non-small amounts" does not go far enough, even though from the perspective of technical implementation of the law he is probably thoroughly right.

In my opinion a decisive weak point is the fact that elite sport is not understood as what it long since represents throughout society as a whole – a specific, for some very lucrative form of economic activity. To make a long story short, it is all about the marketing of services. In my opinion this aspect is in the spotlight of possible legal impairments by doping. This situation is reinforced by the combination of public interests which, although pursuing certain non-economic objectives, basically are nevertheless – similar to the allocation of grants – primarily of an economic nature.

1.4 On the goal of criminal law anti-doping norms

The goal of a criminal anti-doping law therefore has to be another; has to tie up with the central aspect from the perspective of unfair behaviour in sports, as well as the parallel aspect of unfair competition that doping represents with regard to the huge economic interests associated with elite sport. As Adolphsen (2008, 88) correctly points out, to some extend the athlete remains the "central key figure of the doping scene", quasi being the direct and essential protagonist.

The contrasting sample is the following: assuming it's not about top level sports but about bodybuilders who to their own pleasure or maybe to their partners delight are shaping up their bodies by taking strictly illegal substances. And furthermore assuming that several of these "athletes" regularly meet up in a more or less private circle to nominate the winner of the month – without the attraction of prize money or similar. I would say that although this may be a dubious leisure-time activity, even in the light of this anything but trivial form of personal health risk, an intervention of the criminal-law legislator does not seem appropriate. The same would presumably also go for the prohibited consumption of drugs by individual members of a table tennis team on the lower echelons of the amateur leagues. Not because the phenomenon of doping is any different in either case, but above all because no business interests are affected. The fact that producers of harmful drugs ought to be held criminally liable is therefore a mere independent consequence of criminal product liability but not of fighting the doping battle.

If we understand doping in this sense as unfair behaviour, the starting point for criminal reactions becomes clearer: let us first look at the dictate of fair play in a sport-specific context. Contrary to what the Olympic motto "citius, altius, fortius" – "faster, higher, stronger" – would seem to suggest, fair play probably embodies the essence of sport in all its facets. If there is no fair comparison of achievements, it is impossible to be sure whose performance was faster, higher or stronger than that of the competitors. The concept of fair play is thus the counterpoint and limitation of a striving for "achievement at any cost".

And yet fairness is more than simply playing by the rules of the game. The latter can take place on the purely superficial level – fairness appears, at least, to also be an intrinsic value. This concept of fairness can, as we know, be affected in various ways, ranging from blatantly obvious home advantages due to poor field conditions, to past and present soccer betting scandals. Any manifestation of unfair behaviour certainly poses a problem – but whether this at the same time represents a legal problem is a totally different matter.

As I see it, the unresolved doping issue is quasi still at the focus of the concept of fairness. Argumentatively, this topic takes us into a microcosm of the entire fairness discussion. Furthermore, the realization that *doping* represents a *legal* problem meantime also intensified in Germany. The question that interests me most, however, namely how doping ought to be treated as a *criminal law* problem, is still seen controversially.

2 Status quo of anti-doping legislation

Every year has its own doping cases. This also applies to the Olympic year 2006: the first headlines were made by the circumstances surrounding the 20th Winter Olympics in Turin – first of all concerning the Russian biathlete Pylewa, who after being suspended declared the end of her career, and shortly afterwards the events regarding the Austrian cross-country skiing and biathlon team, in whose environment there were numerous disqualifications. Finally, the sporting year culminated in an unprecedented explosive climax over the scandal of the Spanish doctor Fuentes, the subsequent disqualification of almost all serious contenders in the Tour de France and the question of the derecognition of the Tour title afterwards. The Tour in 2007 offered similar incidents. Initially the stage and yellow shirt winner was disqualified and later on the entire Astana Team. Merely pointing out to the Tour de France in 2008 and its lately confirmed cases of suspicion of the cycling professionals Schumacher and Kohl, members of the Team Gerolsteiner. Obviously there have been no structual changes since 2006.

Interestingly, the two "mega scandals" of 2006 originated in Italy and Spain. "Interestingly", because in both countries there are criminal sanctions which allow the prosecuting authorities to enforce criminal proceedings. Although the existence of corresponding criminal standards as such is no guarantee that these will also be implemented, as the repeated dismissal of the "Fuentes case" – probably above all because of the varied influence from the outside – shows. It is, however, the logical prerequisite for any criminal punishment of specific doping violations.

On the other hand in Germany influential voices can still be heard which vehemently reject an application of criminal law beyond the AMG, especially because this would imply a jeopardy to the fundamentally vested right guaranteeing the autonomy of the associations. I intend to pursue the question of whether this is a case of merely putting forward spurious arguments – or whether coming to terms with the doping issue is indeed an internal problem within the associations. From the present-day perspective, I would merely point out that the Jan Ullrich case was also conducted with a certain priority simply on the grounds of investigations by the public prosecution office because of an initial suspicion of fraud. The interim dismissal of the entire Fuentes complex in Spain once again shows limits that could also come into play in Germany if criminal law was to be applied: the public prosecutor's office has controlling competence for preliminary proceedings. This is not an independent authority, but is subject to directives from its superior authority, the Minister of the Interior.

True independence compared to political influence, which sometimes occurs in personal union with influence of the associations, therefore only really exists in the main proceedings under the direction of independent courts. In Italy, for example, doping is a private criminal offence for the athlete hinself. "Provisions to protect health in sports and to fight doping were included in Italy's Codice Penale in the year 2000 (cf. Maiwald, 2002, 400 ff.; Momsen-Pflanz, 2005, 113 pessim). The athlete's personal consumption of banned substances is also explicitly punishable – comparable to the private use of narcotics. Further, the law contains specific statements relating to the object to be protected, for example that sporting activity is directed to promote the health of the individual and the general public. It should be conducted in accordance with ethical principles and educational values.

Apart from the in this respect incomplete Drug Law, there is nothing comparable in German criminal law, even though more recent studies have put forward proposals that point out precisely in this direction (cf. Cherkeh & Momsen, 2001, 1745 ff.; Momsen-Pflanz, 2005, and more recently also Waldbröl, 2006 as well as Jahn, 2006, 57 ff.).

3 Doping as unfair conduct open to criminal charges

This, however, neither *de lege lata* nor *de lege ferenda* negatively answers the question of whether doping as an exemplary form of unfair behaviour constitutes a criminal law problem. Because the criminal liability of doping can tie up with this kind of behaviour and its effects in numerous counts. For example the frequently accompanying damage to or destruction of the athlete's health – catchword bodily harm – or the financial damage incurred to event organizers, sponsors and others, right through to the spectators – catchword fraud or, as I would prefer, distortion of sporting competition with economic relevance – comparable to fraud in tendering processes.

Quite obviously, each of these starting points taken on its own can only cover part of the problem. In fact, an athlete who inflicts harm on him- or herself cannot be charged with bodily harm, since self-inflicted harm – with a few exceptions – is not punishable. Conceivable violations of the drug or narcotics laws still encounter difficulties with the subsumption of "substances used" and above all "other methods" under the respective areas of regulation. And for a culpability on the grounds of fraud, ultimately the full and highly complex subjective offence – among other things the intent on the part of the athlete to damage third-party assets and "not simply to win" – has to be verified in each case.

One reason for this difficulty lies in the nature of doping, not only as a complex form of behaviour on the part of the athlete, but above all as a life process that involves a large number of people: the athletes themselves, their doctors, and other supervisors, coaches, sponsors, the associations, event organizers, spectators – to mention just a few. Thus doping links a large number of actions with a large number of possible imparements.

However, it seems somewhat "wrong", for example, to speak of "unfair behaviour" in the relationship between athlete and spectator. An athlete who obtains a lucrative sponsoring contract solely on the strength of outstanding performances made possible as a result of doping is also in a colloquial manner of speaking behaving "unfairly" towards his or her sponsor; fairness in a distributive sense, however, only applies to a rival athlete who is competing for the same contract but fails to secure it because he or she does not perform as well – and of course only then on the assumption that the rival athlete does not dope. Outside the tournament or competition situation, fairness in sport is therefore only violated in the figurative sense. The same applies in my opinion if the conduct of other involved parties – for example the team physician who distributes drugs to athletes – comes under discussion. The supervisor or physician only behaves unfairly in an indirect way – and according to German law would structurally be punishable for participatory action. Catchword "Fuentes": apparently drugs were dispensed to all interested parties who asked for them. In this sense, no "unfair" conduct.

4 The interests of the doping athlete

For this reason, the focus today should be on the athlete who self-responsibly and consciously behaves unfair in order to achieve competition results that under normal circumstances they would not – or less probably – have been able to achieve. Firstly, only those who participate actively in a sporting competition can, in the narrower sense, behave "unfair". Secondly, I restrict myself largely to the relationship among the competitors themselves because this is where – in a concrete competition situation – the unfair behaviour is directly felt.

To simplify matters, let us first of all assume that our athlete is craving for glory and honour and is not just primarily out to win prize money or conclude lucrative sponsoring contracts. Looking at his potential "victims", in first instance they also "only" lose the achieved honour, the glory of winning or the recognition for a high ranking. Are these the interests that should be protected under criminal law?

5 The doping athlete's motivation

From a criminal sociology point of view, Merton's approach could here be taken into consideration (1968, 283 – 313): the athlete who strives for success under the pressure of the sporting competition, but realizes that, due to the very high level of performance in the absolute top flight, extensive training and talent as well as physical condition and constitution offer no guarantee for top rankings, has to come up with something new: the innovation sought after can be the consumption of banned substances. An illicit path to a socially accepted goal... In this sense: fairness in sport – a criminal law problem?

As we will quickly see, this discussion about the criminal liability of doping touches the basic question of criminal law an in particular the criminal liability itself who's taking a deploying banned substances comparing the argumentation of both parties supporters as well as opponents of new legal regulations of criminal law home and abroad they don't only reflect ancient questions about the aims of punishment but also at the same time those about sense legitimation and limits of punishment by public authorities. But does this consequently mean a loss of confidence in the moral building power of criminal law? On the other hand do we understand the idea of ultima ratio in the manner that criminal law should only be applied where empirically proven all other forms of reaction have failed? Does the creation of new criminal offences always lead to a restriction of action alternatives and hence of the freedom of scope of the citizens concerned – here the elite athlete – or can constitutionally legitimized criminal law also create or guarantee freedom for the individual?

It would be easy to answer all these questions if the criminal-law legislator was able to carry out an experiment on the living object. Criminal law "on probation" is already foredoomed because of its linguistic contradiction. "On probation" means "non committal". However, by its very nature, criminal law cannot be non committal. Quite apart from the fact that due to the non-binding character the "lab conditions" cannot adequately simulate real criminal law conditions. The questions therefore have to be reviewed and answered before the enactment of new criminal offences.

6 The prerequisite of culpability and criminal prosecutability

To have a meaningful discussion at all, we must first ascertain a social need for action. Meanwhile in the case of doping, there ought to be a far-reaching consensus concerning the need for more effective reactions, if we disregard one-sided, interest-motivated approaches and disillusioned supporters of "head-in-the-sand" policies (cf. in more detail Cherkeh & Momsen, 2001, 1745 ff. with further evidence for the development of the discussion).

If criminal law aims to create new offences in the sense that previously non-criminalized forms of behaviour are to become the object of prohibited criminal actions – in other words if we are talking about a true extension of criminal law, then first a legally protected interest has to be identified and defined. Because only the mere existence of an object of protection can legitimize intervention under criminal law – criminal law without legally protected interests would be state limitation of civil freedom of action as an end in itself. But what is the legally protected interest that is threatened by unfair conduct (doping)?

I stated my position for "sporting ethos", elsewhere. However, because of the strong – too strong – morality which is reminiscent here, I would now like to use the term "fairness". The concept of fairness also has the advantage that it is established and outlined with long-term effect in the legal-philosophical and ethical context – not only by the works of Rawls (1975, passim) and Hinsch (2002, passim).

6.1 Fairness in sports as a valuable interest?

Being the cardinal problem, Roxin poses the question right at the beginning of his book: "Are criminal laws which do not protect legal interests null and void?"

(1997, § 2 Marginal Number 25). Fair enough he is not able to find an answer to that, and can only offer a possible solution. Talking about criminal laws which on one hand do not represent themselves as legal interests but at the same time do protect "moral" and certain values and base themselves on moral law; for legitimation you could hardly thought of pulling up with a restriction of the general freedom of action especially facing the Federal Constitutional Court ruling on § 175 StGB (German Criminal Code) (old version) - concerning criminal provision against homosexuality between adults - to conceive of accepting a limitation on general freedom of action, because the opinion that "moral laws" (could) legitimize such an unacceptable or in its acceptance very arguable interference into personal freedom which was represented by former legal practise[158] is out of date and does not deserve any sympathy whatsoever (cf. also Roxin, 1997, § 2 Marginal Number 25 and Jäger, 1993, 240).

Clearly said morals moved ideas or ideologies, which can not be put down to a legally protected interest, and are therefore under no circumstance in a position to claim protection by criminal norms, for the democratic state has to stay as neutral towards the outlooks of life as long as the adoption of the resultant concept of life does not affect authorizations' fundamental freedom meaning not being detrimental to society. The statement that therefore the general freedom of action could only be restricted by elements of an offence and furthermore by those which include such moral norms whose compliance is not only demanded for their own sake but also to avoid damaging effects (Roxin, 1997, § 2 Marginal Number 25) is so far correct, but still not enough.

If this statement already applies for the abolishment of existing standards edged out by social reality, then it applies all the more with respect to the creation of new standards – provided that a changed social reality does not force us to reassess what has to be categorized as "socially harmful". Ultimately the meaning of socially harmful defines itself by the term legally interest however that means the involvement of the entire so called legally protected public interests. In this respect there have to be pointed out exemplarly the environmental (protection) law, competition (criminal) law and parts of the narcotics (criminal) law.

In all cases sur-individual legally protected interests are named: the environment, albeit not in a broad unsubstantiated sense, but in its various media, such as water, air, land and its other outward natures (Bundestag document 8/2382, 10, and 8/3633, 19; Kühl & Lackner, 2004, preceding § 324 Marginal Number 7). It is contentious on the other hand whether a so-called "personal link to legally protected interests" has to be implied, in other words whether the environment is only protected by criminal law for being a general living condition

---

[158] BVerfGE (Federal Constitutional Court ruling) 6, 389 ff. (434) – ruling of 10.05.1957 – 1 BvR 550/52.

for human life or for its very own sake (Bloy, 1988, 485; Kühl, 2002, 245 ff.; Zieschang, 1998, 214).[159]

If, as I do, one views criminal law in a contract theory context, then transferring corresponding sanctioning powers to the state is only rational and meaningful to the citizen if they just in case can also benefit personally from it. Such legally protected public interests are therefore never an end in themselves. Criminal law never protects the state for its own sake. For the state only exists for the greater benefit of its citizens. Consequently, the violation of every public legally protected interest must also carry the potential to cause a violation within the protected status under criminal law of individual legal spheres. Otherwise, the implementation of criminal law would be tantamount to illegitimate state coercion.

Two criteria are thus beginning to form:

(1) Does the public legally protected interest represents a differentiable area of social reality so – that should be added – can potentially affect everyone's interests?

(2) Is the public legally protected interest to be traced back to a foundation of individual interests?

What about fairness in sports? At first glance, the development of social reality would appear to be much stronger in favour of significantly reducing and not continuing to promote the restriction of general freedom of action substantiated under criminal law. For the reality seems to be that doping in the social sub-area of (elite) sport seems to be becoming an almost normal form of behaviour. On the other hand, comparable arguments exist with regard to making possession, consumption and trafficking of narcotics a punishable criminal offence.

However, before we investigate the reasons for existing criminalization under narcotics criminal law and are able to discuss its potential transferability to a possible future doping criminal law, we first need to have a look at the difference between these two sections of social reality:

Narcotics criminality potentially affects every single citizen, whereas doping criminality is in the first place limited to the small number of elite athletes.[160] But does this have an influence on the question of how detrimental to society doping is in comparison consumption and trafficking of narcotics?

As far as it concerns personal consumption the matter has to be stated more precisely. The consumption of narcotics differs from taking doping substances. Above all the respective athlete does not pursue any beyond consumption reaching aims and therefore does not affect third parties. Doping is a totally different matter: here just the act of doping is a means to a completely different and namely to be the victor of the competition. If self-responsible dependant doping

[159] For a critical approach to personal legally protected interest theory Schünemann (1995, 201), for a detailed description on the status of the conflict Kühl & Lackner (2004, preceding § 324 Marginal Number 7).

[160] The reasons why only elite sport is considered as punishable conduct is explained in detail in Cherkeh & Momsen (2001, 1745 ff).

was as equally purposeless as the consumption of narcotics a criminal liability would hardly be discussed seriously. – One may think of the already mentioned border area of sports "bodybuilding". If it is only about building up unnatural packages of muscles and if the indirect purpose is the mere putting on display the very same muscles the blemishing of the consumption of corresponding drugs and the claim for penal protection of the thought of fairness is obviously senseless.

Thus a conclusion *a minore ad maius* for the criminalization of doping then? If it is precisely this purpose pursued with doping and not the act of doping itself that can justify a criminal law response, then why should we not seek an interest worthy of protection under criminal law on the side of this end? If we take this hypothesis further, we could contemplate a definition of a criminal offence that would protect either sporting competition or, even more generally, all possible forms of competition as an idea of human co-existence. Although there seems to be a conceptual link between the concept of competition as such and fairness, the latter route of all-round protection of competition is neither desirable nor feasible for a number of reasons. This approach is, among other things, blocked by the different nature of forms of competition, for example in the economic and non-economic context. Moreover, it is not possible to justify why a disturbance of competition as such should be socially harmful – these can only be consequences in concrete cases, where afforded protection by criminal law must be orientated towards. Whether the legally protected interest adapted itself towards avoiding these consequences (e.g. asset protection) or towards the specific disturbance of competition (e.g. § 298), depends mainly on the typical status of interests. If the offender aims to personally capitalize on certain benefits that are made available in principle by third parties, in other words if the method of distribution is the focus of the offence, then it makes sense to orient the legal protection towards the behaviour injurious to competition. If, by contrast, the aim is to obtain benefits that the third party had no intention of surrendering, it makes sense to link protection to the injurious consequences. In the first case, the focus is on the act, which at the same time determines the typicality of the offence, in second case it is on the consequence. In case of behaviour injurious to competition it additionally makes sense to tie the legal consequences under criminal law into the attack on competition via the method of distribution and to generally only consider the occurrence of one of the above-mentioned consequences during the sentencing procedure.[161] *It is therefore essential to always identify the concrete violation which can be triggered by the attack on the public legally protected interest.*

On the one hand taking a look on the characteristic constellations of doping (Cherkeh & Momsen, 2001, 1745 ff.; Cherkeh, 2000, passim, both with exten-

---

[161] Cf. § 263 on the one hand and § 298 on the other hand (cf. Kühl & Lackner 2004, § 298 Marginal Number 9), as well as in between § 264 (cf. Kühl & Lackner 2004, § 264 Marginal Number 1, 30 f.).

sive evidence) you can see that it's all about a certain kind of influence on athletic competition relating to prize money. For this reason, in the case of doping, legal consequences under criminal law must always be linked to the behaviour injurious to competition. This very influence is being the focus of attention. On the other hand it is not about the distribution of prize money in athletic competitions despite of distortion caused by doping. Therefore legal consequences under criminal law aspects have to be linked to anti competitive acts in case of doping.

Is this interest in sporting competition sufficiently worthy of protection and – if so – is "fairness in sport" the correct term for the legally protected interest behind?

The term "sporting competition" consists of two segments. "Competition" alone just merely describes the instance where a majority of subjects is aligned or hierarchically arranged by means of a predetermined method. The criteria for the arrangement in this very case is to define the attribute "achievement". Strictly speaking, "competition" refers to the thus consummate state of rivalry between subjects within a certain forum.[162] The content of such a concept of competition is obviously too unspecific to be an object of protection under criminal law, as it merely describes an impartial regulatory process. Competition in this sense has no normative implications. The only indirect normative link is the ordering, i.e. controlling function of competition.[163]

The situation with the second term, "sport", is very similar. This describes nothing more than a classification of certain human forms of behaviour subsumed under the characteristic of physical (if so also sheer mental) expenditure of energy.[164] However, "sport" has more far-reaching implications, in particular the feature of personal performance and its observability and comparability.[165] As mentioned above, the only point of reference for a possible criminalization of doping can only be so-called "elite sport". This differs partly from sport in general through the emphasis on the performance characteristic, as well as – a subsequently – much higher symbolic significance, and again as a result is charac-

---

162 Cf. for example Grill (Ed.) 1994, catchword "competition": "rivalry between economic subjects in the respective market."

163 Grill (Ed.) 1994, catchword "competition": "...fulfils the function in a market economy of controlling the economic process."

164 Grill (Ed.) 1994, catchword "sport": "collective term for all movement, games or competitive forms of human physical activity."

165 Grill (Ed.) 1994, catchword "sport": "Sport always includes an externally observable effort (performance) or (artistic) movement that can be attributed to personal skill and enhanced (through training). Due to its easy verifiability, partly objectified as measurability, sport functions both as a possibility for personal confirmation and as a means of social rivalry (*sporting competition* – author's highlighting). A general concept of sport, according to which sporting performance is realized on the self-created reality level of the game as a fictive world, inseparably linked with the spontaneity of the athlete, is contrasted with an absolute concept of sport that sees sporting performance as a work and objective-quantifiable record, detached from the individual."

terized, by an enhanced public interest in the delivery of the performance.[166] That on the other hand and due to general opinion results in a role model and educational function.

In light of the public interest described above, sport as such, and elite sport in particular, could therefore by all means be ascribed to having the character of a legally protected interest. The distortion of sport could, insofar, be classified as detrimental to society. However, as yet the second condition is missing: the chance of repatriation to individual interests.

A more differentiated picture emerges, however, when the thus defined concept of elite sport is combined with that of competition. Without doubt, undistorted competition in elite sport is a legal interest that, demonstrated by means of earlier stated public interest in elite sport, is eligible for protection. Intervention in this legally protected interest through doping strikes its very core. Because it undermines precisely the characteristic attributes of objectivizability, measurability and comparability, so that "elite sport" is deprived of its function and within it its social benefit. Whether the desirable protection ought to or has to be of a criminal law nature is another matter that remains to be seen for the time being.

Is the term "fairness" an appropriate designation for this legally protected interest which is competition in elite sport? First of all, the term fairness in sports does not coincide compared to competition in competitive sports. Because "fairness" is a synonym for "sport ethics", which in turn represents moral and conviction concerning the sport players as a whole.[167] Understood like this, is fairness in sport a substantial and legally protected interest?

According to Roxin, interests which are worthy of protection by criminal law are conditions which serve the individual in its free development in society or rather serves the social system itself (Roxin, 1997, § 2 Marginal Number 9). General legally protected interests belong to the last clause of this definition.

So does fairness benefit the functioning of the system itself? This question has to be answered affirmatively. The moral concepts and value standards of sporting competition are passed on in the context of elite sport to the spectators of the sporting event and, via various mass media, to the general public. Due to the significance of the elite athlete's individual performance, not only how the success was achieved, but also the athlete as an individual becomes a role model and worthy to impersonate for a large section of the public. The topics which are to be subsumed under the term of fairness are not only brought forward in the tight frame of the sporting competition but do altogether gain an exemplary meaning for a general life concept. As the above definition makes clear, sport is

[166] Grill (Ed.) 1994, catchword "elite sport": "Has its essence in presentations (sport events), mostly communicated by the media, of peak performances that as a contest over winning and losing arouse mass public interest. Unconditional performance enhancement, however, frequently goes hand in hand with health risks (doping, stress) as well as personal, social and professional conflicts."

[167] Cf. Regenbogen & Meyer (Eds.) 2006, catchword "ethics".

a symbolic example of how the individual can achieve success in a society geared towards performance and competition. As well as the concept of fairness stands for success through playing by the rules and especially through an objective comparison of the competitors in order to achieve a specific goal, doping at the same time perverts this concept by having success only under the false pretence of performances not actually achieved, in other words, achieving success by unfair means and, in doing so, disrespecting the interests of respective competitors (For more details cf. Cherkeh & Momsen, 2001, 1745 ff.). It is unlikely to be disputed that this role model function of elite sport contributes to a functioning co-existence within society. Although it could be argued critically that the system of values set out in the Basic Law in principle accords every individual the possibility and the right to realize their life concept freely and self-responsibly, nevertheless for young people the guiding function of elite sport for individual behaviour is a fact in wide areas of conduct.

Structurally, therefore, the concept of fairness imparted through elite sport can claim comparable protection to the principle of democracy, the notion of protection of minorities and the threat to public health – albeit without wanting to raise all legally protected interests to the same level. However, it is important to bear in mind that the idea of fairness in this sense fairness is a public interest, which as such cannot be seriously violated under criminal law in the bilateral relationship between two competing athletes.

6.2 Need to legally protect interests under criminal law

In my opinion fairness in elite sports could – last but not least because of its inherent educational and role model function – generally claim protection under criminal law – if also the second criteria is met.

For fairness can only be an interest worthy of protection to the extent and under the conditions that apply to every public legally protected interest, i.e. if the public interest can be put down to recognized individual protected interests; in other words if protecting the public interest at the same time protects, i.e. secures or supports, individual interests.

In short: in terms of criminal law, unfair conduct in elite sport can be no more than a specific modality for what may only be an indirect attack on a traditional individual legally protected interest, comparable with deception in fraud as a specific modality for an attack on third-party assets. Also comparable to the pollution of a body of water as a modality for an attack on the foundations of personal health (anyone who believes environmental offences serve protection of the public legally protected interest "public health" is mistaken, as are those who use this circular argument to legitimize narcotics criminal law).

Because: the right of the state to exist can ultimately only lie in protecting the vital interests of its citizens as effectively as possible – even so-called "offences against national security" do not protect the state for its own sake, but only, because and to the extent that the state rationally and reasonably exists as an instrument to protect its citizens.

If an attack on a public legally protected interest can never lead *in abstracto* to the infringement of concrete individual interests or individual spheres worthy of protection, criminal jurisdiction of the state rightly has to be dropped.

However, this affecting of other individual spheres will frequently only be indirect or conveyed. For it is the indirect consequential effects of distorted competition caused by unfair behaviour – such as doping – that represent the real violation of individual interests. However the "entitlement" to a certain ranking certainly cannot be an interest protected under criminal law. On the other hand good rankings result in earnings possibilities in the form of prize money, sponsoring contracts and much more.

At least as a specific expectancy, the interest in this can fall under assets protected under criminal law.

7 Asset protection as an aim of penal anti-doping offences

This line of thought illustrates two things: on the one hand, where the practice of sport is not associated with assets and earnings, the possibilities for criminal law protection are limited. Insofar this is one argument in favour of only seeing fairness in elite sport as a protected interest under criminal law. Another, for example, is that precisely here the role model function manifests itself particularly intense, regarding the media dissemination of corresponding sporting events – one facet of the aspect of culpability. On the other hand, the need for separate criminal law intervention towards unfair conduct in elite sport can only exist where this protection is not already guaranteed by existing laws – the aspect of criminal prosecutability.

In case of the doping athlete, an appropriate protection of his direct competitor's assets provided the very one had achieved the stated potential earnings, would not have been sufficiently ensured by the seemingly relevant norms of fraud. For it is already questionable whether the rival is the victim of a deception or is deceived in the sense of § 263. Generally speaking – it can be assumed – athletes do not enter a tournament with a clear idea of whether certain other tournament participants are doped to the point that *for that reason* they perform better than themselves. And on the side of the offender – as said in the beginning – the motivation is very often "the victory" in itself, the honour and glory. Only in exceptional cases an athlete is likely to dope in order to aspire assets in form of a certain prize money or a sponsoring contract.

As we can see: the very concrete mediated attack on the assets of a third person as a result of an elite athlete's self-doping at the start of a tournament is, namely, not covered by the offence of fraud – the individual assets are not protected under criminal law against this attack modality. If we take the enormous economic significance of elite sport into account, "fairness in sport" in this case therefore not only represents a *legal* problem, but very definitely a *criminal law* problem!

8 Protection as other than asset-related interests?

This now raises the already posed question of whether "fairness in sports" is only specifically a "criminal" law problem where assets of third persons are adversely affected as a result of unfair behaviour by elite athletes.

Don't other legally protected interests come into consideration? The perhaps initially surprising answer is: no! Physical integrity, in other words individual health, is certainly also adversely affected as a result of taking doping substances; but in this case the elite athlete in question is only damaging his own health – and free and responsible exclusive self-harm is as a matter of principle irrelevant under criminal law – and indeed *has to be* in the contract theory context.

The punishability of the possession of doping substances pursuant to §§ 6a, 95 AMG (German Drug Law) illustrates the already mentioned gaps in the area of unlawful methods and, furthermore, represents itself as a pure symptom therapy. Other individual interests protected under criminal law are – with an appropriately reserved interpretation – as I see it not affected by unfair conduct on the part of the elite athlete – or are covered by existing offences, so that the context of "unfair conduct" in sports is not assigned any specific significance that would substantiate punishment.

One example for the lacking need for punishment of unfair behaviour in sport is the bribery of referees (and players). Here, too, the violation of the fairness principle leads to direct asset impairments. Because however – especially vividly illustrated in the betting fraud constellation, for example the notorious Hoyzer case – the unfair behaviour is specifically motivated and driven by gain at the expense of third-party assets, it is covered by the existing criminal offences of breach of trust and fraud – a perfect example of the lack of a need for criminal prosecutability and corresponding lack of legitimization for creating a new criminal offence.

9 Result

Thus we arrive at a positive result, which, however, turns out to be rather different from what our first contact with the subject of study, "fairness in sport", initially led us to expect. I would like to summarize my results as hypotheses:

- Sports in general, as well as individual sporting competitions in particular, is defined in its socially recognized form through "fairness".
- If the element of fairness is missing from elite sport in particular, this devalues its eminently important role model function – the economic consequences for elite sport and the enormous economic interests associated with it are impossible to estimate.

- Fairness in elite sport is a public interest worthy of protection.
- In order to be eligible for protection under criminal law, it must be possible to attribute this public interest to individual interests. An offence on the public interest must have an inherent potential to violate the concrete legally protected interest.
- Unfair behaviour in sporting competition is a criminal law problem inasmuch as it leads to a threat or infringement of individual interests recognized as being eligible for protection under criminal law.
- Accordingly, fairness in sports becomes a criminal law problem where unfair conduct represents a new attack modality against individual legally protected interests which are not legally subsumable under existing offences, particularly as a result of being embedded in sporting competition.
- In this context "unfair behaviour in sporting represents a penal problem whose remedy will have to be searched for in cheating in tight bordered element of a crime – if necessary a mixture of deception in sports and disturbance of sporting competition with economic relevance".
- To the extent that this threatens legally protected interests under criminal law in the manner described, it goes without saying that beyond possible sanctions imposed by the associations, it's on the criminal law legislator to meet the challenges. Here, the only aspect of interest is the economic relevance of doping.

References

Adolphsen, J. (2008). Der Staat im Anti-Doping Kampf. *Sportwissenschaft 38*, 82 – 88.

Bloy, R. (1988). Die Straftaten gegen die Umwelt im System des Rechtsgüterschutzes. *Zeitschrift für die gesamte* Strafrechtswissenschaft (ZStW), 485-507.

Cherkeh, R. T. (2000). *Betrug (§ 263 StGB), verübt durch Doping im Sport.* Frankfurt am Main (and others): Peter Lang.

Cherkeh, R. T., Momsen, C. (2001). Doping als Wettbewerbsverzerrung? Möglichkeiten der strafrechtlichen Erfassung des Dopings unter besonderer Berücksichtigung der Schädigung von Mitbewerbern. *Neue juristische Wochenschrift* (NJW), 1745-1752.

Grill, G. et al. (Eds.) (1994). *Meyers Neues Lexikon in zehn Bänden,* Mannheim: Meyers Lexikonverlag.

Grotz, S. (2008). Die Grenzen der staatlichen Strafgewalt, exemplifiziert am neuen Anti-Doping Tatbestand. *Zeitschrift für das Juristische Studium* (ZJS)1, 3, 243-255.

Hinsch, W. (2002). *Gerechtfertigte Ungleichheiten. Grundsätze sozialer Gerechtigkeit.* Berlin: Walter de Gruyter.

Jäger, H. (1993). Irrationale Kriminalpolitik. In P. A. Albrecht (Ed.): *Festschrift für Horst Schüler-Springorum zum 65. Geburtstag* (pp. 229-243). Cologne (and others): Heymann.

Jahn, M. (2006). Doping zwischen Selbstgefährdung, Sittenwidrigkeit und staatlicher Schutzpflicht. Materiell-strafrechtliche Fragen an einen Straftatbestand zur Bekämpfung des eigenverantwortlichen Dopings. *Zeitschrift für Internationale Strafrechtsdogmatik* (ZIS)1, 2, 57-62.

Kühl, K. (2002). Anthropozentrische oder nichtanthropozentrische Rechtsgüter im Umweltstrafrecht? In J. Nida-Rümelin, D. v. d. Pfordten (Eds.). *Ökologische Ethik und Rechtstheorie* (pp. 245-263). 2nd edition, Baden-Baden: Nomos.

Kühl, K., Lackner, K. (2004). *Strafgesetzbuch. Kommentar*, 25th edition, Munich: Beck.

Maiwald, M. (2002). Probleme der Strafbarkeit des Doping im Sport – am Beispiel des italienischen Antidoping-Gesetzes. In D. Dölling (Ed.). *Festschrift für Karl Heinz Gössel zum 70. Geburtstag am 16. Oktober 2002* (pp. 399-414), Heidelberg: Müller.

Merton, R. K. (1968). Sozialstruktur und Anomie. In F. Sack F., R. König (Eds.), *Kriminalsoziologie* (pp. 283-313), Frankfurt am Main: Suhrkamp.

Momsen-Pflanz, G. (2005). *Die sportethische und strafrechtliche Bedeutung des Dopings. Störung des wirtschaftlichen Wettbewerbs und Vermögensrelevanz*. Frankfurt am Main (and others): Peter Lang.

Rawls, J. (1975). *Eine Theorie der Gerechtigkeit*, Frankfurt am Main: Suhrkamp.

Regenbogen, A., Meyer, U. (Eds.) (2006). *Wörterbuch der philosophischen Begriffe*, Hamburg: Felix Meiner.

Roxin, C. (1997). *Strafrecht, allgemeiner Teil. Band I: Grundlagen – der Aufbau der Verbrechenslehre*, 3rd edition, Munich: C. H. Beck.

Schünemann, B. (1995). Kritische Anmerkungen zur geistigen Situation der deutschen Strafrechtswissenschaft. *Goltdammer's Archiv für Strafrecht* (GA), 201-229.

Waldbröl, H.-J. (2006). Interview with Britta Bannenberg. Ohne strafrechtliches Dopingverbot geht es nicht. *Frankfurter Allgemeine Zeitung*, 3 March 2006, 32.

Zieschang, F. (1998). *Die Gefährdungsdelikte*. Berlin: Duncker und Humblot.

FSC
www.fsc.org
MIX
Papier | Fördert gute Waldnutzung
FSC® C083411

Kolibri 360 GmbH
Ferdinand-Jühlke-Straße 7
99095 Erfurt, Deutschland
produktsicherheit@kolibri360.de